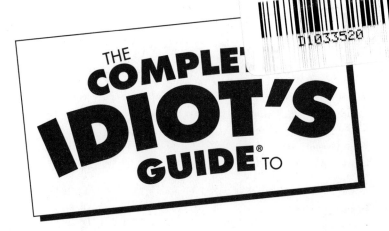

# Indigo Children

*by Wendy H. Chapman, Dir., M.A. in Ed. Psy., and Carolyn Flynn*

ALPHA

A member of Penguin Group (USA) Inc.

# ALPHA BOOKS

Published by the Penguin Group

Penguin Group (USA) Inc., 375 Hudson Street, New York, New York 10014, USA

Penguin Group (Canada), 90 Eglinton Avenue East, Suite 700, Toronto, Ontario M4P 2Y3, Canada (a division of Pearson Penguin Canada Inc.)

Penguin Books Ltd., 80 Strand, London WC2R 0RL, England

Penguin Ireland, 25 St. Stephen's Green, Dublin 2, Ireland (a division of Penguin Books Ltd.)

Penguin Group (Australia), 250 Camberwell Road, Camberwell, Victoria 3124, Australia (a division of Pearson Australia Group Pty. Ltd.)

Penguin Books India Pvt. Ltd., 11 Community Centre, Panchsheel Park, New Delhi—110 017, India

Penguin Group (NZ), 67 Apollo Drive, Rosedale, North Shore, Auckland 1311, New Zealand (a division of Pearson New Zealand Ltd.)

Penguin Books (South Africa) (Pty.) Ltd., 24 Sturdee Avenue, Rosebank, Johannesburg 2196, South Africa

Penguin Books Ltd., Registered Offices: 80 Strand, London WC2R 0RL, England

# Copyright © 2007 by Amaranth Illuminare

International Standard Book Number: 978-1-59257-637-1
Library of Congress Catalog Card Number: 2007922824

09 08 07    8 7 6 5 4 3 2 1

Interpretation of the printing code: The rightmost number of the first series of numbers is the year of the book's printing; the rightmost number of the second series of numbers is the number of the book's printing. For example, a printing code of 07-1 shows that the first printing occurred in 2007.

*Printed in the United States of America*

**Note:** This publication contains the opinions and ideas of its authors. It is intended to provide helpful and informative material on the subject matter covered. It is sold with the understanding that the authors, book producer, and publisher are not engaged in rendering professional services in the book. If the reader requires personal assistance or advice, a competent professional should be consulted.

The authors, book producer, and publisher specifically disclaim any responsibility for any liability, loss, or risk, personal or otherwise, which is incurred as a consequence, directly or indirectly, of the use and application of any of the contents of this book.

Most Alpha books are available at special quantity discounts for bulk purchases for sales promotions, premiums, fundraising, or educational use. Special books, or book excerpts, can also be created to fit specific needs.

For details, write: Special Markets, Alpha Books, 375 Hudson Street, New York, NY 10014.

**Publisher:** *Marie Butler-Knight*
**Editorial Director:** *Mike Sanders*
**Managing Editor:** *Billy Fields*
**Executive Editor:** *Randy Ladenheim-Gil*
**Book Producer:** *Lee Ann Chearney/Amaranth Illuminare*
**Development Editor:** *Lynn Northrup*

**Production Editor:** *Megan Douglass*
**Copy Editor:** *Emily Bell Garner*
**Cover Designer:** *Bill Thomas*
**Book Designer:** *Trina Wurst*
**Indexer:** *Brad Herriman*
**Layout:** *Eric S. Miller, Chad Dressler*
**Proofreader:** *Mary Hunt*

*To my new baby boy, Nicholas Ryan, whose development and arrival coincides with this book. Thank you for your assistance from Spirit in creation of it.*
—Wendy H. Chapman, MA

*To Emerald and Lucas, my stone and my light. Together, we make a new world.*
—Carolyn Flynn

# Contents at a Glance

# Contents

# Introduction

*Who are you, and where did you come from?*

From the moment you first cradle your child in your arms, you are infused with a sense of absolute wonder. This little one seems mysterious to you, yet you marvel at the similarities—the simple miracle that this child came through you to enter this world. Thus the journey begins—a lifetime of getting to know one another.

If you have had the sense from those earliest moments that your child is different—perhaps with unusual spiritual intelligence, a strong sense of purpose, and exceptional gifts—then you may have an Indigo child.

Indigo Children became identified as such as early as 1982, though many were born long before that time. Many psychologists and educators call it "a wave of deep blue," referring to the rich, deep blue light energy for which Indigo Children are named. Experts estimate that more than 85 percent of the children born since 1982 and 95 percent or more of those born since 1999 are Indigos.

Your child may be gifted with an unconventional brilliance or a singular sensitivity. You may be astonished at his or her highly developed sense of self in one so young. At the same time, in day-to-day life with your Indigo child, you also may feel stymied at how best to channel this creative, spiritually wise, and nonconformist soul. Because of these attributes, many Indigos struggle in school and other conventional structures, and some have learning disabilities or extremes of physical or emotional sensitivity. Many days, it may seem that you just have a difficult child.

Whether you know this child as a parent, an educator, psychologist, or family member, you need to know more. The first step in learning how best to channel the unique talents and challenges of an Indigo is to increase your understanding.

In this book, we will take you on an exciting journey. We will help you learn skills to develop, channel, and manage your Indigo child. We'll include practical techniques and tips that will help you most effectively meet his or her needs. And we rather suspect this book will not only help you but also enrich your experience of your child, stretching you in new ways. To know Indigos is to open you to greater self-knowledge and deeper growth. They are here to change you—and make the world a better place. In this book, we will give you a glimpse of how this wave of deep blue will influence the world to come.

## How to Use This Book

This book is divided into a five-part exploration of how to manage and nurture the special children we call Indigos.

**Part 1, "A Wave of Deep Blue,"** introduces you to Indigo Children, helps you identify whether your child is an Indigo and opens a discussion about the changes they will bring to education, politics, health, and spiritual life.

**Part 2, "Indigo's Unique Challenges … and Unique Gifts,"** goes into more depth about the attributes of Indigos and discusses strategies for managing them.

**Part 3, "Mission Incredible: Parenting Indigos,"** provides some hands-on parenting tips for loving discipline, as well as answering the question about whether you are an Indigo, too.

**Part 4, "Thrive: Creating the Right Environment,"** explains that a great deal of parenting the Indigo is facilitating the right conditions for his or her learning, creativity, and health.

**Part 5, "How Indigos Will Change the World,"** develops scenarios of a future where Indigos teach us innovative thinking, tolerance, and compassionate living. In this part, we'll address some of the more metaphysical questions, such as whether Indigos have been reincarnated from past lives.

## Extras

Throughout each chapter of this book, you'll find little tidbits of information that will help you in your journey with an Indigo:

**def•i•ni•tion** _____

These definitions provide more illumination on some of the key concepts about Indigos.

**Crystal Clear** _____

These quotes from various wise people add sparkle.

**Patience** _____

These warnings help you when doubts and obstacles might trip you up.

**Good Counsel** _____

These tips offer easy, quick tips or activities you can do to help your Indigo child.

**Indigo Stars** _____

These anecdotes tell more about a famous person, real or fictional, who has Indigo traits.

## Acknowledgments

From Wendy H. Chapman, MA:

Writing this book fulfills a soul contract for me. I am grateful that I had the opportunity to do this—particularly at this turning point in my life as I am about to have a baby. Thank you to my future son who shared this journey with me from start to finish. He is due to come out about the same time as this book! His assistance and input from the other side was very helpful and appreciated!

I wish to thank my husband for his support of my work and my time spent in creating this book. I also wish to thank my mother for her ongoing support and encouragement always.

I would like to thank Lee Ann Chearney, the book producer who invited me to co-author this book, and Spirit for guiding her to me. I also thank my co-author, Carolyn Flynn, for her excellent input and writing skills. She helped me take this book that had existed solely in my mind for many years finally into print.

To my good friend Patrick M. Jordan, sincere thanks for helping me start up www.metagifted.org, doing all the computer coding, and running the technical part of things for the first five years!

Finally, thank you to Karen Eck and the other list moderators who have been running the Indigo Adults and Metagifted Yahoogroups for me during my book-writing journey and pregnancy time.

From Carolyn Flynn:

The week I started writing this book with Wendy, she found out she was pregnant with her first child. I feel blessed to have worked with Wendy during this special time in her life. She has taught me a lot about raising my two little Indigos, Emerald and Lucas, who decided they would come together, side by side, to be in this world—as twins. I thank Wendy for her sensitivity and her wisdom, her unique and compassionate take on the world.

During the writing of this book, I saw rainbows nearly every day. Once, I got thrown from my bed by a righteous spirit. Another time, I got tapped on the shoulder by an angel. I saw myself connected in a multidimensional web of light. It was Wendy who opened that up to me.

I'd also like to thank Amaranth's creative director Lee Ann Chearney for her role in pushing me and inspiring me to take this book to a higher octave. Many thanks to all the editors at Alpha for their diligence and dedication.

Finally, I'd like to thank the compassionate hearts and brilliant minds of my twins, who give me hope every day that we can meet our challenges, appreciate our gifts, and change the world.

## Trademarks

# Part 1

# A Wave of Deep Blue

If you charted the births of these very special children we call Indigos, it would show they began arriving in greater numbers starting in the 1990s. It was a dramatic climb, to the point where 95 percent of those children being born toward the close of the twentieth century were Indigos. These special children who have arrived with a deep spiritual awareness and a resistance to present-day structures have arrived with a purpose: to change the world.

# Chapter 1

# How to Know If You Have an Indigo

## In This Chapter

- ◆ Attributes of Indigo Children
- ◆ Indigos you may already know
- ◆ Identifying Indigo intelligence, behavior, and aura
- ◆ Indigo child, or just precocious?

Many parents of Indigos have a sense that their child is different long before they come upon the term Indigo Children. They may notice a striking creativity or sense of self, or they may notice an exceptional anger or lack of patience. Or they may observe that parenting this little being is more than the average challenge, when the child questions the rules and demands a voice in shaping structure and discipline. Others notice an uncanny psychic ability—or just a knack for being unusually tuned-in to other people's feelings.

All of these attributes and many more define the Indigo child. So let's take a closer look at who these children are and why they are here.

# What Is an Indigo Child?

If you have picked up this book, it's likely that you are experiencing the challenges of raising an Indigo and haven't known what to call it. Or if you have heard the term, you might have thought it was for New Age kids and not for yours. Maybe all you know is your child breaks the mold. Or maybe you know he or she is brilliant, yet is struggling. Maybe your child isn't doing well in school, or maybe she doesn't get along well with other children, although she seems extraordinarily compassionate. Or maybe your child simply won't listen to you and do as you ask.

Your child may be gifted, yet you don't quite know how to deal with it. Maybe he exhibits an extraordinary knack for understanding the spirit world, talking about getting visits from a deceased grandmother. Maybe she has creative leaps of the imagination or an exceptional gift with language that just don't seem possible in one so young.

Sometimes you simply don't understand your kid. At any rate, you just need to know what you are wrestling with. You may have an Indigo child.

The first thing to know about *Indigo Children* is that they defy categorization. While most are creative, imaginative, brilliant, and unconventional, they don't fit into any mold. Some exhibit high emotional permeability—meaning they are very sensitive and empathetic to others—while others exhibit a peculiar anger or nonconformity that seems quite the opposite. Some may be highly physically sensitive, while others are uncannily psychic. But while there's a wide spectrum, one thing that all Indigo Children seem to have in common is they are unconventionally brilliant, spiritually advanced and strikingly tuned in.

## def•i•ni•tion

Indigo Children are children who are brilliant and creative yet unconventional. Many of them are psychic, highly emotionally sensitive, or highly physically sensitive. Some of them have attention deficit disorder or learning disabilities. Some of them are angry or nonconformist, while others are exceptionally tolerant and compassionate. Indigo Children can be spiritually advanced beyond their years. Your Indigo child may have some but not all of these attributes. The main thing to know about Indigo Children is they don't fit into a mold. They're different, and they are here to change the world.

This is precisely what enthralls and stymies the parents, educators, and psychologists who work with Indigo Children. Each child requires an individualized approach. Indigos want very much to be seen for the unique individuals they are—cookie-cutter solutions don't work with them. You can't be a traditional parent, and you can't educate them in the traditional way.

Whatever the variation, it may be clear to you that your child is tuned into something else, something you may only have a glimpse of understanding about or something that seems completely foreign to you. They are tuned to a higher spiritual vibration.

## The History of Indigos

Maybe you picked up this book because you have always sensed your child was special. But some experts estimate that more than 85 percent of the children born since 1992 and 95 percent or more of those born since 1999 are Indigos. (Wendy thinks this may be too high. More than likely the percentage is about 50 percent of elementary school age children.) In a way, it's a relief to find you're not alone, but then how special is special, if so many children being raised today are Indigos? Understand that most of these children have Indigo traits, but some are more extreme than others. Also remember that each Indigo child is a singular person. As individuals, they defy categorization. As a whole, they have qualities that set them apart from previous generations of children. As a whole, though, what they share is that their "differentness" is changing the world we live in.

The term Indigo Children stems from the belief that these children arrived into this world on a wave of deep blue light energy. Indigo refers to the third-eye *chakra*, which is strong in these children. That chakra's color is deep blue, or indigo. The third-eye chakra is the energy center in the body that governs intuition, a trait that is particularly strong in many

**def•i•ni•tion**

> The **chakras** are energy centers in the body. Seven exist in the body, starting from the base of the spinal cord to the crown. Each energy center governs an area of life, such as personal power, love, truth, or intuition. In Indigo Children, the intuition chakra is strong.

Indigo Children. Many people identify Indigos by picking up on a rich, deep blue light energy emanating from the child's auric field.

In the coming chapters, we'll explain more about light and energy fields and how they figure into identifying Indigo Children, but for now we'll just say that Indigo is the color of deepening knowledge and truth, leading to a higher spiritual awareness. And that, many say, is what Indigos are here to do.

When Nancy Ann Tappe first wrote about Indigos in her book, *Understanding Your Life Through Color* (see Appendix B), she identified the precocious children she was seeing as Indigos because that was the color she saw around them in their life color aura. The life color is the one that determines one's mission on Earth. She first saw children with this life color in the early 1970s (must have been early Indigos!). By the 1980s, she had labeled and started identifying consistencies in the Indigo personality.

Wendy believes that there have always been at least a few early Indigos in the world and that the number of Indigos began to increase in the 1950s, sharply increasing from the 1970s to the 1990s. Evidence of this comes from the thousands of people in Indigo Adults yahoo.com groups who have self-identified as adult Indigos based on characteristics that we'll talk about in Chapter 11.

So you can see that the understanding of Indigos originated from a metaphysical view of the world, but since then, the concept has been embraced and developed by educators and psychologists. They, too, had started seeing children with exceptional attributes, children who were very different.

If you picked up this book already knowing the term Indigo Children, it may be because of a book titled, *The Indigo Children: The New Kids Have Arrived*, written by self-help lecturers Lee Carroll and Jan Tober (see Appendix B), which was the first widely publicized book about Indigos, or *Indigo* (2003), a feature-length film about a fictional Indigo child's experience growing up and teaching her grandfather about Indigo ways. In the film, written by James Twyman and Neale Donald Walsch, the granddaughter says, "I'm not making things up; you're just dimensionally challenged."

That line defines our journey with Indigos. We will be challenged to change the way we perceive the world. As a young woman states in the movie, "It's these kids. They're going to shift everything."

> **Good Counsel**
>
> To find out more about the *Indigo* movie and the movement associated with it, go online to www.Indigothemovie.com. In 2005, James Twyman also directed a documentary, *The Indigo Evolution*, which interviews experts who work with Indigos and examines whether the phenomenon is real. Go to www.theIndigoevolution.com.

## Attributes of Indigos

But first things first—do you have an Indigo? Let's find out!

Not all Indigos have all of the following characteristics, but it's safe to say that if many of these traits are prominent in your child's behavior, you very likely have an Indigo:

- ❑ Your child resists conformity. She doesn't want to be like any other kid.
- ❑ Your child resists authority. Sometimes he can be rebellious.
- ❑ Your child responds to discipline better if she is involved in determining the consequences, or just if she has been allowed to talk about how she feels about it.
- ❑ Your child seems extraordinarily emotionally sensitive. You sometimes wish you could protect him from feeling things so deeply.
- ❑ Your child seems highly empathic. She seems to know what others are feeling without being told.
- ❑ Or, on the other hand, maybe your child is cold and callous. Sometimes you wonder if he has just shut off a part of himself.
- ❑ Your child is intuitive. She seems to just know things.
- ❑ Your child is wise beyond his years. You sometimes think he has a lot to teach you.
- ❑ Your child is physically sensitive or fragile. She has a lot of food allergies, or she seems to respond extraordinarily to sensory input.

❑ Your child carries himself with a sense that he deserves to be here.

❑ Your child developed a strong sense of self at an early age. It may seem to you she has had this all along.

❑ Your child struggles to be patient. Waiting in lines is torture.

❑ Your child resists overly structured situations that require little creativity.

❑ Your child often thinks of better ways of doing things at home or school.

❑ Your child doesn't respond to guilt trips.

❑ Your child gets bored easily with assigned tasks.

❑ Your child seems to have a short attention span. He has difficulty focusing and staying on task. There's a lot going on in his head.

❑ Your child is wildly creative. Sometimes you wonder what she'll come up with next.

❑ Your child exhibited abstract thinking at an early age—that is, the ability to grasp concepts such as hope or God.

❑ You often notice your child daydreaming.

❑ You sense a deep spiritual intelligence in your child.

### Indigo Stars

Olympic gold medal-winning snowboarder Shaun White defines the creative risk-taking Indigo with a strong sense of individuality. White, called the Flying Tomato for his shaggy mane of red hair, is who he is and nothing's going to change him. In a television commercial, White talks about using his computer for downloading guitar chords, designing snowboards, playing online games, and designing a jacket with a gold satin lining. "It's my own little world in there." Like many Indigos, he has a unique definition of his world.

## Famous Indigos We Have Known

Most Indigos are still children, but some are adults, and some early Indigos have already made their imprint on the world. The breakdown of Indigo Children is pretty evenly boys and girls. Here's a look at famous people we think could be Indigos.

In her young life, Alexandra Scott, who died of cancer at age 8, started Alex's Lemonade Stand to raise money for other children with cancer. Another young Indigo was Mattie Stepanik, a published poet at age 9 who was embraced by talk show host Oprah Winfrey because of his spiritual wisdom. Mattie died at age 13 of a rare form of muscular dystrophy but made a mark on his world.

"Nonconformist" defines other Indigos such as Olympic snowboarder Shaun White or Olympic figure skater Johnny Weir. Indigos often are strikingly centered, like Olympic speed skater Apolo Anton Ohno.

Though most Indigos are children, some have shown up earlier in our time. Many experts consider these people Indigos: Apple founder Steve Jobs; film maker George Lucas; film maker Steven Spielberg; comedian Robin Williams; comedian Andy Kaufman; Irish rock star Bono of U2, nominated several times for the Nobel Peace Prize; medical intuitive and author Caroline Myss (*Anatomy of the Spirit*, *Sacred Contracts*, see Appendix B). Other contemporary adult Indigos include spiritual teacher Marianne Williamson (*A Return to Love*, see Appendix B); talk show host Oprah Winfrey; and actress and metaphysician Shirley MacLaine.

Indigos have shown up here and there in history, too: Pilot Amelia Earhart; poet Emily Dickinson; novelist Jane Austen; revolutionary, statesman, and inventor Benjamin Franklin (one of Wendy's ancestors); civil rights activist Rosa Parks; martyr Joan of Arc; education pioneer Maria Montessori; painters Leonardo DaVinci, Vincent van Gogh, and Salvador Dali; entrepreneur and aviation innovator Howard Hughes; poet Robert Frost; essayist Henry David Thoreau; suffragette Susan B. Anthony, who learned to read and write at age 3; film maker Walt Disney; children's book author Dr. Seuss; physicist Albert Einstein; composer Wolfgang Amadeus Mozart; architect Antoni Gaudî; Holocaust diarist Anne Frank; author Lewis Carroll, who wrote *Alice in Wonderland*; puppeteer Jim Henson; politician Bella Abzug; physicist Richard Feynman; Underground Railroad leader Harriet Tubman; and humorist Mark Twain. Princess Diana shows up on Indigo lists because of her high physical sensitivity and humanitarianism. Even the Unibomber, Ted Kaczynski, shows up on some people's Indigo lists.

Fictional Indigos abound, too: Harry Potter and his friend Hermoine; Elliott, the boy who encounters an extraterrestrial in the movie *E.T.*; Jade, the Indigo child who figures in the video game *Fahrenheit*; Joan of Arcadia from the television show of the same name, loosely based on Joan of Arc; the *Farscape* character Chiana; and Dr. Who. Maybe even Junie B. Jones—a favorite of early chapter book readers—is an Indigo. Who knows? She certainly has a strong sense of self.

## How They Are Identified

Indigos are identified in three ways: intelligence quotient tests, aura, and behavior. Wendy thinks aura and behavior may be more useful in identifying an Indigo. That's because, true to form, Indigos resist the conformity of IQ testing. Indigos often have specific intelligence, and IQ tests measure general intelligence. For Indigos, intelligence is measured in creativity and applied intelligence. The behaviors on the previous list are the most definitive indicators of an Indigo.

Indigos have a deep blue light, or aura, around them. An aura is a light that can be perceived in a person's energy field. Auras are projected from all layers of a person—physical, mental, emotional, and spiritual. Indigos often project deep blue from the life spirit layer, though they can also project it from the emotional layer.

 **Crystal Clear**

Before you were conceived I wanted you

Before you were born I loved you

Before you were here an hour I would die for you

This is the miracle of life.

—Author Maureen Hawkins

So what's up with the deep blue? Deep blue—or any color, for that matter—describes the quality of the energy. Because we'll talk about energy a lot in this book, we'll define it here. Energy refers to the essence or animating life force of a living being. It's a universal energy, sometimes called chi, meaning that it's everywhere, in every living person, animal, plant, or place.

## But Really, What Makes Them Special?

Of course, all children are special. We love children because they are imaginative, and they aren't socialized to constrict themselves to the limitations of the world. And there have always been precocious children. So you might ask whether we are simply talking about a group of precocious children.

To be precocious means to be wise beyond one's years, to absorb knowledge faster and deeper. Indigos are certainly that, but one factor that sets them apart is that they appear to have come into this world already with a deep spiritual knowledge. Their unease with this world is that they have come in as children and experience the physical and societal limitations of childhood. There are certain things that they feel ready to do but cannot yet do because they must still grow up. Indigos are mentally and spiritually ahead of the game, but emotionally and physically, they are still children.

In his autobiography, *Chronicles, Volume I* (Simon & Schuster, 2004), Bob Dylan writes about his early music career, "I was at the initiation point of square one but in no sense a neophyte." Indigos are like that. (And now that we think of it, the singular Dylan is probably an Indigo.) Indigos may be starting out in this world, being children who are physically and emotionally immature, but when it comes to spiritual matters and creative intellect, they are not neophytes.

While Indigos can be many things, they universally possess an innate spiritual intelligence, or a metagiftedness. That's a term Wendy coined, and it means "metaphysically gifted"—that is, having a high psychic ability or high spiritual wisdom.

It's clear that their challenges to our established social structures are toward the end of establishing something better for the greater good. They are here on a spiritual mission, something we'll delve into more in Chapter 2.

# A Double-Edged Sword

It's a double-edged sword to be an Indigo—or be the parent of an Indigo. Indigos have many, many gifts, but because they are so different and so very young, they also face many challenges. In coming chapters, we will look further into these talents and challenges to deepen your understanding.

Most important, we'll give you guidelines and simple exercises about how to manage the Indigo in your life. Here's a preview of the Ten

Commandments of working with an Indigo child. Respect, choices, and nurturing are what it's all about with an Indigo. We'll go into more depth with this in Chapter 9.

1. Be honest.

2. Show respect.

3. Practice unconditional love.

4. Empower them though viable choices.

5. Respect their psychic skills. Don't fear them.

6. Teach them energy shielding and grounding skills.

7. Teach them relaxation and meditation skills.

8. Honor their Indigo nature. Treasure their emotional and physical sensitivity.

9. Research alternative therapies for attention-deficit hyperactivity disorder and learning disabilities.

10. Help them develop an awareness of their Indigo nature and mission.

It's important that you value their experience *as it is*. Listen to their feelings and how they are processing them and don't impose expectations from your childhood on them. Indigos are already very much aware that they are singular, and their experiences are different not only from yours, but from that of other children, including Indigos. They will resist incorporating your experience into their psyches. It won't feel right. Their viewpoint is unique. All they want is for you to hear it and honor it.

By no means does this mean you let them run the show. You are still the parent, and you are there to give your children guidance. But guidance that acknowledges, appreciates, and nurtures their unique gifts, while accepting them as they are, even with the challenges—that guidance will get you both where you need to go.

In coming chapters, we'll talk about some innovative and fun ways to parent an Indigo parent. Many of them are simply wise and loving parenting techniques that you would practice with any child; some of them are unique to Indigos. Some techniques may not feel natural to you, and you may not be convinced they are the right strategy. But try them with your Indigo, and you may just find they are not only effective, but rewarding. Remember that respect and choices are integral to parenting an Indigo.

## Indigo Challenges

Let it be said here that Indigo Children is not just a term for children with learning disabilities or attention-deficit hyperactivity disorder (ADHD). Not all Indigos have ADHD, though some do. Some have learning disabilities such dyslexia, or land in the autism spectrum, which includes Asperger's syndrome. We'll discuss ADHD and learning disabilities in Chapter 5.

## Indigo Gifts

Many of the gifts of Indigo Children can prove to be challenging to parents. Their creative approach to the world, their lack of adherence to structure, and their highly developed empathy and sensitivity all add up to children who navigate the world much differently—and less efficiently—than is always practical in day-to-day life. Your Indigo child may demand that you slow down and "take the long way home," so to speak.

# About Wendy, About Carolyn

Wendy has seen many Indigo Children over the years, first as a teacher to gifted children in the public school system for 15 years and then as director of the Metagifted Education Resource Organization (www. metagifted.org). She also is an Indigo.

Carolyn is mother to two Indigos who arrived at the same time—one minute apart—as twins. When she compares notes with other parents in her support network who are raising children of similar age—Carolyn's twins are 7—she finds many others are parenting Indigos.

In the chapters ahead, you'll hear about Wendy's experiences working with Indigo Children, but you'll also learn about adults who are Indigos and find out what it was like to grow up Indigo. You'll hear about the Indigo expressions and challenges of Carolyn's twins, as well as the many Indigo Children who fill her life.

# A Magnificent Journey

If your child is an Indigo, this is a good thing. It may be a difficult journey, but it will be a journey full of wonder. Along the way, you will learn to understand and love your child more deeply, and you will likely learn more about yourself.

## The Least You Need to Know

♦ You can identify Indigos by their behavior, personality traits, and aura.

♦ Among the traits that define an Indigo are spiritual wisdom, high intelligence, strong empathy, and nonconformity.

♦ Early Indigos were pioneers in their time, leaving their mark on history in creative, inventive, or subversive ways.

♦ Indigos are more than just precocious children. They come in with an advanced spiritual awareness.

♦ An Indigo bears a double-edged sword. With the gifts come challenges.

♦ Above all, the rule with parenting Indigos is to listen to them and give them respect.

# Chapter 2

# The Big Picture: Where Indigos Fit In

## In This Chapter

- ◆ Changing our schools and institutions
- ◆ Healing our hearts and minds
- ◆ New paths for social change, new ways of working
- ◆ On the horizon: Crystal Children

You might ask—why these kids, why now? In many ways, this is the most fascinating part. The answer lies in their unique gifts, as well as their unique challenges.

Quite simply, Indigos are here to raise the vibration of the planet. They are here to help us see what needs to change and point the way to how to do it. The world will absolutely have to change to accommodate these wise, creative souls. They are the next step in human evolution.

# Changing Our Schools

Wendy taught gifted children in public and private schools for 15 years, and she quickly noticed that the children had gifts of imagination that were being only minimally tapped. She developed a guided imagery exercise to use with kindergarten through sixth grade children to enhance their creativity and their critical thinking. She called them imaginary field trips.

Wendy gave broad parameters for these imaginary field trips. After getting the children relaxed using soft lighting, relaxing music, and deep breathing, Wendy asked the children to imagine finding an invention in a crystal cave. She instructed them to use all their senses. They had to photograph the invention in their minds so they could come back from the "field trip" and explain how it worked. She gave them paper so they could write and/or draw the invention and describe it.

Over the course of the school year, she did imaginary field trips with every class in every grade in the school. The children started devising their own. It was clear there were several children who were super-advanced in imaginative, spiritual, and creative thinking. Some of them came up to tell her about other visualizations they had had. Some told her about psychic visions or dreams that had come true.

Because many Indigos are making their way through the schools now, that's where they will have their first public impact (and already have). Of course, the very first paradigm they are changing is parenting. Education systems are responding with higher teacher-to-student ratios and more creative approaches to learning.

### Patience

Your Indigo child may not do so well in school despite high intelligence. She may just not want to follow the directions or do the repetitive homework. Many Indigo attributes—imaginativeness, distractibility, compassion—can take your child's focus off the nuts-and-bolts of structured learning. Take care not to assume any lack of intelligence.

As we mentioned in Chapter 1, some, but by no means all, Indigo Children have learning disabilities. Children with ADHD or learning disabilities (see Chapter 5) have required the school systems to devise more customized learning structures. In this way, Indigos are "system busters."

Home schooling is on the rise, increasing from 1.7 percent to 2.2 percent of the school-age population between 1999 and 2003, according to the National Center for Education Statistics. But that might not be the full story. Some experts such as Brian D. Ray of the National Home Education Research Institute think the number might be as high as 7 percent.

Other alternative methods are on the rise as well, such as charter schools or consciousness-based education. Some educational approaches that have been around for a while but often work better for Indigos are Montessori, Waldorf, and Reggio Emilia. These educational methods gain more credence as Indigo Children demand a more individualized approach than the typical public school offers.

What most of these alternative approaches have in common are a focus on the individuality of the student, more teacher autonomy, flexibility in the curriculum, and openness to new ideas. Cutting the children into the deal is very much a part of it. They have a voice in shaping the curriculum. We'll examine the educational options more closely in Chapter 14.

> **Good Counsel**
>
> If your child can see it and say it but doesn't have the writing skills to write it as a paper, you might see if his teacher would let him write a skit, create a video, or draw a storyboard. Let her explore her unique style of expression and have success in that area until her writing skills catch up.

# Changing Our Institutions

Indigos are showing up at a time when many of our institutions are changing. The exponential growth of the Internet and prevalence of personal computers mean that more people can easily access knowledge that otherwise was limited to specialized areas of society. Now you can find out just about anything in an instant. It's easy to bust myths when you can Google to the truth, and myth-busting is exactly what Indigos are here to do.

Indigo Children resist structures that no longer make sense, so they will make us question paradigm after paradigm. They insist on a more collaborative approach, whether it's toward world peace or a more effective creative working team.

Naysayers may also wonder if we are just detecting an emerging *zeitgeist*, seeing it first in the children of the era. As a planet, many people believe, we are moving into an age of greater tolerance and compassion; collectively, we are getting experiences that redefine what political and personal power are and how we use it. Where do Indigos fit in? Can Indigo Children be the leaders for this?

Our take on it is that Indigo Children are already way ahead of the emerging zeitgeist. One may argue that because they are children, they are soaking up up-and-coming ideas like a sponge. But it's clear to Wendy from working with Indigo Children and to Carolyn from raising two Indigos that Indigos already come programmed to carry this new sensibility forward. Indigos come into this world with a vision. They are uniquely equipped. They came in knowing how it is supposed to be, and they expect the structures to change to suit them. They are impatient it hasn't already happened.

**def•i•ni•tion**

**Zeitgeist** is a German word that means, quite literally, spirit of the times. It's the prevailing school of thought, and it usually is associated with an ethic for higher ideals, such as, in the case of the Indigos, more tolerance and more spiritual awareness.

## New Ways of Healing

Indigos will continue to usher in the many alternative therapies that have gained credibility in the past two decades—another change that came in as the Indigos were being born. Many more health care professionals are offering alternative therapies for children, and now there are acupuncture specialists and naturopathic physicians who specialize in children, prescribing homeopathic remedies and Chinese herbs.

Indigos will challenge the paradigms of traditional Western medicine—simply by their body's refusal to play the game. They seem to have a built-in brick wall to taking in any more environmental toxins; many have asthma, chronic respiratory allergies, food allergies, and chronic infections. Their bodies are not going to take it anymore, and they will force us to find new solutions.

Out of this, many Indigos will emerge as healers, like Adam, a twenty-something Indigo healer from Vancouver, Canada, who wrote *Dream-healer* (see Appendix B) at age 19 (and only goes by his first name). Adam got noticed in *Rolling Stone* magazine and other print publications in 2002 when, as a pre-med student, he used distance healing on rockabilly star Ronnie Hawkins, who had terminal pancreatic cancer. Hawkins was told it was inoperable and he had three to six months to live. An MRI test eight months after Adam's Reiki treatment revealed Hawkins was cancer-free, according to published reports in *The Manitoban Online* and other media. Hawkins, born in 1935, has continued to perform. Many other Indigos will emerge like Adam, practicing Reiki (or Shamballa) energy healing, acupuncture, herbal medicine, and other methods.

## On the Political Front

Indigos tend not to be political leaders, but those who do emerge as leaders will bring a visionary, collaborative approach to the political structure, forcing it to bend.

Many Indigos may shrink away from politics because they distrust conventional structures, preferring to be reformers from without rather than refiners from within. They came here expecting that change already to have taken place, and they are impatient with waiting for it to change. They tend to become alienated from politics (among those Indigos of voting age), not voting, out of a sense of hopelessness that it hasn't already changed and a dislike for the existing structures in which politics work. Their approach will largely be from the outside, as a catalyst for change. While some Indigos may become lawmakers, governors, presidents, and diplomats, as a whole, Indigos will be more focused on changing institutions that directly affect their lives, such as medicine and education, becoming leaders in those fields.

Indigo leaders of the future will use their gifts to bring people together to innovative and collaborative solutions that serve the higher good. As they grow into these roles (and grow up!), they will tend not to use the force of their personality to get their ideas across, but rather the power of their vision. They will not wield the power of one, but rather the power of consensus. The will bring an innate understanding of tolerance and cooperation to everything they do.

As the twenty-first century unfolds, expect that Indigos will lend their voices to the current dialogue about the changing marriage institution. Because of their tolerant attitude, we may expect that in the next 100 years, the legal contract of marriage may embrace same-sex marriage or may redefine marriage as a renewable contract rather than forever. But Indigos will not only make their mark by being open to unconventional ideas; they also may prove to be a heart-centered bunch, focused on nurturing family, hearth, home, and authentic intimacy. We may also expect that honesty, compassion, and integrity will guide their intimate relationships and the contracts they make around them.

# Creating a New Culture

Creativity is often squelched in our culture, and Indigos won't accept that. They suffer more than most from it. Many Indigos rebel against a highly structured schedule. They will pop out of that bin no matter how many times you try to put them in it and sit the lid. They need unstructured schedules and blocks of uncommitted time.

It may be very difficult for Indigos to manage their time. This is for several reasons, not just the rebellion against structure. In the case of the emotionally sensitive child (like Carolyn's daughter Emerald), it may be that until there is emotional harmony, she can't organize her time. In the case of the attention-deficit hyperactivity disorder child, the struggle with time management may arise from a fragmented focus and susceptibility to distractions.

Yet Indigos are entirely comfortable with their creativity. What they don't like is having to relinquish it to overly structured schedules. They simply don't accept that that's the way things have to be.

Already there is a burgeoning of creativity in our culture, and many economists and public policy pundits such as Richard Florida (*The Rise of the Creative Class*, Appendix B) point to a growing ethic of creativity as one of the strongest factors in driving the economy of the twenty-first century. Florida, a public policy professor at George Mason University, estimates that 38 million Americans—about 30 percent of the workforce—are working in diverse fields in which they work like artists and scientists, working in collaborative teams on creative projects.

We'll talk more about the entrepreneurial and creative bent of Indigos in Chapter 13.

## Work Environment

Indigos will be more entrepreneurial than corporate—they will want to work for themselves, not someone else. Remember, for an Indigo, it's about not wanting to be molded into any structure.

If they do enter the corporate world, expect them to bring that warrior spirit to the office, making sure there is artwork on the walls, adding color to the environment, and influencing the architecture to create more collaborative environments—no sitting at a desk all day. Indigos will have to be up and about, meeting and socializing and collaborating. And they will expect the architecture to facilitate that—no more cubicle-land. Think Canadian-American architect Frank Gehry, known for his sculptural buildings that de-emphasize societal goals in favor of the personal and interpersonal.

> **Indigo Stars**
>
> Alexandra "Alex" Scott was two days from her first birthday when she was diagnosed with an aggressive childhood cancer. At age 4, in 2000, she founded Alex's Lemonade Stand for Pediatric Cancer Research. As of May 2006, the foundation has raised $6 million for child-hood cancer research. Alex, who died in 2004, is an example of the entrepreneurial and healing orientation of many Indigo Children.

Also expect Indigos to want to be cut in on the rule making in the corporate world, just as they want to have a voice in the privileges and responsibilities within the family in which they grow up.

Some Indigos may carry their interest in healing to the workplace, spurring their employers to be more proactive and supportive to alternative and integrative therapies.

## Their Artistic Style

Indigos will leave their stamp on the world of art, developing new disciplines and original styles. Spiritually influenced artwork will come to the fore, as well as multidimensional or metaphysical art, such as fractals or aura work. Expect live theater to become more improvisational, with a more ensemble approach. Indigos will bring a very communal and collaborative style to everything they do, though some will need to be singular sensations, much like comedian Andy Kaufman or Olympic figure skater Johnny Weir.

The same is true of music—more improvisational. Some types of Indigos will tend to play together, with heavy emphasis on percussion or an orientation to the spontaneity and exploration of jazz; others will be solo acts. They may invent new musical instruments as Blue Man Group has done. Remember, they are tuned into energy—and sound— at a whole different level. Indigos may also use music purely for therapy, forming drumming circles, for instance. Some of the more abstract-thinking Indigos and possibly the ADHD Indigos may groove to multi-dimensional music, such as jazz, or atonal, experimental music.

# Spiritual Agents of Change

Because Indigos come into this world tuned to a higher spiritual vibration, they will require us all to adapt to that. They will be the agent of change that forces us to look deeper within, to live the examined life, to seek a relationship with Spirit. They come with a strong sense of integrity, and they expect everyone around them to adhere to their values and convictions.

If you are the parent or teacher of an Indigo, you likely already know. They question every integrity lapse. They want to understand all the exceptions, all the little gray areas. They will hold you to a higher standard.

Wendy has observed that Indigos have a much deeper awareness of the spiritual plane. Indigos already are more open to this, and they accept these concepts more readily than those of us who rely only on cognitive and rational ways of perceiving the world around us.

Indigos are going to make us all more aware of the spirit world. They are showing us that the spiritual plane is not that far away, nor is it fictional. To Indigos, the spiritual world is fused into their world—not a distant, abstract concept. It's something that they experience.

What Albert Einstein sought to prove—the theory that there is a unified field—Indigos accept as true. The superstring theory, for instance, is one that approaches proving Einstein's theory that all matter is in a unified field. That theory, now sometimes called M-theory, says that all subatomic particles are just different resonances of vibrating super-strings.

We will see more bridges being built between science and reli-gion, in the spirit of Einstein's famous statement, "Science without religion is lame, religion without science is blind." We will likely see more books like Mani Bhaumik's *Code Name God: The Spiritual Odyssey of a Man of Science* and the Dalai Lama's *The Universe in a Single Atom: The Convergence of Science and Spirituality* (see Appendix B for both books); and movies like *What the Bleep Do We Know?* (2004).

**Crystal Clear**

Nature shows us only the tail of the lion. But I do not doubt that the lion belongs to it even though he cannot at once reveal himself because of his enormous size.

—Physicist Albert Einstein

## Elemental Understanding

Wendy remembers one boy in public school who devised a highly spiri-tually advanced game based on rock-paper-scissors. The boy was in first grade, and he told her he wanted to invent a game with fire-earth-air-water. He explained to her that fire and wind were stronger than water. It was reminiscent of the Ko, or regulating cycle, in the Chinese elements (fire, metal, wood, earth, water), in which fire melts metal, metal cuts wood, wood can contain the earth, earth absorbs the water. It was all very spiritually enlightened, very advanced for a 6-year-old— a combination of intelligence and creative, critical thinking with higher spiritual awareness.

## A Word About Crystal Children

You may have already read about Crystal Children, the next wave of spiritually evolved children. Indigos are here as catalysts, to change the world and bring it to a higher spiritual awareness. They have a warrior spirit.

Crystal Children, who are beginning only now to arrive, are here as spiritual healers—in other words, to temper the blow as the Indigos come into their own and start to effect change. Crystals have pure, white energy that may reflect all the colors of the rainbow much like a prism or quartz crystal, and they are here as soothers and healers—so the changes the Indigos bring can come about with more compassion, in a much gentler way. Crystals are more even-tempered than Indigos, while simultaneously being more fragile.

Crystal Children have a higher group consciousness, rather than the highly individualized expression of Indigos. They are believed to be a powerful force for global love and peace.

Often, a Crystal will be born into a family with an Indigo child. One child will be the leader in the family and the rebellious spirit, while the other may be the peacemaker in the family. Can you guess which is which? The first is the Indigo and the second one is the Crystal.

Many people believe that some Indigos can evolve to Crystals, and that some adults will evolve to incorporate many Indigo and Crystal traits. Crystal Children are primarily those born after the year 2000, though some children seem to be blends of Indigo-Crystal.

# Riding the Wave

Clearly, big changes are ahead for all of us, not just the parents, educators, and counselors who will know these children in the early years of their lives. By understanding this wave in human evolution, we can better equip Indigos to do what they are here to do.

## The Least You Need to Know

- ◆ Indigos are here to raise the planet to a higher vibration.
- ◆ Alternative schooling such as homeschooling, Montessori, Waldorf, and Reggio Emilia are among the many types that will flourish because of Indigo Children.
- ◆ Indigos come in already understanding the emerging zeitgeist of tolerance, openness, and more humanitarianism.

◆ Indigos will demand, expect, and develop more holistic and integrative healing.

◆ Indigos are too nonconformist by nature to be politicians, preferring to be reformers, not refiners, but they will bring about change in other ways.

◆ Crystal Children are coming in after Indigos. They are deeply spiritual and are here as healers.

# Part 2

# Indigo's Unique Challenges ... and Unique Gifts

Indigo Children defy categorization. If there is any constant in the definition of an Indigo, it's that the attributes they possess stretch the ends of the spectrum. One Indigo can be highly emotionally sensitive, while another might be wildly angry, and another exceptionally psychic. They can be brilliant, imaginative, and compassionate, or they can be distracted, defiant, and impulsive. And this can be all in the same child ... on the same day. Clearly, they are gifted, but they face unique challenges.

# Chapter 3

# Highs and Lows

## In This Chapter

- ◆ Feeling it all: high sensitivity
- ◆ Creating an energy shield
- ◆ Gotta move: high physical activity
- ◆ Low physical activity and depression

Fine, you might say, I understand that Indigos can be charming and very bright, and it's very noble that they might change the world. But they can also be impossible to live with.

Many Indigos can be precocious and gregarious. They may have an unlimited curiosity about the world. They expect to be active and engaged. Who can keep up with them? Other Indigos are so open to all the information they are receiving—on the physical, mental, emotional, and spiritual levels—that they feel things deeply. You may find it hard to keep up with their feelings. Still others may withdraw or become depressed.

With an Indigo, it's either high or it's low. Here's how to live with them.

# Really Tuned In: High Sensitivity

Many Indigos are like a field of radio towers. They are taking in all signals on all levels—physical, mental, emotional, and spiritual—all the time. Your Indigo could be highly physically sensitive or emotionally sensitive or both.

This fits in with being an Indigo. Indigos are almost always extreme. They hang out at one or both ends of the spectrum. Very rarely will they be average in any category.

# Emotional Sensitivity

Many mornings, Carolyn's 7-year-old daughter Emerald will resist going to school by dawdling. Sometimes she can take a full hour even to get around to getting dressed. Her daughter says things like, "The kids were mean at school yesterday" or "(So-and-so) doesn't want to be my friend anymore" or "I don't have any friends at school." Yet when Carolyn drops off her twins at school, her daughter is greeted with a swarm of girls who want to hold her hand and make her their special friend for the day.

When the first-grade teacher told Carolyn that Emerald always seemed to know the work, but sometimes had trouble completing assignments on time, that provided another piece of the puzzle. Then Emerald's second-grade teacher said Emerald would be an excellent candidate for the gifted program if only she could focus less on her friends and more on class work. When Carolyn checked it out, she learned that Emerald was trying to help every other kid around her with class work, coaching them about writing.

Carolyn's daughter is a harmonizer. She is so tuned in emotionally to what's going on with her classmates that she has to take care of their emotions before she can do her own work. She has taken on an extra job—making sure everybody else is happy—in order to protect herself.

Emotional sensitivity is often high in Indigos. They are wide open to other people's energy. They are going to feel the dominant emotional energy in whatever room they enter. Some might take on that energy and not recognize that it's someone else's. For example, when parents fight, often the child can take on the anger.

According to Elaine N. Aron, author of *The Highly Sensitive Child* (see Appendix B), highly sensitive children account for 15 to 20 percent of the population. These children are highly aware and quick to detect subtle emotional changes. They are easily affected by others' emotions.

Other highly sensitive Indigos can cry at the drop of a hat. It doesn't matter if it's an appropriate time or place. Others direct their angst outward, flying into a rage. Still other children become manic with joy, bubbling over. And some Indigos may have all those emotional outbursts at different times or even almost all at once. Wendy recalls as a child going from laughter to tears of sadness in seconds, or into a fit of rage, or as quickly from a rage into tears and then almost as rapidly, into joyful energy.

Overexcitability is a decidedly Indigo trait. Polish psychologist Kazimierz Dabrowski (1902–1980) developed the Theory of Overexcitabilities, which described children with a high abundance of energy and what he called supersensitivities. He observed that gifted children had an abundance of these intense reactions to stimulus. He broke them down into the following categories:

◆ Psychomotor (surplus of physical energy)

◆ Sensual (heightened sensory awareness)

◆ Emotional (exceptional sensitivity)

◆ Intellectual (an active mind)

◆ Imaginational (lots of free play, vivid dreams and fantasies)

Indigos will most commonly demonstrate overexcitability in imagination, sensory response, and emotions. This theory is gaining more attention at conferences on gifted children and with organizations such as Supporting the Emotional Needs of the Gifted (SENG; www.sengifted.org).

Just as Indigos take in a lot more energy than the average child, they also can project out a lot of energy and affect a whole room full of people. Sometimes they can be bright, dazzling lights; other times, they can be black holes, sucking all positive energy out of a room. Just imagine the kind of challenge this presents to a teacher who has five or six Indigos in the classroom—or more.

If you have a child like this:

◆ Help her shield herself from others' energy.

◆ Give her opportunities to talk about her emotions and release what she's feeling.

◆ Release her from the job description. Help her understand she doesn't have to take care of everyone else's emotions every day. She can take care of herself without having to take care of other people first.

◆ Don't make her attend social events that are truly optional, especially if her emotions are raw that day.

### Good Counsel

An energy shield will help your child through times of high sensitivity. To help your child create an energy shield, lead her through a guided meditation. Ask her to sit quietly, close her eyes, and imagine her center; you may want to use a symbol to help her imagine this, such as a butterfly, a golden orb, or a sparkling spider web. Guide her in imagining her body connected to earth as well as connected to Spirit. Help her imagine a sphere of light around her body that creates a force field that will protect her. As she practices this, let her fill in the picture of what this force field looks like and how it moves. Encourage her to envision the force field in action, with color and light. Ask her to draw it later. This will help her remember it.

A guided-image energy shield may help protect your child from these extreme emotional highs and lows. Many Indigo Children are so emotionally sensitivity that they haven't developed a shield, or if they have, it's very thin.

Wendy has worked with children to develop their own energy shield. The simple act of visualizing a force field in your mind will activate it. She advises children on how to put it into action, projecting it out and empowering it. The children Wendy works with often develop multiple layers to their energy shield visions. There can be a layer to manifest things, another layer for luck. Some children have a "KEEP OUT" layer.

Some children imagine their energy shields like machines, with in-out valves. One 10-year-old boy Wendy worked with had a silver chrome energy shield that shot out lasers like a video game. Sometimes his energy field would project out roses for love to his family. His energy field was abundant and had many layers, but your child's does not have to be. The energy field doesn't need to be complicated to be effective. Your child only has to believe in it and activate it.

The mother of the boy with the silver chrome energy field reported to Wendy that it worked and he loved it! She and her son would use the visualization in the morning, and suddenly the problems that came up every day during the morning getting-out-of-the-house drill dissipated. The rage beneath the struggles was gone. They were able to generate a successful energy shield—one that shut out negative energy but did not leave the boy shut down. Instead, he felt protected and empowered.

**Patience**

Energy shielding can be an effective technique for many of the challenges Indigos face, but it's important for your child not to completely shield himself. Your child's force field should be more like an eggshell—permeable but still keeping unwanted energy out. If the child shuts down entirely, he or she may not be able to feel love or show compassion. A filtered shield will allow Indigo Children to be protected, but still connected to others.

# High Physical Sensitivity

High physical sensitivity often goes hand-in-hand with emotional sensitivity, but not necessarily. A child with high physical sensitivity has a greater awareness of all information on all sensory levels—sight, hearing, taste, touch, and smell. All of this fits together with being more open. A high physical sensitivity child is more aware of how everything interacts with her—body, mind, and spirit.

Wendy notes that if the toe seam is off line in her sock, it will drive her nuts, but her husband would be oblivious if his socks weren't on straight or even if they were the same kind of socks at all. Carolyn remembers as a child, walking downtown with her grandmother and insisting that she couldn't take another step because of the way her sock was crammed in her shoe. And Carolyn's daughter is the same way, too—a regular "Princess and the Pea," who can feel the pea beneath a ceiling-high stack of mattresses. Carolyn's daughter will complain about clothing tags scratching her skin, and frequently gets rashes unless Carolyn uses Dove soap in the bath and Dreft in the laundry.

Many of the people listed on a website (www.sensitiveliving.com/famousHSP.htm) as highly sensitive people are Indigos, including poet Emily Dickinson; comedians/actors Andy Kaufman and Jim Carrey; and painters Leonardo DaVinci, Vincent van Gogh, and Salvador Dali. Also highly sensitive (and possibly Indigo) are film director Woody Allen; poets Sylvia Plath, Anne Sexton, and William Butler Yeats; musicians Tori Amos, Enya, Bjork, and John Lennon; and visionaries such as mythologist Joseph Campbell, the Dalai Lama, and Marianne Williamson. Then there is one real-life princess: Princess Diana.

Wendy says she's not sure she'd want to change this blessing of high sensitivity about herself, though it was a challenge when she was a small child. If chocolate tastes better to her than the average person, she wants to appreciate that gift. Possessing a highly refined sense of taste or smell truly is a gift in most situations, except maybe when you get sprayed by a skunk. It's a double-edged sword, so help your child learn to appreciate the positive aspects. If your child fits this description, you could have a future culinary whiz or *Consumer Reports* mattress tester on your hands.

### Indigo Stars

Mahatma Gandhi was highly physically and emotionally sensitive. As a boy, he ran home from school to avoid hearing the other boys make fun of him. As a young husband, he had to sleep with the light on because he feared the darkness. He also was highly sensitive to food.

The first step to handling your prince is to help him appreciate the gift. You must learn to accept it, not change it. (Take this from Carolyn, who can remember her own sensitivity but still has to remind herself not to change her daughter.) You can make small adaptations that will improve both of your lives greatly. You are not spoiling your child. Indigo Children don't perceive the world as you do, unless perhaps, you're an Indigo adult.

When parents struggle to accept their child's high physical sensitivity, Wendy relates an analogy she used with a parent of two children. One child was physically sensitive, but the other was not. She asked the parent to think of the sensitive child as a raw egg, the other a hard-boiled egg. If you drop a hard-boiled egg, the eggshell cracks. But if you drop a raw egg, the eggshell shatters and the yolk spills. Some children can hold up to adversity and show only a few cracks; others are devastated.

By the way, Indigos tend to have more food allergies than the average child. Most of them are to chemical additives. Many Indigos are very sensitive to sugar. Highly processed foods, foods high in monosodium glutamate, better known as MSG, milk with growth hormones—all of these hit an Indigo hard. Many Indigos do best on an organic, whole foods diet. We'll go further in depth about nutrition in Chapter 15.

### Good Counsel

If your child insists that scratchy clothing labels are torture, you may end her suffering without losing the information on the tag. Don't just cut off the tag or rip it out; it's best to remove the stitches holding the tag using manicure scissors rather than leave the stub of a tab, which may scratch more. Take the tag and affix it to a notebook, making notes about which shirt it goes with. That way, you have all the laundering instructions and the size. And you have a much happier child. (Also, some clothing manufacturers make tagless garments.)

Nutrition is yet another way Indigos are forcing our society to change. Indigos' bodies simply won't accept the way we are growing, producing, and processing our food. It's not healthy for them. The Organic Center's second State of Science Review estimates that cancer-fighting antioxidants are 30 percent higher in organic foods. The global market for organic foods was expected to increase from $26 billion in 2001 to $80 billion in 2008. In the United States, sales of organic food increased 19 percent from 2000 to 2001 and were expected to increase another 30 percent by 2008.

Another type of physical sensitivity that many Indigos seem to experience is that of electrical sensitivity. Many will be uneasy during a thunderstorm or feel a buildup of excess energy they need to release. These Indigos will blow out light bulbs at almost twice the expected rate merely by sitting near them, or they may notice that streetlights go out as they walk under them. Similarly, some children are so "charged" that electrical appliances in the house short out in their presence.

# Frustration: It's My Party, and I'll Cry If I Want To

Indigo Children have high expectations of themselves. They come into this world believing they deserve to be here, and they often have an inner sense of their purpose. Yet they are still children with limited physical capabilities. They are developed mentally and spiritually, but not emotionally and physically. Often, this is a recipe for frustration.

Indigos have very little patience with themselves and with others. Because they are creative, imaginative, and smart, they expect other children to keep up. Because many of them are unconventional, they are smart, but misunderstood. It's frustrating to know on the inside that you're smart, but understand on one level that it's not apparent to the rest of the world. This is the peculiar frustration of Indigos who don't do well in school because they resist the structure and/or have learning disabilities.

Often children channel their frustration toward one end of the spectrum or the other—high physical activity or low physical activity.

## High Physical Activity

Some Indigo children are hyperactive. They are go-go-go. They have abundant energy, but they don't necessarily know where to channel it. These Indigos operate at high volume. They have a wider amplitude of emotions, and they express them in a big way. When they jump, they jump high.

They may have trouble focusing, unless they are doing something physical simultaneously. Wendy saw a recent report that children with

ADHD who knit in the classroom are able to stay more focused and attentive to the lesson, so this may be an idea for high physical energy Indigos, too.

Indigos with high physical energy swing fast from highs to lows. They are spirited. They can be exasperating. Along with this goes more creativity, more risk-taking. They can be dramatic or explosive or grand. They can be charismatic—or manipulative. They are often opinionated, and they may show leadership abilities. These are the future rock stars or governors among the Indigos.

When Indigo Children are happy, they glow. Your job as a parent is to find productive ways to channel this into physical energy. Your child will need to be outdoors, and you will likely want him or her to take up a sport.

## Low Physical Activity

Other Indigos have low physical activity. They are so overwhelmed with the quantity and magnitude of information they are taking in that they are in a state of emotional and physical paralysis. They walk around as though their cup is too full and they are afraid they will spill over if they take in another drop of information. Many of these children are autistic, have Asperger's syndrome, or are very depressed.

 **Crystal Clear**

> Bitter are the tears of a child: Sweeten them.
>
> Deep are the thoughts of a child: Quiet them.
>
> Sharp is the grief of a child: Take it from him.
>
> Soft is the heart of a child: Do not harden it.
>
> —Author Pamela Glenconner

These children may be frustrated about not being able to change their world, and they turn it inward, in the form of depression. The depression Indigos experience is primarily existential—"why am I here?" They wonder what their purpose is here on Earth and why they have to endure the life they are living. These Indigos feel disconnected from purpose. Their physical and emotional frustrations have piled up. They feel like caged birds.

You can help your Indigo by facilitating his or her spiritual and psychic connections. A good balance is key. Children with low physical activity levels may feel better about themselves and the world if they begin some regular exercise they enjoy such as swimming, karate, outdoor games, or body-mind movement such as tai chi or yoga. This would give them more energy, reduce depression, and let them feel more productive.

Naturally, if your child is beyond feeling blue, and you think he may be depressed, you should seek the attention of a health care professional.

# Calming the Storm

With Indigos who fall into these extremes, your focus as a parent is in tempering them. Start by appreciating your Indigo for who he is, focusing on the strengths of these traits. Begin building your Indigo's skills so she can gradually start setting healthy boundaries for herself, knowing to ask for what she needs to gain ease with any situation.

## The Least You Need to Know

- Indigos often fall in the extreme ends of the spectrum. Some can be highly sensitive, while others can be highly insensitive or shut down.

- Many Indigos care so much about creating harmony in their environments that they take on too much of other people's energy. Energy shielding can protect them.

- Simple modifications can help your highly sensitive Indigo be more comfortable in her daily life.

- High physical activity Indigos may have difficulty focusing and controlling their behavior unless they have a physical outlet.

- Teach your low physical activity Indigo ways to enjoy light movement, such as tai chi or yoga.

- Remember that many highly emotionally sensitive Indigos are artistic and creative.

# Chapter 4

# A Peculiar Anger

## In This Chapter

- ◆ Where does the anger come from?
- ◆ Rage: releasing the pain
- ◆ Unconditional love: restoring the calm
- ◆ Gut-check: examine your own anger

All children get angry, and of course we must help them learn to manage their anger. But with Indigos, the anger seems to go deeper. It's more than a defiant child trying to figure out how to exercise her will on her world. The anger of an Indigo child has at its root a sense of injustice. It's a very peculiar anger, indeed.

Let's examine this anger and look at ways to manage it more effectively.

## A Great Divide

Indigo Children seem to have come into this world with a strong sense of how things should be. They understand somehow that the systems in place are not at their peak functionality. They know it, and they experience it. And because they are small, there's only so much they can do about it.

If your Indigo's anger feels like outrage, you are probably right. An important place to start in understanding your child's anger is getting a good fix on what your Indigo perceives is not right about his world. All in all, your task is to transform anger into love. If you address Indigos' defiance at that level, it will change the energy into a loving focus.

Here are some of the sources of the anger for Indigos:

♦ The world they live in has not yet reached the point of spiritual advancement they expect.

♦ The structures of society must change to accommodate this spiritual advancement. Paradigms must shift.

♦ The structures of society do not serve them—they do not take into account each individual's uniqueness and creativity, and do not promote tolerance and compassion.

♦ They have a baseline understanding of how things should be, but they can't articulate it yet and they aren't in a position to change it without some help from you.

♦ They are spiritually and mentally mature, but emotionally and physically immature. They are impatient about the time and effort required for those aspects to catch up—the growing-up process.

♦ In some cases, they have shut down their ability to empathize. They feel shut off from the feelings of others and from their own feelings.

On a deeper level, Indigos know they are here to change the way things are. They know that the systems in place are not functioning at peak. They know they are charged with changing those systems. They are impatient that it's not happening yet and don't want to wait for the time—when they are grown up—when they can usher in change.

Many Indigos resist being spiritual beings in a physical body. You have to remember—that's an adjustment for them. Until this point in time, they have been just spirits. These Indigos may be awkward in their bodies. They may be so cerebral that they are clumsy, and their gross motor skills may lag behind. These Indigos are in a bit of a state of shock at discovering they must live and dwell in these bodies that get banged and scraped so easily.

Other Indigos—especially the ones with highly tuned psychic abilities—may feel so connected to Spirit that they just don't understand those who are not. Being able to experience that connection to Spirit so naturally makes it difficult for these Indigos to understand why everyone can't be that way. One thing you can certainly do for them is to strengthen your own connection with Spirit, making a point to tend to that area of your life more. If this doesn't feel natural to you, be open and let them teach you.

**Patience**

Indigo Children are often physically and psychically sensitive, which means that when they're angry, they can feel the energy much more strongly than the average child. The energy reverberates. They also are highly aware of their angry thoughts and those of people around them. As young children, they may fear the power of these angry thoughts, and this may further fuel their outrage. Remember when they are angry, they are deeply scared. A hug may be just the thing to bring down the energy.

What presents a challenge for the grown-ups in an Indigo's life is that this isn't run-of-the-mill anger. It comes up as rage. The emotions can play out big. So let's try to understand the ways the anger comes out.

## Compression and Release

Many Indigo Children shut down their emotions to protect themselves. When they do, they lose their connection to other people, and that hurts. The energy of the emotion becomes compressed inside them, and it doesn't have a way to be released because they have lost touch with their feelings. This can feel very frightening.

To help your Indigo child, look for ways to channel the energy into positive outlets—physical activity or a creative project. This channels anger into a positive form—something less to be feared. It helps your Indigo to feel more comfortable with the fierceness of the anger. You are training your child to use anger as a productive force, not a destructive one.

To prevent anger from building up ...

◆ Give them regular physical activity.

◆ Give them creative outlets.

◆ Let them speak their minds. Create an open forum.

When anger does erupt ...

◆ Teach them to take a "time out," or a "calm down."

◆ Remove the audience. For example, if the rage comes up in the grocery store, remove the child from the store.

◆ Follow through. Have them write down the issues they want to talk about. Make sure to address them at a family meeting.

### Crystal Clear

Anger is a great force. If you control it, it can be transmuted into a power which can move the whole world.

—Scottish writer William Shenstone

In Carolyn's house, the "time out" became a "calm down." Time out was too connected to punishment—a failure in her son's mind and something imposed from outside (the parent decides when this is necessary and how it will be done). Reframing the technique as "calm down" helped Lucas see it as taking care of himself. It's still often imposed by the parent, but as Lucas matures, it's something he chooses as a way to manage his feelings.

Creating an open forum will work for prevention and damage control. When Wendy taught in a second-grade classroom, she had a clipboard mounted to the wall where kids could raise issues. She would check in regularly, asking, "Is this still an issue for you?" Sometimes the two or three days of waiting until the meeting would allow the issue to be resolved on its own, or the children would make an extra effort to resolve it. Other times, the same issue would come up every week.

Buddhist teacher Thich Nhat Hanh recommends a similar practice in his book, *Anger* (see Appendix B). He advises couples to set aside Friday evenings to talk about any conflicts that come up during the week. The two people agree that on that evening, they will address any unresolved conflicts. They will take the time out of their schedules to listen actively to each other.

Set up a regular, consistent time to meet as a family. Designate one parent to be the organizer, setting the agenda (and change roles every so often). Doing this regularly and consistently assures your child that he can bring up a topic and it will be handled. He can trust when he hears "Okay, I understand you have strong feelings, but let's start to calm down now so we can look at this" that you will follow through—and it's imperative that you do. Sticking with it will go a long way to calming his frustrations and fears. Also be willing to have emergency meetings if necessary, following a similar agenda.

## Physical Solutions

Carolyn's Indigo son Lucas is easygoing and gregarious—most of the time. Sometimes anger builds up, and he rages. When this happens, he just can't get unstuck. Talking to him doesn't work. He's in a funk, and he's spitting angry. It became clear to Carolyn that he needed a physical release of the anger energy, so she gave him two techniques—the Anger Dance and Legs-on-Wall, a yoga pose.

The Anger Dance amounts to stomping, jumping, running fast and hard in a circle, pounding a pillow, and screaming, "I'm angry! I'm angry! I'm so mad!" All Lucas has to do is keep it up until he doesn't have any more energy. This worked quite well when he was toddler and preschool age, because the anger was beyond his capacity for words. Now that Lucas is 7, Carolyn adds more talking it out. After he's calm, the two of them (or three of them, if the dispute involved his twin sister, which it often does) meet at the two pillars in the foyer of their house. They sit across from one another. Each person gets a chance to speak and takes a turn listening.

Yoga offers many poses, called asanas, that can calm your body, mind, and spirit, and you'll see in coming chapters that we recommend them often. In the case of anger, yoga can create a place of safety in the body

## Good Counsel

Set up a raves and rants box. Of course, it is human nature to rant about something that's wrong rather than take the time to rave about what's going right. But let your child (or children) make this their place to speak their minds. Have regular, consistent family meetings, and set an agenda that includes time for the raves and rants.

that allows the anger to emerge in a less volatile way. Let's remember the anger is trying to tell us something. Creating a sense of peace in the body is a way to create a safe place so you can concentrate on hearing that message.

Legs-on-Wall is a yoga pose Carolyn does with Lucas for calming. It's worth trying, even if it means marking up your wall. The two of them, mother and son, lie on the floor side-by-side with their legs extended up the wall, taking in deep breaths and releasing. There is no talking.

This is a good preventative or restorative pose. It might not work in the heat of the moment, but if you sense some anger and frustration building in your child, Legs-On-Wall is a good one to do. It can be particularly effective as a routine pose to do when you arrive home if you know your child is prone to anger after a long day at school, or is quite simply a grump. Add in your tough day at work and nasty traffic on the way home, and you may both need this inversion pose as a transition. Inversion is the key word here. Your blood flows in a different direction. Your head is below your heart. Being partly upside down helps you calm your body and mind and often leads to a spiritual shift in perception.

Another yoga asana that Wendy recommends is called Cleansing or Woodchopper Breath. In this pose, you are pretending to chop wood. Stand with your feet about hip width apart. Interlock your fingers and raise them overhead. Fall forward, breathing out with a "ha!" Let your arms swing back through your legs. Your knees should be slightly bent. Inhale, lifting your arms overhead. Repeat three times. CAUTION: Avoid this pose if either one of you has high or low blood pressure.

# Vocal Solutions

Giving your child permission to scream—as in the Angry Dance—can be a good way to release tension. It's not culturally acceptable to be angry; admitting that from time to time we *are* angry can be a big relief for your child. Vocalization works well with Carolyn's daughter Emerald because she's highly verbal (likes to talk), kinesthetic (likes to move), and musical (likes to sing). Emerald sometimes screams and then she's over it.

Drumming can help, too. Drumming is proving to provide significant health benefits as well as being effective therapy. In *The Healing Power of the Drum* (see Appendix B), psychotherapist Robert Lawrence Friedman presented research that showed benefits for at-risk adolescents, stressed-out employees, Vietnam veterans, and people with Alzheimer's disease, Parkinson's disease, and multiple sclerosis. He says drumming brings us back to simplicity, linking us back to a time before technology separated us from our souls. It releases negative emotions and anchors the drummer in the here and now. Friedman believes drumming works because it increases Alpha brain waves, which increase one's sense of well-being.

# Creative Solutions

It's good to channel your Indigo's anger into a creative project. You might see some angst in the creative work, but that is quite necessary for the process of releasing feelings of anger so that these angry feelings don't become rage out of control.

Your child can channel angry energy into visual art, a poem, or a journal. It doesn't matter if it's full of angst—likely it will be—just let it out.

**Patience**

If you sense your child or teen's art, poetry, or journaling is full of too much angst, don't dismiss your misgivings. If it feels disturbing to you, it probably is. Trust your intuition. While you want your child or teen to express herself, you are responsible for making sure the exploration doesn't go too far off the deep end. Talk to your child or teen. Seek professional help.

# How Love Can Transform Anger

One of the most loving steps you can take with your child is sending her the message that anger is not bad. It's informing her that something is out of balance. It's what you do with the anger that's important.

Rage is an unfocused energy—a violent and uncontrolled anger or a fit of violent wrath—burning out of control. It comes from a very intense feeling—of outrage, of not being heard—and it is closely linked to a deep fear, something that feels more like terror inside. It's only with love that you can begin to focus rage. First, use the techniques previously mentioned to cool the flames. Then, in love, with your child, begin to focus the anger and attempt to resolve it.

This will be a process, not a one-time event. Remember from the first part of this chapter how deep the anger might go. That's not easy to articulate or understand, even for a grown-up, much less a child. But you can begin to focus it on specific instances where your child sees that things aren't right or aren't working for him. By acknowledging that it's hard when this thing isn't right, you have taken a big step. Empathy goes a long way.

You can help your Indigo by listening, letting her tell you how she sees her world, without correcting her or judging her. If it doesn't feel right or good to her, it doesn't. She's the authority on that. Telling her to ignore it or adapt or assimilate won't work. Her feelings about whatever is happening must be acknowledged before she can be willing to adapt.

## Hugs, Hugs, and More Hugs

Sometimes your child simply needs to be held. It probably won't work in the heat of the moment. But hugging your child every day can build up love and trust and lay the groundwork for honest, open, respectful communication.

In Carolyn's home, she and the twins call it "filling up the love tank." Carolyn's twins know that she will check in with them at the beginning or end of the day to ask whether their love tank is getting low. Her daughter will often hold her hand low near her ankles, wearing a sad face. "My love tank is down to here. My brother's getting all of the attention."

If your child's anger is not physically or emotionally violent, you may want to reach out and hug him when he's raging. You don't need to say anything. Just love him. Carolyn found this worked well with her son when he blew up at soccer practice. He had lost his temper the week before at practice, ardently and articulately (and unceasingly) arguing his point, which was about a perceived injustice. Carolyn and her son discussed in advance some calm-down techniques to use the next time a similar situation came up. The next time, Carolyn came over to Lucas and invited him to go on a walk with her. They didn't talk about why he was angry. She merely walked with him, her hand gently on his shoulder. They were connected. Not talking about it right at that moment shifted her highly verbal son's focus to the physical activity of walking and the light touch from his mother. When they returned to the field, he was ready to practice again.

Touch or hugs can work with children who are not too physically sensitive or physically active. But often if your child has high physical sensitivity, a hug will set off all of the alarm bells, as is sometimes the case with Carolyn's daughter. And if your child is highly physically active, it may feel confining when so much physical energy is pent up. That child may need to run it off. The best course of action depends on your child. Trust your intuitive knowledge. Let that guide you.

## Listening

Empathic listening can go a long way to keeping anger from building up. Listen without engaging—getting wrapped up in dispensing parental advice or presenting solutions. Reflect back what your child is saying. One day, Carolyn's son was getting worked up about finding his swim goggles. He was convinced his life was going to be ruined if he did not find them. He was grouchy and touchy and snapping at his mother and sister. He alternated between the blame game and a woe-is-me lament. But the solution was this simple: Carolyn said, "I hear that your goggles are important to you today. I'm sure we can find them, especially now that we know how much you need them." Her son was relieved when he understood Carolyn knew his concern was important. After that, all of them were part of the solution. And guess what … they found the goggles in the next place they looked!

Don't argue with the anger. Instead ask, "What do you need, and how can I help you?" Sometimes the response is simple, "I'm sorry that happened." Honor that you hear your child. Make sure she knows you're listening. "That's an interesting idea. I'm sure we can talk about it later." (And be sure to do it!)

## A Word About Anger and Rage

The difference between anger and rage is that the energy of rage gets bigger and becomes more chaotic. Often, rage is an unfocused release.

If you could see the aura around a person who is in a rage, there would likely be a red shell. Or there can be energy shooting out like fire. Sometimes the aura is black and red. Sometimes, the rage is so palpable you can even feel it. If the rage is being directed to you, it can almost feel like arrows or spears being chucked at you.

> **Indigo Stars**
>
> Perhaps it's more accurate to call them "fallen" Indigo stars: one of the best-known examples of angry, hurt Indigos are Eric Harris and Dylan Klebold, the teens who carried out a shooting massacre at Columbine High School in Littleton, Colorado, on April 20, 1999, killing 12 students and a teacher. The event kicked off a debate about violence in film and video games, as well as gun control. The inner turmoil that led to their actions gives us insight into the peculiar anger of Indigos at its most extreme.

What it feels like on the inside, to the Indigo, is like a heat rising in the body. It's like a writhing snake rising up through the spine. Some children describe rage exploding like a firework.

When your child explodes, you can't grab back the energy. Let it explode and dissipate, then help your child restore his center.

Use this three-step process:

1. Help your child recognize the thoughts that were irrational. Listen to his fears without judgment. But put those fears into perspective without discounting them.

2. Help your child recognize he did have a point. The rage might have gotten out of control, but he and you together may need to address a certain problem.

3. Devise some action steps. Come up with tasks or assignments that he can do to address the problem.

Many of these techniques take much effort and patience to take hold. If you have a child who is in a rage much of the time, it may take time before you turn the tide. And don't be afraid to think outside of the box. We know one family that solved its challenge by combining these techniques with nutritional therapy.

## How You're Feeling

It's important as a parent to take note of your own experience around your child's rage. Indigo parents often feel confused, frustrated, and guilty. Rage is a powerful emotion, and it can trigger a lot in us to be in its presence. It can be frightening.

Many parents feel helpless around their child's anger. Carolyn knows one Indigo parent who was so near the end of her rope during yet another episode of her 6-year-old child's rage that she was minutes from checking him into the inpatient psychiatric clinic. That's how terrifying it can be to live with something that you don't understand and can't control.

### Patience

You need to keep yourself and your family intact. You and your spouse are the emotional foundation of the home on which your child depends. It's important to restore your home life to equilibrium, because these angry episodes affect you, your marriage, other siblings, even your pets. If you feel you can't go it alone, seek professional help. It's important to gather as much information, resources, and allies as you can.

Parents often feel very responsible for what's happening—that is, that they may have caused it. Parents need to understand that their child's anger is not their fault, and it's not a criticism of their parenting, as much as it might feel that way. It can become super-volatile when parents let their own anger be sparked. In some marriages, it can be divisive, when each parent blames the other for the child's behavior.

Don't let yourself go there. Remember first that the source of the anger is about something beyond your parenting, even if the trigger may have been something related to you. It's about having a strong spiritual sense that Indigo Children must deal with and change what is here—and they just don't like it.

The best thing you can do for your angry Indigo is work on yourself. If you find your child's rages shake loose some personal issues for you, or if they put undue strain on your marriage, get some support.

## Choices and Rules

An Indigo child's anger is a cry for love and respect. It's a message that she feels helpless. Indigos want to be seen as equals even though they are younger physically and immature emotionally. When they do not feel respect, it sets them off. Children and parents get into a stalemate when children are saying things like "Why aren't you listening to me?" or "You don't respect me. Why should I respect you?" and parents are saying things like "You don't know what you're talking about. You're just a kid."

But don't go there. To react that way is to take your child's frustration personally. What your child is asking for is a voice, to have his feelings and opinions heard and respected. Allowing your child to have a voice doesn't mean he gets to make the choice. You give him limits, and you determine the consequences of exceeding those limits. Within those limits, he makes choices. The level of choices depends on his age and development.

Let's say your child gets it in his head that you must take him to the amusement park *today*. But you know that he has swimming lessons, and his sister has a soccer game, and somewhere in there you have to get to the grocery store so you can make dinner tonight. You can calculate the time commitment, and you know there's a crunch. But your child's logic is that the amusement park is right on the way to his sister's soccer game, and he asks every time.

Walk your child through the choices and the consequences of those choices. Start with empathy ("I know that the amusement park looks like lots of fun, and I'd love to do that with you someday"). Up front, set limits on the choices, explaining the logic behind the boundary ("Our schedule is committed today"). What are the consequences of those choices, and why are they important? Why is his sister's soccer game important? Why is dinner important? Let your child take part of the process by brainstorming solutions, knowing the limit ("if not today, then maybe tomorrow" he might say). Empower him in the decision-making, and he will not feel so helpless or angry about the situation ("so if we were going to pick another day, which day could we pick when we wouldn't be so busy?").

# Radio Signals

Anger is a signal that something is out of balance, and while you cannot change the world that feels out of balance to your prescient Indigo child, you can equip him to navigate that world. Help your child learn to set boundaries and develop good anger management techniques, and give her lots of love, and you'll find you have a child who can channel her sense of justice in productive ways.

## The Least You Need to Know

- ♦ The root of anger in Indigo Children very often is a disappointment that the world's current systems lag behind their expectations.

- ♦ Channel the powerful energy of your child's anger into physical activity or creative projects.

- ♦ Listen to your child with respect so he knows he has been heard.

- ♦ Teach your child body-mind relaxation exercises to use as a way to head off or calm down anger.

- ♦ Always let your child know that anger is healthy and normal, but teach her that it's an emotion that needs to be expressed appropriately.

- ♦ Be aware of your own response to your child's anger, noticing what it triggers in you, and be responsible to yourself to address what is out of balance for you.

# Chapter 5

# ADHD and Learning Disabilities

## In This Chapter

- ◆ Indigo? ADHD? Or both?
- ◆ Characteristics of ADHD
- ◆ Other learning challenges
- ◆ Alternative solutions for ADHD

Not all Indigo Children have ADHD; nor are all ADHD kids Indigo Children. What is certain is that Indigo Children's brains are wired differently. These children can be exceptionally and unconventionally brilliant, yet many of them have difficulty learning in school.

Teachers may describe these Indigos as arrogant, distracted, or bright but unfocused and sometimes disruptive. These Indigos— whether it's ADD/ADHD, autism/Asperger's or dyslexia— possess some very special attributes, including a novel approach to solving problems. With some key strategies, you can learn how to channel your child's potential.

# Not Fitting In

With Indigo Children, it's built in to their core that they will not fit in with structures that exist. They are by their very nature nonconformists. This means the way their minds operate is quite different—and often means ADD/ADHD, autism/Asperger's, or a learning disability such as dyslexia is present. While ADD/ADHD is not a learning disability, it often results in learning difficulties. However, we're not so sure we even want to use the term learning disability so much as learning "diffability"—*learning differently from the norm.*

Indigos tend to have a higher sensitivity, lots of energy, and bore easily, when means they can appear to have a short attention span—traits associated with ADD/ADHD. Not all Indigos are ADD/ADHD, which means that some Indigos have the ability to channel their excess energy. These Indigos direct their high sensitivity into tuning in to other people's emotions, as well as cultivating their inner life or psychic awareness. Or, if they have lots of energy, it's channeled into exploration. They may love to explore the garden or go for a hike, returning with bugs, flowers, peacock feathers—you name it. Or if they bore easily, they pour their creative energy into many endeavors at once. You may be amazed at how prolific they are.

The ADD/ADHD child may struggle with this energy, working in spurts, starting many projects but not completing them. You may be amazed at their enthusiasm when it's in high gear, but wonder why all the projects are unfinished. The ADD/ADHD Indigo may exhibit a lot of frustration that he has all this energy and excitement but few techniques for sustaining the focus to complete projects and feel gratified about the results.

On the other hand, an ADD/ADHD child is not necessarily an Indigo unless other attributes are present, such as great empathy and high sensitivity, which can manifest as high emotional intelligence, emerging psychic skills, or a wise compassion.

According to a Harvard Medical School publication, anywhere from 1 percent to 6 percent of Americans—adults and children—have ADD/ADHD. At the high end, 6 percent represents about 10 million people. The online encyclopedia Wikipedia.org, citing government studies, puts the number of American *children* with ADHD at 4 million, or about 5 to 8 percent of all children. Neurologist Fred Baughman places the number of ADHD kids between 5 million and 7 million, compared to 500,000 in 1985.

Let's take a closer look at what defines ADD/ADHD.

## Indigo Stars

Actor Jim Carrey is reported to have ADHD. He starred in movies with nonlinear plots such as *Eternal Sunshine of the Spotless Mind* as well as slapstick roles such as Ace Ventura, the lead character in *The Mask*, and the Grinch in *How the Grinch Stole Christmas*. Interestingly enough, Carrey also portrays Andy Kaufman, another Indigo, in the movie about Kaufman, *Man on the Moon*. Many other brilliant and unconventional thinkers and artists also had ADHD, such as Russian composer Rachmaninov, prophet Nostradamus, astronomer Galileo, and surrealism painter Salvador Dali. A nonlinear understanding of time is one of the many creative gifts of ADHD.

# An ADD/ADHD Checklist

Remember that ADD stands for attention deficit disorder and ADHD stands for attention deficit hyperactivity disorder. The primary difference is that hyperactivity is not seen in ADD.

The diagnostic manual that psychologists use breaks down ADHD into three areas:

- Inattention
- Impulsivity
- Hyperactivity

Inattention is the distractibility that many often associate with ADD/ADHD. Impulsivity is the tendency to act without thinking. Hyperactivity generally fades as the child grows up.

Most children exhibit signs of inattention and impulsivity. That's part of growing up. But the ADD/ADHD child has these behaviors to a degree that is inappropriate with his or her age and developmental level.

The National Institutes of Health has developed guidelines to help parents and psychologists sort out the difference between growing pains and learning disabilities. (Go online to www.nimh.nih.gov/healthinformation/adhdmenu.cfm for more.)

**Crystal Clear**

ADHD should stand for Attention Dialed into a Higher Dimension.
—Author Doreen Virtue

Here is a checklist that can help you identify whether your child might be ADD/ADHD. Mental health professionals recommend that if your child has seven or more of these attributes, you have your child checked out for ADD/ADHD.

**Inattention**

❑ Does your child avoid or dislike tasks that require sustained attention?

❑ Is your child disorganized at home and at school?

❑ Is your child easily distracted by peripheral noises or sights, such as refrigerator noise or other people's conversations?

❑ Is your child forgetful?

❑ Does your child fail to complete tasks or struggle to sustain an activity?

❑ Is it hard for your child to listen?

❑ Is your child careless? Does he make a lot of mistakes?

❑ Does your child daydream a lot?

**Impulsivity**

❑ Is your child physically aggressive?

❑ Is your child clumsy, often stumbling or breaking things?

❑ Does your child often interrupt you or others?

❑ Does your child often blurt out things?

❑ Is your child highly impatient at having to wait?

❑ Does your child often intrude on others?

**Hyperactivity**

❑ Does your child have difficulty sitting still?

❑ Does your child appear to be driven—to be in constant activity?

❑ Does your child make a lot of noise when she plays?

❑ Does your child fidget a lot?

❑ Does your child talk excessively?

❑ Is your child restless?

❑ When you are in a place where your child cannot run or climb, do you have to rein him in many times? Have you ever had to leave a situation because he just couldn't stop himself from running or climbing?

# Learning Disabilities

While many ADD/ADHD children do have *learning disabilities*—experts say it's about 25 percent to 50 percent—ADD/ADHD is not a learning disability. A learning disability is a neurological disorder, while ADD/ADHD is a behavioral disorder. While medications can help an ADD/ADHD child, medication does not change the wiring of a learning-disabled child. ADD/ADHD children are able to learn in conventional classrooms when treated, but learning-disabled children often stay on the special education track.

**def•i•ni•tion**

A **learning disability** is a neurological disorder. Children with learning disabilities are smart—sometimes smarter—than their classmates, but they are wired differently and processing information differently. The biggest challenge learning disabled children face is with basic reading and language skills. The online resource center LDOnline.org estimates that 80 percent of children with learning disabilities struggle to read.

Learning disabilities began to be identified in 1963 when Samuel Kirk, a professor of special education at the University of Illinois, spoke to a group of concerned parents, first using the term learning disability.

The National Institutes of Health estimated in 2001 that 15 percent of the population in the United States—one in seven Americans—has a learning disability. The online resource LDOnline.org estimates, citing the NIH, that as of 2001 2.9 million school-age children in this country had learning disabilities.

Learning disabilities include:

- **Dyslexia.** These children struggle to decipher written words. Often the letters or words appear transposed as the mind attempts to translate what the child sees on the written page.

- **Dyscalculla.** These children struggle to solve arithmetic problems and grasp math concepts.

- **Dysgraphia.** These children struggle to form letters or write within a defined space.

- **Auditory and/or Visual Processing Disorders.** These are sensory disabilities. The child has normal hearing and vision but struggles to hear or understand language.

- **Nonverbal Learning Disabilities.** This is a neurological disorder in which brain functions such as visual-spatial, intuitive, organizational, evaluative and holistic processing are disrupted.

Learning disabilities are not the same as autism, Asperger's syndrome, or behavioral disorders such as oppositional defiant disorder or ADD/ADHD.

Many Indigos fall into the category of learning disabled-gifted in which they are weak in some areas, but in other areas, they are super strong. An LD-Gifted child may go unnoticed as needing help because he may be able to compensate for his weaknesses by drawing upon his strengths. These children might be given attention for their learning disability but not for their giftedness. Many children are not identified as LD-Gifted because it's difficult to discern. As a result, most twice-exceptional children are not served for both exceptionalities, even though those who are identified and served have been shown to thrive.

## Autism and Asperger's Syndrome

Asperger's syndrome is a developmental disorder that experts estimate occurs in about 71 of every 10,000 births. It looks and feels a lot like autism, in which children insist on a routine, resist environmental change, and appear to be absorbed in self-stimulation. Children with Asperger's have above-average intellectual function and language skills, but they struggle to reciprocate in conversation and are often challenged in social interactions.

Autism is a developmental disability that affects social interaction, communication, imaginative play, and cognition. Autistic children might have unusual responses to people and strong attachments to objects. They often have high sensitivities—in sight, hearing, touch, smell, and taste. It's the same sensitivity present in Indigos, just dialed to the higher end of the spectrum.

# Innovative Problem Solving

If your Indigo has a learning disability, you have a challenge. But Wendy likes to think of ADD/ADHD as a gift as well. The great distractibility of the ADD/ADHD child is something that allows your child to be very aware of the world. ADD/ADHD children notice instantly when things change, and they are often very empathetic. An ADD/ADHD child is very random in his or her thinking, which allows for creative thoughts to pop up and inspire them.

### Good Counsel

Your child may not necessarily be ADD/ADHD but may not have found her place. If your child is capable of putting in sustained focus on projects she loves without getting distracted, she is probably an Indigo resisting the structures and authority figures that hamper her creativity. This kind of child will thrive instantly in educational systems such as Montessori or Waldorf that allow children to choose their activities.

If your child is having trouble fitting in and getting required tasks done, you must first of all help your child accept it. Help him value himself the way he is. Many ADD/ADHD children grow up to create their own place so they can function optimally, carving out a special niche and working for themselves. You can help your child lay this foundation, as well as help him adjust to the world in which you both live.

## Alternative Solutions

Stimulant drugs such as Ritalin are the standard treatment for ADD/ADHD, but many people resist it because Ritalin, while it changes certain behaviors, also shuts down a child's creativity and intuition. It gives parents and teachers what they want—a child who can listen and focus and complete tasks—but there is a cost. The Drug Enforcement Administration reports a 500 percent increase in prescriptions to treat ADHD since 1991. (ADHD was first accepted into the diagnostic manual psychologists use in 1987.) IMS Health, a health care information company, reports about 20 million prescriptions were written in 2000 for stimulant drugs such as Ritalin.

Many alternatives exist if you are willing to be patient as you try different therapies to see what suits your child. The alternatives take more time to explore, but they might be worth it, if you still have your creative and innovative thinker. (A good resource for further research is *Managing the Gift: Alternative Approaches to Attention Deficit Disorder* by Kevin Ross Emery)

- ◆ **Meditation, visualization, and hypnosis.** All of these techniques use relaxation to train the mind.

- ◆ **Nutritional adjustments.** Eliminate processed foods, and emphasize whole foods. That means more fruits and vegetables, less meat, and more whole grains. Research the use of supplements such as blue-green algae, chamomile, and St. John's wort. We will discuss alternative remedies and ways to research them in Chapter 15.

- ◆ **Vibrational adjustments.** These are flower essences, taken internally; aromatherapy using essential oils; or aurasoma.

- ◆ **Behavioral training.** Teach your to make to-do lists and set priorities. Reward them when they get tasks done.

- ◆ **Magnet therapy.** Research shows that self-esteem in ADD/ADHD children improves with magnet therapy, and parents report anecdotally that it helps. Practitioners believe techniques such as wearing a magnetic bracelet work because it changes the polarity in the brain and helps ground you. Wendy does not recommend magnetic mattresses, nor any magnet therapy worn 24/7, however, because she believes the body would adapt, and then the magnet as tool for therapy would be useless. As with any therapy, do your research, ask questions, and talk to other parents before you try it.

♦ **EMF balancing.** This technique balances the electromagnetic frequencies in the body. It is a form of energy shielding. The recipient lies on a massage table, while the practitioner performs Tai Chi-like movements.

♦ **Biofeedback and neurotherapy.** This is a technique that trains a person to become more conscious of thinking and behavior and change it by being more aware of brain activity.

♦ **Neuromuscular integration.** Psychotherapist Karen Bolesky perfected this technique for ADD/ADHD. It is sometimes called *soma*, and it works to recondition the nervous system. She bases her technique on the theory that left-brain functioning dominates in the ADD/ADHD brain, which creates a state of being overwhelmed. By integrating brain function between left brain, right brain, and core brain, the technique creates more ease and expansion, increasing the ability to concentrate. The technique works to create a safe place in the body for the ADD/ADHD child who feels out of control.

♦ **Rapid eye technology.** Psychotherapist Ranae Johnson is the founder of this technique, which uses blinking, eye movements, breathing, and stress reduction energy work to access and release negative emotions that the body is storing.

# Energy Healing

Energy healing, such as Reiki and its many variations, including the Shamballa Multidimensional Energy Healing that Wendy teaches, can be very effective not just for ADD/ADHD but all Indigos. It helps to

calm and focus the ADD/ADHD child, but it also protects the psychically aware or highly emotionally sensitive child.

Shamballa is similar to Reiki, which is an energy healing technique that
uses hand movements and light touch to redirect energy in and around
the receiver's body to regain balance. Shamballa uses more intuition
and operates at a higher frequency of energy.

Dr. John Armitage, also known as Hari Das Melchizedek, channeled
Shamballa from St. Germaine about 10 years ago. It incorporates 352
symbols, or energy calling cards. Wendy believes there are 360 symbols, a full circle. Practitioners draw these energy calling cards in the
space around a person, which can activate healing. Some are specific to
healing cancer, relieving depression, or energizing creativity. Each symbol has a name and a vibration, and most of them come from Sanskrit
or Japanese kanji.

## Good Counsel

Shamballa symbols remain secret to nonpractitioners because until
practitioners are fully trained to be attuned to the symbols, they
may misuse them. Wendy equates it with tuning your radio to a certain
station. When you become a practitioner, you have an attunement ceremony, in which you are in deep meditation as your teacher channels
energy into you. The ceremony clears the channel, cleaning out toxins
from all levels (physical, mental, emotional, and spiritual), and allows you
to be a pure channel of light, as well as encoding the symbols.

Wendy coached the parents of a hyperactive child, using Shamballa
energy healing. The 8-year-old boy was struggling in school because he
wasn't complying with teachers' requests. The parents would do energy
healing with their son at bedtime, balancing his energy so he could
sleep better. One parent stood at the head of the child, the other at his
feet. They balanced the energy by sending it back and forth between
each other, above, through, and around the child. During the session,
they visualized bringing in protection and healing energy. This was
very helpful to him the following day after receiving the healing, and
he reported he slept well that night. His focus at school improved as a
result.

Wendy also recommends clearing out clutter from your child's bedroom—really, from your whole house. It will minimize the distractions. Using feng shui, the Chinese art of balancing chi, to organize your home will help balance the energies as well. Feng shui harmonizes the chi, or life force energy, in a space.

## The Novel Approach

All of these approaches are unconventional, but your ADD/ADHD Indigo may find them much more natural to his way of thinking. That's because it's built-in to ADD/ADHD Indigos to come up with novel approaches to their challenges. They have already put in some time trying to figure out how to navigate their worlds differently from the other children. It's been quite necessary for their survival.

Cut your ADD/ADHD Indigo in on the discussion of the solutions, even if she's quite young. Let her participate in presenting ideas and making choices. It will let her know you appreciate her unique gifts, and it will help her understand them for herself.

# Creating a Safe Place

With ADD/ADHD Indigos, energy shielding can shut out distractions and create that peaceful place in the mind and the body where ADD/ADHD children can access their brilliance and gain confidence. Innovative approaches can open them up to self-directed and self-generated solutions. As you'll see in the chapters ahead, energy shielding and other techniques can help to temper the other challenges of being an Indigo, as well as enhance their gifts.

## The Least You Need to Know

- ◆ Not all Indigos have ADHD; not all children with ADHD are Indigos.
- ◆ ADHD is defined by inattentiveness, impulsivity, and hyperactivity.
- ◆ The gifts of ADHD include a unique awareness of the world. ADHD kids notice subtle changes and think more creatively.

- Other learning disabilities that Indigos may have include dyslexia and Asperger's syndrome.

- Alternative therapies can help you avoid the negative side effects of drugs.

- Shamballa, an energy healing technique, can help Indigos with ADHD—and those who don't.

# Chapter 6

# Psychic Ability, Leaps of Language, and Abstract Thinking

## In This Chapter

- ◆ Your child's psychic gifts
- ◆ From the collective unconscious
- ◆ Protecting your child
- ◆ Abstract concepts and language mastery

Indigo Children often have a great ability to make intuitive leaps and engage in abstract thinking. They tend not to think sequentially but holistically. They see the big picture, and they do not have a linear definition of time. They seem to understand that time can collapse and expand, and they are open to ghosts, spirits, and angels.

These unique attributes add to a child who has innate psychic skills. Whether your child is psychic or demonstrates an early grasp of abstract thinking and ability with language, know that it's one of the gifts of being Indigo.

# Is Your Child Psychic?

Maybe you have noticed that your child seems to know things, and you don't know how he can know them. Maybe your child gave you a message that the road to school was closed and you needed to take an alternate route. Later you heard there was an accident on that road. Or you ignored it because you didn't understand it, and you got snarled in heavy traffic because of the accident.

Often, the psychic child will talk about a deceased relative. She can tell you things about a maternal grandmother she never knew. Sometimes your child will tell you stories about fairies or angels. She might even swear there is someone in the room, sitting on the corner of her bed or in the rocker.

Carolyn has learned to heed it when her son Lucas states something she doesn't understand. Sometimes it's something he knows, sees, or smells. By age 3, he already knew things he had no way of knowing, and often talked of seeing angels. Once when Carolyn and the twins were driving by a restaurant that was under construction, her son said Carolyn's friend who stained concrete floors was working there. Carolyn had just caught up with this friend recently and her friend hadn't mentioned anything about a new project at that restaurant. But sure enough, the next time they talked, Carolyn's friend had landed a contract to do the concrete staining for that restaurant.

Lucas has the same blue eyes as his paternal grandfather, who was born in the Ukraine. When her son was a newborn, his grandfather rocked him in his arms, singing patriotic songs for his homeland. One day when Lucas was 6, he drew a picture of a guitar with a hand playing it. Out of the guitar, the words, "Oh my old Ukraine, my old Ukraine," lilted across the page. Ten days later, Carolyn learned that the grandfather was near death and had been taken to the hospital—10 days before. Carolyn believes Lucas has a strong psychic link to his grandfather, who did pass away, and he was getting the message—long before anyone else—that his grandfather was preparing to leave the material world and enter the spirit world. This is *precognition*, the ability to see into the future.

Children in general are more open to experiencing an awareness of something beyond the material world. A friend of Carolyn's tells the story of 7-year-old twin sisters who were given a fairy ball. They played in the courtyard for a while, then a grown-up asked them—facetiously—if they had seen any fairies. "No, of course we didn't see any fairies," they reported. "But we did see a hand." They described a hand emerging from the wall holding a larger fairy ball. Okay ….

**def•i•ni•tion**

> **Precognition** is the umbrella word for many different ways of receiving psychic information. It is the ability to know about events that have yet to transpire: someone is coming to see you, someone is going to die, you will meet someone.

Being psychic is a higher level of awareness that there is something beyond the world we can touch. A psychic person is less bound by physical space and has learned ways to open up his awareness to other times and other dimensions. The psychic child is crossing time/space boundaries and is aware of events yet to come or long past. Some are in touch with spirit guides, spirits of departed loved ones, angels, fairies, or some other spirit kin.

## Psychic Undercurrents and the Collective Unconscious

If all that's too much for you, you might want to think about it in terms of Swiss psychologist Carl Jung's collective unconscious, the reservoir of our collective human experience—a built-in knowledge we have from birth. Think of it as your emotional inheritance. Jung said we can never be directly conscious of this knowledge, but it influences all of our experiences and behavior. We know about it indirectly, noticing how it influences our emotions through our subconscious.

We may experience this awareness as a synchronicity, the occurrence of two seemingly unrelated events at the same time. A grandfather is dying, and his grandson hears him singing a patriotic song. A train hits a father; the watch that he gave his son stops ticking at that instant.

Other experiences that point to evidence of the collective unconscious at work include:

♦ Love at first sight—the sense that you know this person or you are meant to know this person.

♦ Déjà vu—the sense that you have been in a place before.

♦ Immediate recognition of symbols.

♦ Archetypes such as the warrior, the victim, the sage or hermit or guru, the universal mother, the divine feminine, the coyote or trickster, which show up in fairy tales and myths, as well as in our personal journey of life.

Jung describes these experiences as "the sudden conjunction of our outer reality with our inner reality of the collective unconscious." We see this in the creative experience that all artists and musicians share, when they tap into their muse, or in the spiritual experiences of mystics from all religious traditions. We experience it for ourselves in our dreams, fantasies, and cultural mythologies, from ancient Greek myths to modern-day myths such as *The Lord of the Rings* or *Harry Potter*.

### Indigo Stars

One fictional Indigo who is exceptionally gifted in the paranormal is Harry Potter. He is connected to both the light side (his parents) and dark side (Lord Voldemort and the scar he left on Harry's forehead) and has to find balance between the two. In *Prisoner of Azkaban*, he uses energy shielding when he learns to master the dementors. He gets in touch with his father through animal spirits when the deer across the lake connects him to the light energy of his father, who he believes protects him from the dementors. In *Chamber of Secrets*, he displays leaps of language in his mastery of parseltongue, the snake language.

In light of hit television shows such as *Medium*, about a suburban housewife who is a psychic detective, it's clear that many Americans are fascinated with psychic abilities. Harris Interactive conducted a poll in November 2005 that found that one in five Americans believes he or she has been reincarnated. About 40 percent of Americans believe in ghosts, while 68 percent believe in angels, the poll showed.

# Forms of Psychic Awareness

Indigo Children may display psychic awareness in reporting visitations, hearing voices, and sensing presences. They may appear to see angels, or they may say they do. Some parents report noticing a sphere of light surrounding their child in many of the photos they take. This kept happening to Wendy; in many photos taken of her since she was a child, there is an orb of light near her head. And in every photo from her wedding, there are multiple light spheres. Other signs of the presence of psychic energy manifest around electricity. Some Indigo parents notice that electrical devices are sensitive to the presence of their child. Light bulbs burn out faster than average, and electronic devices shut off or blow out when the child is near. Watches may suddenly stop working.

Here's a closer look at forms of psychic awareness:

- **Clairvoyance.** Clear sight, the ability to see into the spirit dimension or into the future.

- **Clairaudience.** Clear hearing, the ability to hear sounds "broadcast" or spoken from the spirit realm. Receiving writings, as in the handwriting on the wall, falls into this realm but is sometimes called clairscrivence.

- **Clairsentience.** Clear feeling, the ability to perceive feeling without an external physical cause.

- **Clairgustance.** Clear tasting, the ability to taste something without putting it in your mouth. The taste comes to you as a precognitive message—something that will happen—or as something from the spirit world (the taste of your deceased grandmother's rhubarb pie, for instance).

- **Clairaroma.** Sometimes called clairscence or clairolfaction, it's the ability to smell clearly. You sense a fragrance that is not present but comes from the spirit world.

**def•i•ni•tion**

> **Clair** is a root word from French that means clear. When we use the term clairvoyance, we mean clear seeing. Clairsentience is clear feeling, while clairaudience is clear hearing. People with psychic gifts usually have one or two traits more strongly developed than others.

- **Clairempathy.** Clear emotion, the ability to experience precognitive empathy.

- **Clairtangence.** Clear touching, more commonly known as psychometry. It's the ability to know, by holding an item, about the owner of the object or about its history.

Other forms of psychic abilities include:

- **Telekinesis.** The ability to move objects with your thoughts.

- **Psychic teleportation.** This includes astral travel in dreams, or to have the awareness of being in one place physically but another place spiritually at the same time, which is bilocation.

- **Telepathy.** The ability to communicate mind to mind—that is, to read minds. It often happens between Indigo parents and children.

- **Channeling.** The ability to receive the thoughts of enlightened spirits or angels. It's also used sometimes to define inspiration for artwork and music or automatic writing or sudden knowing.

# What Parents Can Do

Understanding that your child is psychic may be exciting yet troubling for you. It's important that you see that your child has a gift. See it as a gift from God (use the term that is appropriate for your spiritual beliefs), not from evil. It is a tool, and you must help your child learn how to use it.

How your child develops this gift is all in how the parents handle it. Be matter-of-fact about it, and don't overreact. If you are fearful of your child's skill, she will sense it and may choose to suppress her skill. Several books listed in Appendix B may help you nurture your child's skill and learn to cultivate your own. Remember everyone is psychic. It's just a matter of activating the skill. You may want to find a mentor to work with your child to develop this ability if you don't feel prepared for the task.

Here are some practical ideas for helping your child manage his psychic ability.

## Third Eye Filter

Many parents consult Wendy because they are concerned their children are too vulnerable to visits and voices from the spirit world. She suggests putting a filter, using creative visualization, around the third-eye chakra, the energy center in the body that governs intuition. The third-eye chakra is located in the center of the forehead, about one inch beneath the skin, and its color is indigo—the indigo from which Indigo Children derive their name. You may direct your child to say, "I'm only going to receive messages about events that directly affect myself, my family, and my friends," or "I'm only going to receive information about something I'm connected to or something I can directly change." Then visualize a filter around your child's third eye, shutting out all of the extraneous information.

> **Crystal Clear**
>
> The most beautiful thing we can experience is the mysterious. It is the source of all true art and all science. He to whom this emotion is a stranger, who can no longer pause to wonder and stand rapt in awe, is as good as dead: his eyes are closed.
> —Physicist Albert Einstein

This can be helpful if your child gets psychic messages about plane crashes or earthquakes—something she can do nothing to prevent. Wendy used to get very distracting ringing in her ears, similar to tinnitus, about three hours before major earthquakes. Other Indigos told her about experiencing similar psychic early warning systems before global earth changes, which helped Wendy understand the same thing might be happening to her. It appeared to be a psychic warning system for severe earthquakes, but it was not anything she could change or help, so she decided to filter it out before pursuing other treatments. It worked! She set up a psychic filter, and now her ears don't ring.

**Patience**

If something dire happens—you get in a car wreck or a grandparent dies—and your child predicted it, this may be quite frightening for your child. It may have seemed very vivid to him, as though he saw it on a video screen. The child may think he caused the incident. He may fear it and shut down. Put the event in logical perspective. Always remind your child that he has a special gift to be able to know what was going to happen, but he did not cause it to happen, nor could he have prevented it.

## Intuitive Protection

You can also use the third-eye chakra for energy protection, helping your child visualize a beam of light emanating from her forehead, protecting her like a laser sword. Imagine a force field of light to keep out bad energies. This is a form of energy shielding.

One of the "rules" of the spirit world is that humans set the boundaries. You may ask them to leave by saying, "Only spirits of the light may enter here. Any spirits not of the light must go now!" You may also call upon spirits of the light, such as angels, to protect your child.

One visualization technique Wendy uses is the Merkaba, a star-shaped double tetrahedron, also called a stellated octahedron—that is, two interlocking tetrahedra of light, one pointing up and the other down. To do this, imagine the Merkaba in your heart center and then visualize it expanding to encompass your whole body. By activating the Merkaba around you, astral journeys happen more easily and a constant level of spirit body protection is empowered.

The website www.crytalinks.com/merkaba.html defines Merkaba as a symbol of divine light used by ascended masters to connect with spirits attuned to higher realms. *Mer* means light, *ka* means spirit, and *ba* means body, all coming from Ancient Egypt. The star tetrahedron represents a spirit-body surrounded by whirling fields of light, rotating in different directions. The Merkaba comes from the Hebrew tradition and is linked to the chariot of fire that scooped up the prophet Ezekiel and took him to heaven. That's why the Merkaba is used as a symbol of ascending to heaven.

# Core Self

It's important to help your psychic Indigo define her core self. She needs to be grounded in a firm understanding of who she is. You may guide her through a meditation to find a safe place in her body—visualizing a core self that the spirits can't touch, see or talk to. You may also create a ritual of a safe place in her room—a place she can go when she receives spirit visitors she doesn't want. You might give her a stuffed animal or doll she can hold when she goes to this safe place.

Many therapists use sand trays to help children define that core. With sand trays, a child creates her own world, arranging plastic figures and objects in sand, and she tells a story about it—how she fits into her universe (this is my house, this is my family, this is my school, these are my friends, this is my church). Help your child carry over this exercise into her psyche, visualizing her sand-tray universe as a place she can go in her mind any time she needs to anchor herself in her core self. Talk to her about the people and objects she set up on her sand tray and how they are related to her.

Movement practices such as tai chi, qi gong, and yoga also can help your child develop a strong core self so that he is not so permeable and vulnerable to the intuitive information he receives. Tai chi helps your child imagine a force field of protection around him and develops his confidence. Yoga helps ground your child in her body. The cat-cow sequence relieves stress and regulates breathing, while sun salutations are a good way to connect with spirit and earth. In sun salutations, you can envision your body as the connector between heaven and earth, reaching toward heaven with your hands, grounding yourself to earth through your feet.

# Clearing the Space

Ghosts and spirits with negative energy or evil intent are often drawn to bright spirit lights, such as Indigo Children, so it's important to put some energy protection on your child's space through meditation, visualization, prayer, or energy shielding.

Forms of protection you can use include amethysts or citrine, crystals that have a cleansing, purifying energy; hanging lavender and eucalyptus leaves at doorways; placing other charged crystals such as quartz points at key places of a room or house; setting Reiki seals on any openings to the house.

### Good Counsel

Keep your child's space clear of clutter. Feng shui is the Chinese art of arranging your space to attract good energy and repel bad energy. In feng shui, chi is the life force energy of the universe. The techniques of feng shui are built around the five Chinese elements—wood, fire, earth, water, and metal. By keeping your home free of clutter and paying attention to how you arrange objects such as fountains (water) and mirrors (metal), you attract the good spirits and send the others away.

# Abstract Thinking

Abstract thinking is imaginative thinking, in which you grasp intangible concepts such as love or peace. Indigos often understand these concepts earlier than the average child, putting them into practice, acting on them. They might understand they can channel healing to someone, or they might have a concept of an afterlife.

Indigos as toddlers often understand object permanence early—the ability to hold an object in mind even though you cannot see it and know that it still exists. An example: when Mom drops off her Indigo child at preschool, her daughter is calm because she knows Mom still exists even though she is gone, and she knows she will come back. Indigos are so connected with Spirit that they know and feel Mom even though she's not physically present.

As a result, they have less difficulty processing death. Carolyn's twins readily accepted that their grandfather was in heaven. Heaven is an easy concept to buy into because they experience the material and spiritual worlds as more permeable.

Indigos also exhibit more holistic thinking. They can get their minds around big concepts, and they can see the whole because their view of time is not linear. They are more open to understanding the elasticity of time—it can collapse and expand. Two moments in time separated by a calendar year are close together in their minds when they think spiritually. It is only when they feel the restrictions of the body's need to move one day at a time that they feel frustrated by this delay, even more so than the average person. The future has already happened in one dimension, but in the third dimension of the physical body, is it still very far away.

# Leapin' Language

Indigo Children often exhibit gifts with language associated with gifted children, which is in tune with the faster intellectual development often seen in Indigos. They quickly learn to speak in whole ideas and sentences, and when they learn to read and write, they develop a huge vocabulary and complex sentence structure. They often pick up other languages very quickly.

Sometimes Indigos will invent an imaginary language. This often happens with twins (though not with Carolyn's), who invent a language only they share. (It's more common in identical twins than fraternal.) Some soul family members who meet as toddlers may also experience private invented languages.

Sometimes Indigos will speak in sudden spurts of a language they don't know and haven't been exposed to—that is channeling a language. That happened to Wendy when she was about 4 or 5. One day she came down the stairs, speaking fluent French. Her mother recognized the language as French, though she did not know French and the family had not been around anyone who had spoken French. Wendy's mother said while Wendy was telling this story, she was not responsive. Wendy and her mother, as well as a psychic they consulted, believe it was a past life she was re-experiencing. We'll talk more about past lives in Chapter 20.

# Keep the Lines Open

Whether we are talking about psychic skills, leaps of language, or abstract thinking, all are gifts. Preserve your Indigo's openness to these experiences by practicing grounding and energy shielding. Tap into your own abilities, and above all treat your child with acceptance. Teach him to treasure these gifts and not to fear them.

## The Least You Need to Know

◆ Many Indigo Children exhibit psychic abilities at a very young age.

◆ Precognition—the ability to know about future events—may come through all the senses—sight, touch, smell, taste, and hearing.

◆ The way your child reacts to his psychic abilities depends on how you react. See it as a gift—and a tool he can learn to use effectively.

◆ Use a third-eye filter to protect your Indigo child from receiving too much psychic input.

◆ Help your child develop intuitive protection and cultivate a strong core self to protect herself.

◆ Many Indigos understand abstract concepts such as God early; others have an extraordinary gift for language or may develop an imaginary language.

# Chapter 7

# Compassion and Tolerance

## In This Chapter

- ◆ Shielding your tender-hearted child
- ◆ Teaching your child to set boundaries
- ◆ Opening up the child who has shut down
- ◆ Implementing practices that promote tolerance

Indigo Children possess a unique brand of compassion and tolerance. They are quick to empathize and reach out to others. They have a built-in sense that we are all doing the best we can. Though it's a cliché, in many ways, they would like to teach the world to sing in perfect harmony.

Indigos can be tender and forgiving, yet sometimes they can be too vulnerable. At the same time, they can be impatient that others aren't the same. As a parent, it's your job to help them cope with this gift.

# Reaching Out

In the movie *Indigo*, the Indigo girl encounters the mother of an Indigo boy at a park. She reaches out to her and touches her breast gently. The girl's grandfather is taken aback by her forward behavior, but the woman explains it's okay. She had learned recently that she had breast cancer. The girl intuitively sensed the woman's pain, and the movie implies that the Indigo girl's touch healed the woman.

Whether or not you believe that some Indigo Children have the healing touch, it's true that many operate on a high degree of compassion. They may be so emotionally perceptive that it may seem they are psychic—and maybe they are. Who's to say where the line between emotional perceptiveness and telepathy lies? Again, even if it's a stretch for you to believe that mere touch can heal cancer, you certainly know that compassion goes a long way to promote emotional healing.

*Compassion* is distinguished from empathy, which is when you *feel* another person's emotions. It's not merely sympathy, which is a feeling of sorrow for another person's struggles. Compassion is a feeling *with*, feeling the emotion alongside another person, but it is almost always paired with the need or desire to mitigate the other person's pain. Empathy and sympathy can both be present in compassion.

## def•i•ni•tion

Compassion is the awareness of another person's pain, and it is closely linked with action. Out of compassion, we want to end another's suffering. Often, compassion is concern that is empathic. We don't just see it and understand it—we feel it, too. And we want to do something about it. It's what we're talking about when we say, "have a heart." Compassion is loving from the heart.

When we say someone is compassionate, we mean that the person is focused on others, soft-hearted, and tender. That person is aware of the other person's suffering and is concerned about his welfare. Tolerance, which we will discuss later in this chapter, takes that concept to a more universal level, focusing on a preservation of dignity and protection from suffering for all people.

A highly compassionate Indigo knows when you have had a rough day, even without your saying so. She will come over to you and hug you.

Or he may put his hand on your forehead when you have a headache. Some parents have told Wendy that sometimes their headaches go away after their child touches them, because many have come to believe their Indigos have the healing touch, much like the girl in the movie.

Compassionate Indigos will be kind to children with disabilities and will not shun them. They strive to include them and help them. They are not hesitant to relate to people with autism or Alzheimer's or other conditions that inhibit the ability to communicate. That's because they still can and do communicate. In the movie *Indigo*, the girl communicates telepathically with the elderly Alzheimer's patient.

Wendy knows of some Indigos who will go out of their way not to step on the grass so as not to "hurt" the blades of grass. They will humanely capture the bugs they find in the house to free them outdoors instead of squashing them. They may insist on humane traps for critters—much like the live traps Carolyn and her twins set for the mice in the garage and freed in the arroyo, a dry riverbed.

Compassionate Indigos will test your own compassion. They will bring home stray animals. They will want to give money to homeless people, and then they'll invite them to dinner. They will want to hunt up and down the street for the cat that went missing from their friend's house. They will ask for more snacks in the lunchbox because they know a classmate doesn't get treats in his.

## Why This Is a Good Thing

Recent research suggests that self-compassion is more important than high self-esteem in helping us weather life's rough waters. Wake Forest University psychologist Mark Leary presented three studies in 2005 that showed that the ability to be kind to oneself even when you fail or face rejection is more crucial than self-esteem.

It may be that self-esteem is situational, while self-compassion is a universal trait—treating yourself with the same kindness you would treat a friend, no matter whether you feel good about yourself or not. The ability to think this way equips your child with a buffer against negative events. It's: "I love myself even when I goof up" rather than "I'm such a loser." The study also showed that because people were more compassionate with themselves, they were more likely to admit their mistakes and address them.

If you see your Indigo child practicing compassion toward others, you more than likely see him practicing it with himself. Encourage these thoughts in the way you guide your child through life's setbacks. Voice them when you experience rejections and defeats so that you set an example for your child. With good judgment, you might use examples from your work life; doing so may give your child a template for turning a less-than-perfect test grade into a learning experience.

## My Heart's Wide Open

Is there a downside to trying a little tenderness? Unfortunately, yes. It means that your child's heart is wide open. She can be vulnerable to another person's suffering to the point that she doesn't take care of herself and she can't function. Carolyn's daughter is like this. She must know that everyone is all right before she even notices what's going on with herself.

Sometimes your Indigo child will need more than the average coaching on not approaching strangers. He may want to help everybody. Not everyone wants to be helped or can be helped, and some mean harm. The concept of harmful people may be so foreign to your Indigo child's frame of reference that it will be difficult to teach him. So you will have to go the extra mile to educate him about stranger danger. You'll need to explain that some people mean harm, and you may need to be uncomfortably specific for the message to get across. Explain it, with enough detail that your child understands the need for the rule. Many parents hold back on how they explain it because they don't want to scare their children. Explain it without fear, in a calm, firm manner. Let your child know he will be safe if he follows these guidelines. In the larger sense, telling your child "Don't talk to strangers" is not as useful as teaching your child how to identify whether someone is trustworthy or not, whether that person means harm. Help your child develop good instincts about people.

Sometimes your child's sense of compassion can be downright annoying. The child who will not walk on the grass when the rest of the family is crossing the field can seem noncompliant or rebellious. Of course, you must choose your battles, but if it's important to keep the family together because it's unfamiliar territory or there's a crowd, you'll need to address it. When this is the case, offer acceptance with limits. Keep the discussion short and be firm about what you will do and won't do. Make it clear she will need to find a workable solution within those limits.

Don't belittle your child, and don't tell her she's abnormal (even if it briefly crosses your mind to think so!). Resist explaining the science of the life of a grass blade unless your child is older (8 is the average age of logic). Logic most likely will hold no sway. Unless you allow a scenario that acknowledges and includes her compassion, you won't persuade her with logic. Explain that it's important for her to stay with her family. Say, "Your father and mother want to keep everybody together. We're responsible for all of our children, and we want to make sure you're safe." Let her know that the solution must fall within the boundary of "the family is crossing this field together" (you might want to add "today"). You can say something like, "How do you think you could stay with the family and still not hurt the grass?" Suggest something that includes an acknowledgment of her compassion: "What if we sent a blessing to the grass, thanking it for allowing us to walk across as a family?"

It's very likely that your inventive Indigo will come up with a solution when she understands the limit—and the compassion behind the limit ("the family must stay together"). It could mean going barefoot across the grass so as not to disturb it as much—a compromise that you can probably live with if it's a hot summer night. Your child could send healing energy to the grass after crossing it, or cast a magic spell so that special stepping stones emerge that create a shield to protect the grass—an imaginative solution.

# How You Can Help

These Indigos feel *everything*. They take everything to heart. They feel responsible. Here's how to help your Indigo child develop a thicker skin.

Many of these Indigos are born with a natural sense of Reiki, an energy healing technique similar to Shamballa. Reiki, developed in the early twentieth century in Japan, has grown in popularity in the United States and gained more acceptance. A 2005 study in the *Alternative Therapies* journal found that in 2002 more than one million Americans had experienced a Reiki treatment. In the United Kingdom, Reiki is among the complementary alternative therapies approved by the National Health Service.

More and more people are experiencing Reiki and Shamballa and becoming convinced the techniques make a difference. The Reiki Research Foundation, for instance, has found that Reiki reduced lethargy for 90 percent of the people, reduces depression for 87 percent, and reduces pain for 74 percent.

Whatever you may think about energy shielding techniques such as Shamballa or Reiki, or crystal healing, many Indigo parents swear by them. Wendy has worked with many a parent and child who find that these techniques help them establish boundaries. Some are reluctant converts.

Here are some techniques that can help your child from being too vulnerable with others:

♦ Use energy healing to get your child centered.

♦ Teach your child energy shielding to protect herself.

♦ Create a safe environment for your child to express his feelings.

♦ Guide your child in determining how to decide who is okay to open up to, who is not.

♦ Model for her how to determine if someone is trustworthy.

♦ Dialogue with her about how you decide what information you share with others versus what you keep private (personal emotional matters, for instance).

Above all, don't be afraid of your child's vulnerability. Don't dismiss negative emotions such as sadness, jealousy, or anger. It's important that you honor these emotions in your child and in the way you speak of them in others.

**Patience**

Boundaries between private and public, family and world, may be a hard one for compassionate Indigos to grasp, because to them, everyone is family. They don't always feel the separation from others that you do. You'll need to emphasize the importance of not trusting strangers, giving them specific guidelines. Cultivate your Indigo's natural aptitude for intuition and strong sense of self to help your Indigo learn how to set good boundaries that don't feel like they are based on fear or mistrust.

# Energy Shielding

Many energy shielding techniques involve creative visualization, using your imagination to envision a scenario where the energy is diverted. Pair the visualizations with affirmations that you develop, and you reinforce the intention of the techniques—and therefore, their effectiveness.

Methods include:

- **Reflecting the energy.** You simply reflect the energy coming at you back to the other person. A note, however: some people feel this may have karmic consequence as it only sends back the negative energy and is not the most enlightened way to handle things. It is the spiritual "eye-for-an-eye" method.

- **Healing the energy.** Send healing energy back as a way to resolve conflict. This can mean sending back forgiveness.

- **Equalizing the energy.** If someone attacks with hate, send love.

- **Protecting yourself from the energy.** Certain crystals that Wendy uses in crystal healing can provide protection and can enhance your child's energy field. Imagine a sphere of white light surrounding your child. Focus on a golden rim of light to seal the sphere around your child. This rim of light allows good energy to enter and repels negative energy. (We'll talk more about crystals in Chapter 12.)

84

You and your child may develop any energy shielding visualizations that work for you. One technique is envisioning a wet blanket to throw over the energy that is threatening to you. Or you may envision a Star Wars force field around you. Or you can picture garage doors that slam down on any bad energy trying to enter your psyche. Or perhaps you can visualize a shield sending out spears or thorns.

## Setting Compassionate and Clear Boundaries

It's difficult to help the compassionate Indigo child understand that she doesn't have to be nice to everybody. It's not her responsibility to help everyone. Nor can she.

Recently, Carolyn's 7-year-old daughter Emerald started getting calls from a boy in her school who had a major crush on her. Carolyn's daughter—rightfully, in Carolyn's opinion—thought she was too young for a boyfriend. She told him that she only wanted to be his friend. He protested, telling her that she was so beautiful. Her sense of justice kicked in, and she said, "You should not love someone for what they are on the outside. It's the inside that matters. I'm beautiful on the inside." This, of course, only made the boy love her more, and he kept calling and calling and calling ....

Finally, Emerald asked Carolyn how she could get the boy to stop calling her. (She was very upset when her twin brother invited the boy to their double birthday party!) Emerald was very concerned that she not hurt the boy's feelings. Saying "Please don't call me anymore. You're bothering me," felt mean to her. Carolyn advised her daughter that she didn't have to keep taking phone calls if she didn't want to talk to him. She also told her not to "duck" him by not returning his calls or having her mom give an excuse for why she couldn't come to the phone. "You can't just let him keep hoping," Carolyn said. So they decided she would let him know she appreciated him as a friend and she liked talking to him at school, but she did not want him to call her at home. This was the boundary. This felt good to Emerald; she held her head high when she arrived for the first day of second grade, reiterating her message to the boy. (Carolyn reports all is well on that front now!)

This anecdote gives us some good general guidelines for establishing boundaries:

◆ Emerald let the boy know what she appreciated about him. She was kind.

◆ She also let him know she was open to limited contact (talking at school).

◆ She drew a line (don't call me at home).

◆ She let him know where she stood (too young for a boyfriend).

◆ She didn't go into a long explanation—a mistake she made in the first conversation with her statement about inner beauty. A long explanation invites the person to engage you in a debate about changing your mind, which the boy did. When you set a boundary, your mind is made up.

◆ Yet she wasn't overly rigid. She didn't engage in either-or thinking. It wasn't black-and-white, as in "I don't want to be your girlfriend, so I'm not going to ever talk to you."

◆ She didn't make it personal. It wasn't about whether the boy was a nice person. It was about what she was willing to do (talk to him at school) and what she was not willing to do (talk to him on the phone all the time).

## The Other End of the Spectrum

What if none of this sounds like your Indigo? Some Indigos have shut down so much that they are actually apathetic to others. They may seem impervious to others' emotional needs. These are the Indigos in crisis who desperately need to be reached and opened up again. They have learned to use an energy shield in the "on" position but not to regulate it yet. They may close off from negative people, but that also can extend to friends and family. To be able to take down that wall and yet still stay protected is very important for them. Teach them basic energy shielding and find ways to connect with them to help.

You may also want to introduce them to touch and movement therapy, such as massage or Tai Chi. This will help them activate their body awareness and create a safe "bubble" of personal space. Massage and other touch therapies can help your child create a safe, centered place from which she can open herself to others' emotions without feeling all shook up. The reason these Indigos shut down is because they do feel it so deeply. They really just can't take in any more of another person's pain. So they shut down.

> **Crystal Clear**
>
> The whole idea of compassion is based on a keen awareness of the interdependence of all these living beings, which are all part of one another, and all involved in one another.
>
> —Thomas Merton, American Trappist monk

Tai Chi is a Chinese mind-body set of movements, considered to be one of the "soft" martial arts. The movements are relaxed and performed in slow motion. Tai Chi training teaches balance—physical and emotional. In Tai Chi, you learn to be aware of your emotions and the way external influences affect your emotional balance, as well as understanding the same in others. You also learn how to moderate extremes of behavior and attitude—something from which many types of Indigos will benefit.

# A Brave, Tolerant World

Indigos feel very different, so they already understand embracing differences. Yet at the same time they can be tolerant of people of difference races and abilities, they can have a very low tolerance for mediocrity. That's because their tolerant nature stems from idealism. They strive for moral integrity and believe in human dignity. They generally have a very humanitarian view and are able to look at situations from a global perspective. It's easy for them to grasp the concept how of our impact on the environment affects the globe, in terms of the water and energy we use and the garbage we generate.

The most tolerant Indigo Children may be the ones who emerge as leaders. They may serve as guides for others who are not accepted for who they are. They may emerge as the advocate for those who are shunned, and it may come out of their own experience of not being accepted for who they are. They are able to view with compassion those who do not accept their uniqueness and move to action—to attempt to enlighten them, not to shun them or shame them.

### Good Counsel

Pair your tolerant, compassionate, and highly functioning Indigo with a low functioning child. Or simply pair an older Indigo with a younger. Have them work as a team on a project, either at school or at home. This can present an opportunity for the gifted Indigo child to stretch himself, for while these types of Indigos embrace diversity, they still struggle with being tolerant to those who aren't as quick to learn what they know. It can be a rewarding experience to help your Indigo develop more compassion and emerge as a leader.

Traditionally, gifted children (which many Indigo Children are) are in separate class groups because gifted children often feel the slower members of the group hold them back. But these Indigos might prefer group activities and accept them as a challenge—seeing their role as that of helping the other members of the group. Indigos will thrive if they have the opportunity to be in both kinds of groups—as helpers and leaders in some instances, and in others, groups where they can go as fast as they want and really go deep into the subjects that interest them.

With so many Indigos flooding the school systems now, it's interesting to note the number of programs developed to give children opportunities to develop more tolerance. This type of Indigo child is already programmed for tolerance, and these programs will help cultivate this attribute. For a collection of ideas, go to EverythingESL.net/inservices/teaching_diversity.php, which lists 25 resources to teach about peace and tolerance. Here's a sampling:

- Collaborative, noncompetitive activities that promote helping others. The Caring School Community Program has a program called That's My Buddy, which pairs older and younger students in activities.

- Getting out of the blame game. Instead of focusing the effort on who did something wrong, focus on justice and fairness. One program that may be offered in your school is "Beyond Blame," developed by the Educators for Social Responsibility. The curriculum for middle and high school students focuses on justice, fairness, and mislaid blame.

♦ Planet X is a study unit available on the Internet that guides kids in working together to establish a Bill of Rights for a new planet. It helps students practice negotiation skills.

♦ For younger children, there is Ask Eric, which provides lessons on cultural sensitivity for kindergarten through third grade students.

## Indigo Stars

Princess Diana of Wales could very well have been an early Indigo because of her deep emotional sensitivity and her role in promoting tolerance and compassion. She grew into her role as princess and diplomat, arising from a childhood where she took her parents' divorce hard and triumphing despite the strain of a cold, loveless marriage. She turned her compassion out to the world. She is credited with shattering the stigma of AIDS in the early days, when she held hands with AIDS patients.

# The Big Picture

We weren't just joking about teaching the world to sing in perfect harmony. These compassionate and tolerant Indigos really do want the rest of the world to think as they do. These Indigos feel a stronger connection to the Universe, all of its people and all of its beings. They are more aware of the spirits of animals and plants. They also have a higher awareness of the imbalances and inequities that exist and want to correct them.

We may also see more consensus building among these children. These children want situations to be fair. They care very much about getting to the truth and establishing peace. They find peace in knowing the truth. Our classrooms may become more collaborative.

As Indigos grow up and make more of a contribution to the world, they will raise the level of compassion to a higher level. They will seek to reduce poverty, homelessness, and joblessness. They will seek a health care system that is universally available and affordable. All of this points to a future world—a world with more (if not perfect) harmony.

## The Least You Need to Know

◆ Indigos may display a remarkable level of compassion, the awareness of the pain and suffering of all living things.

◆ Tender-hearted Indigos benefit from energy-shielding techniques that help them stay centered.

◆ Teach your Indigo ways to set clear and compassionate boundaries that honor self and others.

◆ Some Indigos have such a sense of compassion that they are overwhelmed and shut down. Touch therapy and movement may help.

◆ Indigos have an innate orientation toward tolerance, which stems from their compassion and idealism. Some of these Indigos may emerge as leaders.

◆ Give your Indigo opportunities to learn in collaborative, noncompetitive situations, and he will thrive.

# Chapter 8

# Nonconformity, Independence, and Self-Reliance

## In This Chapter

- ◆ Reaching out to the self-sufficient child
- ◆ So misunderstood: the downside of nonconformity
- ◆ Rebellion and peer management
- ◆ From self-reliance to interdependence

Indigo Children are independent souls. Some of that is because they feel so different, being at the extremes of behavior, sensitivity, and sensibilities about the world. Many of them pride themselves on nonconformity. Many of them are completely comfortable with being lone rangers.

Some of them are focused on independence from an early age. They may seem uncannily self-reliant for ones so young. They want to do it for themselves. They don't feel the need to follow the crowd. While such independence is a good trait, it can present you and your Indigo with some challenges. In this chapter, we'll discuss strategies for dealing with this gift.

# Your Independent Thinker

Out of the Indigo child's independent thinking style come many benefits. Your child has a strong sense of himself, and that means he knows what is right for him—and what isn't. He already has an appreciation for his singular qualities. It's your job to support this consistently. Honor his resistance to conformity but do teach him the art of compromise. He must choose his battles. Not always does he have to hold himself out from the crowd. Not always does he have to be different for the sake of being different.

You may think sometimes that your Indigo child is being different to make a statement, but more often than not, she is being different because she is. She is an original. She's simply going to do her own thing.

Your Indigo may be perfectly content to play by herself, even amid a crowd of other children, much like Carolyn's niece, who can completely take herself out of the fantasy play all the other cousins are involved in and go exploring butterflies and beetles in the back yard. She only zones into the group play every so often.

Your independent Indigo may not need a lot of your attention, and if he's part of a larger family, you may find that you have to go out of your way to make sure he doesn't have an unvoiced need. He may play separately from other siblings for long stretches of time.

Your independent Indigo may also have a highly active imagination, developing an imaginary friend, keeping that friend around past the ordinary age of development when children move on. Because she's tuned in to the spirit world, she may be completely comfortable playing elaborate games with imaginary beings, and this won't get socialized out of her as early as it does with non-Indigos.

Bear in mind that your Indigo may actually have a spirit friend who is not entirely imaginary. She might talk to one of her spirit guides or to a fairy being who seems entirely real to her, even if no one else can see it.

Remind your child that because others can't see her invisible friend, it is better to talk to that friend when others are not around so they won't be confused and won't tease her about it. Of course, your independent-thinking Indigo may not care what others think!

# The Gift of Being an Original

Your Indigo is truly original. He may be a delight. He's always coming up with inventive games—you never know what he'll come up with next. All children are by nature inventive, but the Indigo breaks the mold.

For instance, Carolyn's son Lucas, from first grade on, became the master of creating intricate and elaborate board games. Because he is highly proficient in all levels of math, many of the games involve solving multiplication or division problems, blending them with elaborate geometrical and non-linear mazes. (Upon entering second grade, he quickly made the case for being in the gifted math program.)

Since he was 3, Lucas also has specialized in what Carolyn terms "cataclysmic climatological phenomena performance art," which amounts, basically, to her son acting out and painting an earthquake or volcanic eruption on a mural-size piece of paper, using multiple media.

If your Indigo is constantly coming up with stuff that makes you say, "Never would have thought of that …," you have this type. Your Indigo may channel this into art or inventions, or he may be a budding mathematician or entrepreneur.

## Indigo Stars

When the late comedian Andy Kaufman was a child, according to the Andy Kaufman home page, he would not play ball with the other children. He stayed in his room, where he imagined there was a camera in the wall, and he would perform for a television show that he imagined was being broadcast to the rest of the world. Kaufman would not call himself a comedian—he resisted all labels. Many considered him eccentric, including fellow performers, who often were not in on the joke. The online encyclopedia Wikipedia says Kaufman was considered not a comedian so much as a practitioner of anti-humor, or dada absurdism.

# All By Myself

"I do it myself," is the phrase for which Carolyn's toddler-age niece is best known. Your Indigo may have this in the extreme, insisting on trying everything without your help. It may be frustrating for you at times, because you can see she needs your help. It also can prove to be isolating for your child—others may be so accustomed to her remarkable self-sufficiency that they don't notice when she really does need help. As she grows up, she may be so accustomed to taking everything on solo that she doesn't know when to ask for help—or even how.

More than likely you won't be able to help her head on. You may have to find lateral ways to help her—maybe play alongside her and ask questions about how the game or project works, treating her as the expert. When you see an easier way to do it (independent Indigos don't always do it the easy way), you may educate her by asking her questions about why she does it the way she does it. Appeal to her sense of expertise when you say, "What do you think would happen (if you did it this other way)?"

Don't overestimate your child's ability because of his independent attitude. It's easy to expect a lot of your Indigo child when you see how much he is willing to learn and able to accomplish. You may inadvertently give him too much responsibility—something he can handle most of the time but from which he occasionally needs relief. Always let your child know that he has a voice in how far he wants to go with a talent or activity. Always let him know it's okay to rely on you, even when he thinks he can go it alone. "I'm watching your back" might be the way to play it with the independent Indigo.

**Patience**

Some independent Indigos can really be hard on themselves when they doesn't learn something right away. Unlike the more compassionate Indigo child, this type may have a high futility factor that is hard to detect beneath a "can-do" façade. You can help him by reframing some of the negative self-talk that results when he stumbles while learning something new. Give him new, self-compassionate talk. And keep reminding him that we all have a learning curve.

And when your independent Indigo does turn to you, showing good judgment about what challenges to share, validate his judgment as a strength. He may perceive needing to turn to you as a weakness, but the truth is that knowing when to share a burden is indeed a strength. This falls into the "catch them doing something right category." Any time your child demonstrates behavior that you want to encourage, make sure to give specific praise.

# Nonconformity

Here's the upside of *nonconformity:* your Indigo won't follow all the other lemmings over the cliff. She will avoid trends, but rather be a trendsetter. She may always be "out of the box," suggesting to the teacher that she write about a topic of her choosing rather than the assigned homework. This stubborn commitment to be different may keep her out of a host of teenage trouble—drugs, depression, sexual rebellion.

## def•i•ni•tion

Nonconformity is defined as the failure or refusal to conform to accepted rules, standards, norms, or conventions. A nonconformist disagrees with the rules and may challenge them directly or indirectly. Those who are nonconformists see that the rules need to be changed. They are the impetus for bringing about better ideas and guidelines for society. As Ralph Waldo Emerson said, "To be great is to be misunderstood."

And here's the downside: sometimes your nonconformist is simply rebellious and hard to live with. She may refuse to do tasks you expect her to do. She may shun joining the rest of the family in activities. She may be uncooperative and disagreeable. In other words, she may act like a teenager long before she hits age 13.

Make an effort to bring your rebellious Indigo into the family fold by encouraging her to join in or suggest family fun ideas. If she comes up with the idea, and she gets your okay to "run with it," then she will likely stay engaged. She might carry over her enthusiasm to plan the next family fun event. If she doesn't have ideas, brainstorm together as a family, and let her be the main organizer of the event. Say it's a family barbecue. Ask her what she would like to contribute to this. What would make it fun and different—different being the key word here? Party games? Exotic foods? Maybe she's on a health kick or she loves everything about Italy. Let her make smoothies or serve antipasto. Get her interested, give her some power, and you have her attention!

## Separate Yet Together

To really understand the effects of nonconformity in Indigos, let's take a closer look at what it is. German psychologist Erich Fromm, in his book *The Art of Loving* (see Appendix B), said we feel lonely and isolated because we feel separate from other human beings; we feel separate when we don't conform to family and cultural norms, even if that's our choice. Thus, we face the pressure to conform to others' ideas of who we should be in order to be loved. There is a condition on whether we are loved.

These feelings go deep. Fromm says, "The awareness of human separation without hope of reunion by love is a source of shame."

That's the nonconformist's existential dilemma. While most of the time your independent-thinking Indigo behaves as though the last thing he cares about is what people think of him, that's not always true. Deep down, he cares what *you* think. Your love and acceptance are key to his comfort level with his independent ways out in the world. Like Fromm writes, he must have the hope of reunion by love. That means that you're still home base, even when he's saying, "I do it for myself," he wants to know you're there. You must let him know you love him for who he is. Make the effort to really know him—not to change him to conform to your idea of who he should be, but to know him as he is. The family climate determines how your child integrates his independence with the need to be loved as he becomes a teenager and an adult, interacting with the rest of the world.

## Different for Different's Sake

On the other hand, some nonconformist Indigo Children may do things for the sake of being different, including drugs. Yeah, we know, we just said some Indigo Children will resist those teen pressures because they are stubbornly individualistic and won't follow the crowd. But there's a certain Indigo type who likes to experiment—and will. You'll know which one you have soon enough. Your Indigo likes the feeling of being different—and likes it when others notice he is different.

As a parent, help your Indigo carve out a unique niche—that's safe. She won't want to do anything conventional—unless the conventional is so out of favor that it's become unconventional—such as girls choosing cheerleading over soccer. Your Indigo will want to swim against the tide. He may give Buddhism a try—then join a Southern gospel choir. He may shun playing electric guitar and be enthralled with the harp.

Give your Indigo the opportunity to develop interests that tap into a community, so that she can feel a part of a group yet have the sense that she's among others who also are unconventional and freethinking. That way, she will not feel so isolated (or be as susceptible to the experimentation that you want to head off). Indigo Children are vulnerable to negative influences when they don't feel understood. It's important that they feel you understand them, and it's equally important that they have other adults and peers who do, too.

From an early age, you can teach your child to stop and think about whether a new friend is a good influence. When your child is quite young—say in preschool—this conversation often comes up around bullying or teasing. Keep it simple. How does he feel when this friend is a bully—good or bad? Tell him friends are supposed to make you feel good most of the time—not the other way around. And good friends don't get you to do mean things, such as tease or bully other children.

Later, as he enters elementary school, where friends become a big part of his life, you can take the dialogue to the next level. How does he feel about himself when he is with this friend? Does he feel smart? Valued? Stronger or weaker? Listened to or talked down to? Included or excluded? Lay the groundwork through the preschool and elementary years. This is when children form their ideas about friendships that lead to good choices in the teen years, both with friends and with dating. As your child becomes a preteen and teen, you can carry the same questions to her media input. Did this book, movie, song, or television show make you feel good or bad about yourself? What did the characters value that you agreed with? What did you disagree with? Would you be friends with these people?

**Good Counsel**

The best thing you can do for a nonconformist Indigo is to allow her to explore her unique talents. Abandon any preconceived notions about what she will grow up to be. Support her exploration, and help her find activities in which she excels.

Don't be surprised if it feels like you have a bit of a dilettante on your hands—that is, a dabbler. Combine the imaginativeness, free thinking, and curiosity with nonconformity, and that's often what you get. We know that dilettantes can be expensive. One week you're signing up for horseback lessons. The next you're buying a trumpet. Set limits up front about activities. Establish how many you will do, set a budget, a geographical range, and agree on a length of time that your child will pursue the activity. Give your child ways to get a taste for the activity. Maybe she plays a friend's trumpet or rides a friend's horse before you sign up for lessons.

## The Isolation of Being Different

The danger of nonconformity is that your Indigo child may feel lonely or isolated. As a younger child, she might separate herself from other children, and that may lead to anger or depression that intensifies in the teen years, when she may become more isolated. Some Indigos who feel too different and too isolated may become bullies or may shut down.

Teen suicide is a huge problem in our time. Here are some suicide warning signs in teens:

- Your Indigo is nonresponsive to a show of caring from you or other family members.

- Your Indigo seems to have no friends.

- Your Indigo is not making future plans and won't discuss the future.

- Your Indigo is giving away important personal items.

- Your Indigo is talking about having no reason to live.

- Your Indigo has commented about life being better "on the other side."

- Your Indigo seems overly reckless—seems to have a death wish.

- Your Indigo has experienced a recent loss, especially a relationship.

- Your Indigo has lost interest even in her favorite hobbies.

- Your Indigo recently faced humiliation or failure.

- Your Indigo is using alcohol or drugs.

- Your Indigo's sleep patterns have changed.

- Your Indigo feels out of control or fears losing control.

- Your Indigo shows signs of depression.

If you see these signs, here is how to help:

- Connect. Show you care by spending time with her.

- Tell her you love her.

- Show an interest in her skills and talents.

- Help her focus on the positive. Have her collect positive stories about the challenges she's facing.

- Help identify activities and people who have brought her joy—in the past and the present. Help her reconnect.

- Together, make a talents list of her positive attributes.

- Get out and do something together that helps another person.

- Send your teen energy healing or bring him to an energy healer.

- Use crystal healing (more about that in Chapter 12). Give him grounding stones such as hematite or pyrite.

- Encourage him to take control of his energy shielding, allowing positive energy in and blocking out negative energy.

- Spend some time with pets or other animals.

- Never hesitate to ask directly if he is thinking about suicide.

- Get professional counseling for your teen.

If your teen is showing these signs, it may be difficult to have the conversations around taking these steps. We encourage you to take these conversations to a professional setting—do not delay—with a psychotherapist.

Assuming you have laid the spiritual groundwork with your teen, one breakthrough conversation is to talk about what she wants her life to be that it is not. How does she envision herself in the afterlife, or the next life, if she believes in reincarnation? If she did commit suicide, how would Spirit respond to that choice? Would her next life be *more* difficult? What, then, are the spiritual gifts and lessons of this life? Help her consider the challenges she has now and the ways she can turn those into blessings. What spiritual gifts does she have now that she may have lost sight of? Her senses, her health, her intelligence, her spiritual awareness, to name a few. Encourage her to start over again in this life, changing what she can change and accepting what she cannot. Encourage her to strengthen her reliance on Spirit, less on self. What is Spirit giving her to work with in this life?

This is a hard one, and we advise you do it with the guidance of a therapist or spiritual adviser. It's an exceptional conversation, but something that isn't out of the realm of possibility with an Indigo. Remember, they are highly attuned to spiritual matters. And that may be what resonates for your teen, cutting through the isolation and despair. Coming together with a new acceptance for her and a goal of sharing spiritual enrichment together may be the breakthrough for both of you.

**Crystal Clear**

Man's task is to give birth to himself.

—German psychologist Erich Fromm

Nonconformity is, by definition, disharmonious. It means that you don't fit in. It's the refusal to conform to accepted standards, rules, or laws. Inherent in nonconformity is a dispute. The person who does not conform is disagreeing with the rules—and that's okay. Some of the rules may need to be challenged.

The free-spirited Indigo may not challenge the rules directly. He may behave as though he never knew there was a rule in the first place. An Indigo with leadership skills may have the charisma to challenge the rules using conventional techniques. She may know how to talk the talk and walk the walk, but she's not going to do it in the same old way. An antisocial Indigo is withdrawn and often displays a mistrust or even hostility for the rules. His holding himself out is a statement in and of itself. All styles are agents of change.

# Self-Reliance from Day One

Transcendentalist Ralph Waldo Emerson urged us in the nineteenth century to "Trust thyself." Emerson writes that there is a time when each individual recognizes the worth of his own judgment. He says, "There is a time in every man's education when he arrives at the conviction that envy is ignorance; that imitation is suicide." At some point, each individual reaches an acceptance of who he is. What's different about Indigos is that they are already well on their way to accepting themselves as they are. They are programmed for self-reliance.

## The Least You Need to Know

- ◆ Honor your child's strong sense of self and resistance to conformity, but teach him the art of compromise.

- ◆ Channel your original thinker's inventiveness into art, entrepreneurship—or inventions!

- ◆ The independent child may have difficulty asking for what he needs. Play alongside him or ask him to instruct you in how he does something so you can stay in touch with his needs.

- ◆ Give your nonconformist Indigo room to express herself as a trendsetter, but give her ways to participate in the family and other communities, expressing her uniqueness.

- ◆ Some nonconformist and independent Indigos are susceptible to depression. Be alert to the signs, and know how to reach out.

- ◆ Self-reliant Indigos are well on their way to the self-acceptance that can lead to leadership roles.

**Part 3**

# Mission Incredible:
# Parenting Indigos

Feel honored that you are the parent of this very special child.
Along with the territory come new ways of developing discipline
and a challenge to love unconditionally and maintain integrity.
In this section, we'll give practical tips for parenting Indigos—and
we'll ask the question of whether you might be an Indigo, too.

# Chapter 9

# Setting Limits: All About Discipline

## In This Chapter

- ◆ The value of respect
- ◆ How to determine consequences
- ◆ Setting up choices within limits
- ◆ Sample dialogues

Respect is the byword when it comes to setting limits for your Indigo child. Including your child in the solution is not to relinquish your role as parent, nor is it to be a soft, permissive parent. Rather, it means to treat your child as you would anyone, respecting his wisdom and his right to make the decisions he is ready to make.

It's all in the communication style. While you always recognize that your child is a child, and she needs your direction, you communicate that she is part of a partnership, in which she shares a responsibility for learning and growing. In this chapter, we help you get clearer about your mission as the parent of an Indigo child.

# A Little R-E-S-P-E-C-T Goes a Long Way

Indigo Children will demand respect. That's why respect is at the top of the list of the Ten Commandments we gave in Chapter 1. If you give your Indigo child an adequate measure of respect, you'll find you have a child who takes responsibility for his thoughts and actions. Your child will grow up with a solid understanding of the consequences of bad decisions. And this is the best form of discipline of all—teaching your child self-discipline.

This is a lifetime curriculum, and each day contains lessons—lessons that add up as you go along. As Carolyn's sister often says, "Ninety percent of parenting is knowing what they are ready for when." A 3-year-old Indigo who needs a nap simply isn't going to be able to temper her frustration when denied a Popsicle. She is not ready to understand deferred gratification. And it will do you no good to explain impulses or work through the logic of why we nap. You may just need to tough it out, all while maintaining grace and respect for your little creature.

But the 6-year-old who got in trouble at school when he punched the bully on the playground is capable of understanding there are other ways to resolve conflict. He can contribute ideas and solutions, and he can take responsibility for his behavior. He can understand far more subtleties.

Listening to your child is the key to knowing what role your child is ready to play in learning to take responsibility for his actions. Listening is one of the first components of respect.

> **Crystal Clear**
>
> To respect a person is not possible without knowing him; care and responsibility would be blind if they were not guided by knowledge.
>
> —German-American psychologist Erich Fromm

## A Deeper Respect

*Respect* with an Indigo is a particular brand. It goes deeper than the average respectful relationship. It goes to understanding your Indigo's unique nature. Here are some guidelines for cultivating mutual respect:

◆ Listen to your Indigo child without judgment and with empathy. You don't have to agree with his ideas. You may want to correct his ideas, but first listen. You have to hear him and know him, and this puts you on solid ground for correcting him. For now, delight in how his mind works. Be an anthropologist. Try to figure out what makes him tick.

## def•i•ni•tion

To **respect** someone is to show regard for, to hold in high esteem, to feel appreciative toward. When you respect someone, you honor his dignity. Respect in action is listening and showing consideration for the person's feelings. Tolerance is built in to respect, as in this anonymous quote, "To be one, united, is a great thing, but to respect the right to be different is even greater."

◆ Let your Indigo child know that you want to know her for who she is.

◆ Let your Indigo child know that you will take into account his needs, wishes, and desires. This is not the same thing as submitting to them. You will still decide what is valid and what is appropriate for your child. But do let your child know that even if a decision doesn't go his way, you considered his wishes.

◆ Ask your Indigo child for his ideas. Let him know you value his ideas by doing this consistently.

◆ Be truthful.

◆ Accept your Indigo child's idiosyncrasies. This hooks into the eighth commandment, to honor her Indigo nature.

◆ Show respect through the care with which you provide for his basic daily needs—feeding him, providing a home—taking into consideration his emotional and physical sensitivity. If there is a lot of honor that goes into this, it doesn't matter how rich or poor you are. Your child needs your love and attention more than anything else you could give.

◆ Don't interrupt your Indigo child when she talks, and expect the same courtesy from her.

- Accommodate your Indigo child on his wishes when you can—when it's small stuff. This is not necessarily about getting them things, but more about doing things together. They do not have to get every object they want.

- Allow your Indigo child to give you feedback—without being defensive. Allow that because your Indigo child is a child, she may not necessarily do this tactfully or respectfully. But when you treat your child with respect, you are teaching her the way to give respect to others. It will come in time.

Children do not feel respected when:

- They are manipulated.

- They are coerced.

- Their ideas aren't included or sought.

- Their ideas are invalidated.

- They are interrupted.

- They are laughed at.

- They are judged without being heard.

- Their feelings and needs are not taken seriously.

- They are underestimated.

These principles are universal. They don't just apply to Indigo Children; they apply to all children. And they don't only apply to children. These statements are true for all of us. But Indigo Children take to heart these trespasses on respect. That's what sets them apart. They reject any paradigm that accepts these behaviors, and they are forcing us to change.

## Guidelines for Consequences

Think of each parenting challenge as a training moment. While consequences might be merited, it's important that the consequences teach the child values and principles that she can use when she faces future situations. For that reason, the best solutions are consequences that arise naturally from the situation.

It's important that the consequences be memorable—something that gets through to the child on a deep and lasting level. There is no better way to do this than to make the child think about it for himself. That's why it's beneficial to include your child as you determine appropriate consequences. Yes, your child will more than likely recommend consequences that don't take away anything too dear or don't cause too much pain. On the other hand, some children will recommend consequences that are far more harsh than you had planned. Be amused, then walk your child through more appropriate consequences and your reasons for them. Use these guidelines:

- What was the effect of your child's actions?

- How did it hurt someone else or herself?

- How did it not live up to the principles you value?

- What's the long-term effect if this continues to happen?

Let's say your child missed several math questions on his homework because he rushed through it. Normally, he aces this stuff. It's your job to help him connect all the dots: because he wanted to play with the magnetic building blocks, he raced through the addition and subtraction problems, thinking he already knew the material, and he didn't double-check his work. That's the cause and effect.

The person it hurts is himself: he won't learn the material and he won't get good grades. That doesn't support the value the two of you share: getting a good education. If he continues to be sloppy with his homework, not only might he not do well in school, he might not learn skills that he will need to know later in life. Help paint the picture. Where does learning math skills fit in, and why is it important? You might connect it with the activity in which he's shown interest: building things. How does someone use math to build a building? To really bring this home, you might measure the magnetic building blocks, then ask him how many it would take to build a structure 18 inches tall. It's a high concept to get across to a child that a series of addition problems on a page of arithmetic homework might come in handy as an adult who wants to build skyscrapers. But put it down on a level where he can experience the results, and he will get it.

# The Parent-Child Partnership

Cutting your child in on the solutions and the consequences is not relinquishing your role as the parent. Ultimately you're the one responsible for your children maturing into self-sufficient adults. Involving them in discussions is a way to teach empowerment and responsibility. You teach them that they have many resources to solve their problems. You communicate that you expect them to take responsibility when they make mistakes. And you get buy-in. A child who thoroughly understands the problem participates in the solution.

### Good Counsel

After you discuss solutions with your child, establish accountability—for both of you. Let your child know you'll be checking on the situation—whether it's talking to the principal about the bully, asking the teacher to check in with you a week or two later about whether she's seen a change in his work habits, or checking the time he's putting in on his homework.

## What Doesn't Work

It's very tempting as a parent to say, "I'm the parent, you're the child. You will do as I say." What parent hasn't let those words leap out of her or his mouth? It certainly gets to the point. But this logic simply isn't enough for an Indigo child. Nor do Indigos accept the idea that because you have more life experience, your solution wins the day. As much as this may take you aback, it's important to stop and think about why they won't accept it. You may have 30 or 40 years of life experience on them, but to Indigos, it's a different world. What worked before won't necessarily work again. Indigo Children are quick to recognize that the circumstances of your life don't necessarily translate to their experience: it's already built in to them that their experience of this world is singular.

Let's say your Indigo is acting out a lot, and you think he needs anger management counseling. A logical solution might be to schedule him to see a psychologist, asking for referrals and interviewing prospective counselors to find a good fit. Makes sense, doesn't it? But your Indigo may think out of the box. For instance, if you have already been having a dialogue with your child about his psychic abilities and awareness, or about energy healing, he might suggest that this is too conventional an approach for him. He might suggest that instead of or in addition to a psychologist, he go to a psychic or energy healer. A few intuitive-oriented psychologists integrate psychic information in their work, and that can be a good match for your Indigo. As Wendy and Carolyn were brainstorming this book, Wendy suggested this approach to anger management.

Synchronistically, this conversation came up right after Carolyn had scheduled her 7-year-old son Lucas with an anger management counselor, though this was news to Wendy. Carolyn had informed Lucas that they had an appointment and had portrayed this casually—as "this is someone who can give you some good ideas about your anger," not as in "you have a problem, and this person will fix it for you." Still, Lucas was apprehensive. Wendy's suggestion for this book reminded Carolyn to factor in Lucas' ability to tune in to psychic undercurrents—something that sets him apart from other children. It gives him a challenge—the challenge of being more intuitive than many of his boy peers—and a gift—another channel in which to get guidance and insight to meet his everyday challenges. Perhaps, it occurred to Carolyn, he can use his intuitive powers to notice when people aren't treating him right and his anger is building up.

Another example of ways the Indigo approach to life may provide more innovative solutions is in the case of Indigos who have ADHD. Many conventional schools push for those children to go on medication. Parents struggle with this decision—they want a quick fix for the short term so their child can focus and improve in school. Depending on your child's age, you may include your child in this discussion. An older Indigo child may have learned about herbal or homeopathic remedies for ADHD or be willing to adjust his diet before resorting to conventional medication for ADHD.

An older Indigo may assist in your research for solutions. If your Indigo surprises you with solutions you wouldn't have thought of, consider giving it a trial period. As always, set up ways to measure the success of the solution and be accountable.

By the way, you are not admitting a weakness when you acknowledge your child's anger or disappointment. Old-style parenting might sound something like "I'll give you something to cry about" or "I'm really doing this because I love you" (far too complicated and guilt-inducing for a child to grasp). But Indigo parenting responds with empathy with limits: "I know you are disappointed because ..." Acknowledge anger, jealousy, distrust, hurt. These are uncomfortable emotions, but letting them be out in the open takes away the power they have over us. Acknowledging them helps your child overcome them rather than repressing them and letting them enslave her.

### Indigo Stars

Keki Mingus was the editor-in-chief of the one-time parenting magazine *Violet*, which advertised itself as being for alternative-living, green-friendly, creative parents who have "grown up but haven't grown old." Mingus describes herself on the website as the "tone-deaf, flat-footed, spastic daughter of a great musician"—Charles Mingus. Mingus says the most important thing her father conveyed to her was to approach art with honesty. *Violet*'s editorial ethic was very much for singular parents and children, many of whom are likely Indigos.

## Choices Within the Limits

The parenting style we are discussing is more open than the style you may be accustomed to. It may be very different from the way you grew up, and it may not feel natural or right to you. It's important to distinguish that when you are offering choices, you are not failing to establish good limits for your child. You establish limits, and you give choices within those limits. The degree to which you allow your child to participate in shaping the choices depends on his development—*what he is ready for when.*

When you offer choices, make sure that all are acceptable solutions. You may prefer one choice over the other, but let her test it. If taking the time to allow your child choices, listening to her, and respecting her ideas seems like a lot of attention to life's daily transactions, it is. But that's a reminder of how much time and effort is required for loving another living being. Getting to know someone is an intricate project. Part of the mission of Indigo Children is to call us to attention with them. They compel us not to turn away and to invest in loving.

With Indigo Children, the more expedient "because-I-said-so" methods of parenting won't work. The child compels compassion and originality, something that goes beyond the reflex of caring to the new territory of knowing them as singular individuals and loving them deeply for their uniqueness.

Right now, you can shift this paradigm. When your Indigo child demands you know her uniqueness, it's a call to love. You are being challenged to love her better, but also to know yourself better. You are being challenged to develop more self-awareness and self-compassion.

# Indigos and Limits

Accept that your Indigo child will test the boundaries—and will want to change them. And don't read this as an affront to your role as parent. It's not a reflection on your abilities as a parent. Instead, it's a reflection that you have an Indigo.

Remember that what you resist persists. If you are resisting change because your child is pushing the limits, and you think this should not happen because you're the parent, and you know what's best, you are not doing anything to change the situation. The more you read it as being all about a challenge to your authority to a parent, the more the situation will present itself.

If instead, you see it as an opportunity to develop a wiser, more peaceable solution—and possibly an opportunity for personal growth—you will be much more successful.

Change your attitude to one of acceptance and unconditional positive regard. Use the following statements as affirmations:

*I accept that my Indigo will test the boundaries. I understand this is not about me.*

*I accept that when my Indigo pushes the limits, it's because she wants to know the limits. The limits make her feel safe in a world that doesn't understand her as much as I do.*

*Sometimes, when my Indigo pushes the limits, it's toward the end of gaining higher understanding and seeking a singular, more workable solution.*

*I am equipped to work with my Indigo child to find break-the-mold solutions to his challenges. I know it is my responsibility, and I know I have the skills.*

*I love my child unconditionally. I regard her highly. I see her strengths, and I know her weaknesses. I love her still.*

*I know my child is not being willful just to make my life hard.* (Repeat often!)

*I understand that parenting an Indigo requires more patience and a lot of listening. I see the beauty in this, and I accept this.*

## Hear What's Beneath the Resistance

When you get resistance to life's day-to-day chores, though, it can be quite difficult to slow down and work it all out. Both Carolyn and the twins' father find themselves saying to their children, "Let's keep it simple," because their imaginative, energetic twins often want to throw in every idea but the kitchen sink to what the adults think should be a routine situation.

For instance, Carolyn couldn't quite understand why her daughter Emerald, who loves to dance, was giving her an endless stream of complaints about a hip hop dance class. Of particular importance was getting the right socks. It took much doing to get the right pair—the pair that would make her daughter happy. Carolyn wondered, "What's so complicated about this? What am I not getting?" It led her to think that perhaps Emerald didn't like to dance as much as Carolyn thought. *We won't sign up for* that *class again*, was what Carolyn was thinking.

This story is a reminder that it may seem simple to you, but not to your child. Once Carolyn stopped to listen, she learned that the heart of the matter for Emerald was that the hip hop dance teacher had set the bar really high, and it was challenging her to keep up with the class. Emerald believed if she wore the right socks, she could keep up, but more important, she needed to know she was being heard about her specific need, which then allowed her to open up and talk about her struggle to try something new. Once this was uncovered, it was much clearer to

Carolyn: it wasn't that her daughter didn't like the class for which Carolyn had signed her up; it was that she *liked it, so much* she wanted to try harder to do something that was challenging her. She needed support—and socks! It was a lesson for Carolyn to take her sight past the thought that she had made a mistake (signing Emerald up for a class she didn't want to take) and get to a truth (equipping her child to face a new challenge and allowing her to speak her needs).

Know that sometimes when your child is resisting, it's about making sure something is in order—maybe because the situation is uncertain or challenging. Know that sometimes there is a lot of emotion behind the situation, and you need to stop and talk about it. Listen, listen, listen. That's the underpinning of respect. Listening was what was in order here, no matter whether the answer was that Emerald liked the class or didn't like the class. Listening was its own success. Even if you don't have all the solutions, you can solve 90 percent of the problem simply by listening.

## A Sample Dialogue

Let's take this sample dialogue to show how to move from resistance to acceptance, all while guiding your child in making good choices. The situation is the child does not want to wear the clothes the parent set out for school.

Resistance: "You must wear the white polo shirt and skirt. Now get it on. We're running late."

A screaming fight ensues.

Instead:

Acceptance: "Maybe we can pick out something else that's okay for a warm day and works for school. Give me two ideas, and we'll decide which works best."

In this case, the parent gave the child some parameters. She knows up front that she can't come back with a sundress in winter or red corduroys and a sweater in summer. The parent also set a limit on the number of suggestions. If you are running late, set a time limit. Put two minutes on the kitchen timer, and get an agreement that if she doesn't come up with a better option, you'll go with the original pick for that day and you'll discuss it later.

Acceptance and Change: "Tonight we'll choose together what you're going to wear the rest of the week."

Another scenario: The child says he hates what you packed for lunch. He comes across in a way that really pushes your buttons. His tone is disagreeable and accusatory.

Child: "I hate peanut butter and jelly. I'm so absolutely sick of it. That peanut butter is goopy, and that bread is just gross. Today there's pizza in the cafeteria. Why can't I ever have that?"

Resistance: "I already packed your lunch, and that's that. The pizza is bad for you anyhow."

Instead:

Acceptance: "Really? I'm sorry to hear you don't like peanut butter and jelly. I'm glad you told me."

Child: "It's okay, I guess. But I would like to try the pizza at school sometime. It looks delicious."

Acceptance: "It could be. I wonder what it's like. Do you think it's nutritious, too?"

Child: "It's got pepperoni and a thick crust and ... only a little cheese. It's probably not good for you, but I just like it."

Acceptance: "That happens to me, too. I sometimes want to try things that look delicious but might not be good for me."

Child: "Could I try it, please? Just once?"

Acceptance: "I suppose it wouldn't hurt every once in a while, but today isn't a good day. I've already packed your lunch. Next time, could you tell me in advance when pizza day will be?"

Acceptance and Compromise: "Maybe we can have pizza for dinner this weekend. We can make one that's better than the school pizza."

Acceptance and Change: "I'm sorry you don't like what I packed. I've got an idea. Sometimes I get in a rut about what to pack for your lunch, and I really need some ideas. How about this weekend we plan a lunch menu, and you can help me prepare the food? It's important to me that you get something healthy and tasty for lunch, and that would help me a lot."

These examples are geared toward younger children, but acceptance dialogues can also work with teenagers. One line that comes in hand to neutralize arguments (many thanks to Jim Fay of Love and Logic parenting) is, "I love you too much to argue with you about that." With teenagers, especially Indigo teenagers, you will want to learn to get pretty clear pretty fast about what your resistance is to the situation. What part of this do you need to control, and why?

Get clear on what you need to respond to and what you can leave untouched. When your 14-year-old storms at you that you're too uptight, you can say, "You might be right about that," and go on to what you really need to say. Fay recommends this one with teens: your teen threatens that if he doesn't get a bigger allowance, he might have to start selling drugs. To this, say: "That might be an option." What are the consequences of this option? Let your teen reason it out. Let him realize the potential consequences of taking that option (getting hooked on drugs, going to jail for dealing) and take ownership for it (what does he really want in life).

Tell him you are sorry he's having this problem, but you think he's ready to make more decisions for himself. Let him know you are there for him if he needs more resources and information to make a decision. Asking him, "What do you think you'll do about your problem?" gives him power—and keeps the dialogue open.

 **Crystal Clear**

No matter how calmly you try to referee, parenting will eventually produce bizarre behavior, and I'm not talking about the kids. Their behavior is always normal.

—Bill Cosby, American comedian

# The Bottom Line

Being the parent of an Indigo requires a more open style. It means changing some of the ways you think about the role of a parent. Greek philosopher Aristotle defined tolerance this way: "It is the mark of an educated mind to be able to entertain a thought without accepting it." This can be your guideline for listening with empathy—true, engaged listening.

Shift your focus away from who is the absolute authority with your child—where the buck stops. That point is really not up for debate. Instead, shift your focus to how you're going to be responsible to the relationship. Show up, listen, respect your child and be responsible *for* him and *to* him. Make getting to know him your lifelong project. Hear the call to attention. Heed his desire to be more loving, more accepting, more engaged with him. Take the care and respect to grow this brilliant, imaginative child into a self-sufficient, responsible adult.

## The Least You Need to Know

- Truly respecting your Indigo child will earn his respect.

- Including your Indigo in decisions teaches empowerment and responsibility. Offer choices within limits that are acceptable to you.

- Be open to your child's innovative suggestions to solve problems in ways you may not have thought about.

- Set up natural consequences that are appropriate to the situation.

- "Because I'm the parent!" won't work with Indigos, but "Because I hear you and respect you" will.

- Change your attitude to one of acceptance and work out compromises.

# Chapter 10

# Unconditional Love and Integrity

## In This Chapter

- Loving the sensitive child
- Dialogues in compassion and constancy
- Isn't behavioral correction conditional?
- Establishing an integrity ethic

All children thrive on unconditional love, but the Indigo child needs more diligence to this principle than the average child. It's likewise when it comes to integrity. Many Indigos have an uncanny ability to see through anything that is inconsistent with love and truth. They have a way of keeping you honest and unmasking any agenda you might have.

You won't be able to operate with your Indigo child on anything less than high integrity and unconditional love. His demand for both will nurture in you an expanded expression of a higher love. And guess what? You get what you give, and you very likely will find you receive an exquisite measure of unconditional love from your child. In this chapter, we help you practice a purer form of love, truth, and integrity.

# It's Unconditional

Why do Indigo Children demand unconditional love? It's because they are unconventional. They don't fit into the mold, so they need to hear they are loved for who they are more than the average child. They need it because they are stretching the limits, and they need to feel that it's perfectly okay for them to be on this quest to define themselves—as they redefine the world we live in. Your love is the tether that keeps them from floating off, weightless, like a helium balloon.

If they sense you are trying to change the way they operate without respecting their style, they will not feel loved. Yes, you must help them adapt to their world, and that does mean they must compromise and adjust the way they operate. If you do this with acceptance of who they are, you will get a lot further faster. If your child picks up that you fundamentally want to change what is so unique about him, he will resist. He will keep testing it, because what he wants to know before he can wrap his mind around changing is whether you really appreciate him as he is. Honor him.

> **Crystal Clear**
>
> I believe that unarmed truth and unconditional love will have the final word in reality.
>
> —American civil rights leader Martin Luther King Jr.

Give voice to your feelings about the adaptations your child is making to work within existing structures, such as the educational system. "I know it's hard for you because … you're so creative and unconventional, and I appreciate that about you. We do need to find a way for you to get this done. What might feel good to you?" This is the place from which you can come, a place of acceptance and respect.

Give them empathy for their struggles. See the rightness in it. They may be entirely right. Give them some admiration for their effort to change the structure. Give them guidance in accepting what they cannot change. Also give them validation for their effort to adapt despite the flaws in the structure.

Let's take the struggle of the emotionally sensitive Indigo. Wendy knows this one well. When she was a child, other children often picked on her. It was difficult for her to develop a thicker skin. Wendy's mother would tell her that the other children were jealous because she got good grades. She told her to ignore the taunts from other children. This advice was good for Wendy's ego—the unconditional love and support was vital. Wendy's mother gave her empathy: "I know it's hard for you to ignore it when other kids tease you." What Wendy would have liked to have known then was how to make an energy shield force field to prevent the teasing from hurting her so deeply. Teach your child that her sensitivity is a treasure. Help her see the gifts. And give her tools that will protect her yet allow her to be the sensitive soul that she is.

# A Tall Order

Unconditional love is a high ideal. Your child experiences your love every day, and you know you're not perfect. What the research shows about effective parenting is that you only need to be a good enough parent—you are there for him as much as you can be, emotionally, spiritually, and physically.

The key to unconditional love, then, is consistency—not perfection. Your steady-on, focused approach to loving and supporting your child is what, in the end, will register with her, even if you stumble day-to-day.

Marriage researchers Benjamin R. Karney and Lisa A. Neff of the University of Florida found that spouses who love each other compassionately while fully aware of their spouse's specific qualities, good and bad, had longer, more satisfying marriages. Love compassionately, knowing and honoring your child's qualities, good, bad, or otherwise, and you are well on your way to loving unconditionally.

**Good Counsel**

Unconditional love may seem like a big job, especially in a world that falls short. Remember that your child isn't going to get unconditional love from everyone. If a child has one person giving unconditional love to him, he is very fortunate. As the parent you can be that person for your Indigo and help him consistently feel strong and supported.

Notice how you react to your Indigo child's perceived negative qualities. How do you characterize them? In particular, examine your attitudes about your Indigo child's challenges. Make a list of your Indigo
child's gifts and challenges. Identify the ways he or she is different from
other children. What are the good points and bad points about each of
these qualities? How do you feel about them? If you feel angry, sad, or
scared, ask yourself why. What are you afraid will happen? It may be
that you are concerned your child will not do well in school or will not
be accepted by her peers. Often the fear arises from the desire to spare
your child any emotional struggle. Get to the root of your fear, and you
will be able to love from a more enlightened and empowered place. Try
reframing these attributes:

> Resistant > strong-willed

> Hyperactive > dramatic, spirited

> Distractable > ability to do many things at once

> Stubborn > persistent

You get the idea ...

⭐ **Indigo Stars**

For more than 45 years, Albanian nun Mother Teresa comforted the
poor, the dying, and the unwanted. Joan Guntzelman, who wrote a
biography of Mother Teresa, describes her as her own person, "startlingly
independent, obedient, yet challenging some preconceived notions and
expectations." When the Roman Catholic Church beatified her as a
saint, Pope John Paul II remarked on her strength in placing herself completely at the service of others. She was undeterred when others criticized
her or rejected her, chief among them the communist country where she
was born.

# Defining Unconditional Love

Let's look more closely at the components of unconditional love:

- Compassion (which we defined in Chapter 7).

- Knowledge of the other.

- Consistency and constancy (which we'll cover later in this chapter).

- Commitment to growth. You are committed to learning from your mistakes.

- Tolerance (which we defined in Chapter 7).

- Unity. Choose to join as allies. Strengths make both of you stronger. Weaknesses are made strong because you are united. Weaknesses do not bring out adversarial behavior, but rather bring you together.

It's important to note what unconditional love is *not:*

- Unconditional love is not fear-based and does not exploit fear. Fear is present in manipulation, using guilt or coercion to get your child to comply.

- Unconditional love focuses on inclusion, not separation. Unconditional love does not create dualities—right or wrong, win or lose. It focuses on win-win solutions.

- Unconditional love focuses on growth and learning, not on authority and power.

## Resolving the Eternal Paradox

It may seem like a huge paradox to say on the one hand to love your child unconditionally and to say on the other hand that the parenting responsibility requires guiding and correcting your child. Isn't correction conditional?

Correction is about behavior. Acceptance is about the essential core of who your child is. Your child's behavior, good or bad, doesn't change whether you love him. Correcting his behavior doesn't mean you don't love him; it means you *do*. You correct your child *because* you love him.

It's *how* you punish your child when she misbehaves that determines whether there is static in your consistent message of unconditional love. It may seem incongruent to your child that the consequence of her unwanted behavior is less attention and less tenderness from you.

The incongruence comes in how we typically define love: attention, tenderness, harmony, praise, and approval. These are all superficial definitions.

Constancy and compassion make the difference in the paradox between correction and unconditional love. Here's what constancy looks like: even as you set up consequences for behaviors you don't want, you constantly attend to and support your child in learning and growing. You remain engaged with your child. Here's what compassion looks like: even as you correct your child, you show compassion for the thoughts and feelings that led to the behavior. You tell your child it's normal and okay to have those thoughts and feelings. But you also show him a better way to act on those thoughts and feelings.

Children want to test whether you love them unconditionally. Understand that that's a given. How can this help you reframe your inner dialogue when your Indigo child tests you? It's only human to react to your child's testing of these limits by seeing it as struggle between parent and child. If you're thinking, "Why does he have to test me all the time?" you're in reactive mode. But reframe it with love, as in, "When he tests me, he's asking me for love. He's seeking my guidance. I'm so glad he's asking *me*." If you reframe the test as a request for love, not a challenge to your authority as a parent, it's remarkably different, isn't it? He's seeking your wisdom. Your child feels uncertain about his way, and he needs you to show him the path, complete with guardrails to ensure his safety. The guardrails—the limits—help your child know the route to take.

# High Integrity

How can you establish a high ethic of *integrity* in your family? It begins by setting an example. Then give voice to what you value, as you set the tone. Catch your children in moments of integrity and validate them. Keep a dialogue going so that you each understand what integrity in action looks like and feels like. Create a common ethic in the family: this we believe.

## def·i·ni·tion

Integrity is defined as steadfast adherence to a moral or ethical code. But more importantly, it's a wholeness—an undivided or unbroken state of completeness. If your ethic is the truth, you do truth across the board, not telling the truth in one instance but not another. Someone who acts with integrity is unimpaired. It's a solid state of soundness.

Let's start off by defining integrity:

◆ **Be honest.** This doesn't simply mean telling the truth; it means fully disclosing information that needs to be known. Of course, children cannot yet understand adult topics. Tell them the truth as much as is reasonable—as much as they can grasp. Keep it simple, but keep it open. Allow your Indigo to ask for more explanation. Let her know that it matters to you that she fully understands.

◆ **Be specific.** Your explanations for why you want a certain behavior don't have to be given in exhaustive detail. But notice when you are being vague. Vagueness will feel like lying to an Indigo child. Instead of telling your child not to run around screaming, let him know, "It's hurting my ears. I'm getting a headache. Can we find another way to get this energy out?"

◆ **Be true to your word.** That means your child can trust that you say what you mean and you mean what you say. When you set up consequences, you follow through with them. When you make promises, you deliver.

◆ **Be willing to admit when you are being less than you want to be.** If you promise your child something and you can't quite deliver, explain it. Own it. Take responsibility. Maybe it will take longer to accomplish. Maybe it wasn't the right thing for your child and when you thought it through, you saw it differently. "I know I said we would … but after I took into account … I reconsidered what's really important to us." Always return to your values, and give voice to those in your dialogues with your child.

◆ **Follow through.** Back up your intentions with action.

◆ **Be consistent.** Listen, meet with your child, follow up. Practice, practice, practice. Be reliable.

◆ **Keep the end in mind.** The end is that your child grows up to be a person who feels unconditionally loved and makes decisions in alignment with his values. Keeping the end in mind will help you take struggles out of the temptations of the moment. (Buying another piece of chocolate may get you out of a heated sibling exchange, but what does this teach your child? Is indulgence a value?)

Many of the items from this list mirror those from Don Miguel Ruiz' book, *The Four Agreements* (see Appendix B): be impeccable with your word; don't take anything personally; don't make assumptions; and always do your best. Not taking things personally is especially important for highly sensitive Indigos who take everything to heart. Ruiz says, "Nothing others do is because of you. What others say and do is a projection of their own reality, their own dream. When you are immune to the opinions and actions of others, you won't be the victim of needless suffering."

### Patience

Indigos will know if you lie to them. That will set up a distrust, even for the most seemingly harmless lies, such as Santa Claus or the stork that brings babies. Establish a more organic truth, an understanding that can be true for a 3-year-old and evolve for a 9-year-old. An organic truth is something that doesn't have to be denied later on. Instead of depicting Santa Claus as an immortal human in a red suit, you may portray him as "Santa is a wonderful, giving Spirit" or "Santa has many helpers." Later, your child can grasp the concept of a spiritual and cultural symbol.

## Praise, and Praise Again

Sincerity is the place to start with praise that has integrity. When you compliment your child, your compliment is sincere, specific, and believable. Make your praise specific and well-chosen. Specificity has a way of proving it. It's the evidence that this is true. Well-chosen praise has meaning. You don't need to preserve every mediocre achievement to the point of hilarity, much like the Wall of Gaylord in the movie *Meet the Fockers* (2004).

Because Indigos are highly intuitive, they know when someone is being dishonest. They know when you are buttering them up. They know when you have a motive—you want them to behave in a certain way.

Of course, you do want your child to behave in a certain way. (This is what we mean by being honest!) And we know positive reinforcement works. It's an excellent motivator. We also know it works a whole lot better if it's not just your approval that your child seeks—if she also shares that value. When you use positive reinforcement, guide your child toward understanding the sense of self-satisfaction she can derive from doing it right. When she cleans up her room completely—not just giving it the once-over—and she gets to enjoy an uncluttered space for herself and she gets to have her friends over—she will internalize the positive reinforcement. When he gets his homework organized and maintains a disciplined schedule on working on it, he gets the satisfaction of getting better grades and feeling better about himself because he's overcome the challenge of being distracted and disorganized. He gains a better self-image.

It's also important to note that messages of positive reinforcement go over better when your child is receiving more praise than criticism—not the other way around. If your child hears three criticisms for every praise, she will come to hunger for every morsel of praise and shrink from every criticism. Your child will be approval-oriented, not self-motivated. She will see your love as conditional.

But try it the other way—three praises to every one criticism. Your child will already have a solid base on which to stand to receive and hear the criticism. He will already know what you want, why you want it, and why he wants it, too. He will be more motivated to achieve it.

Praise must be sincere, specific, and free from an agenda, even a hidden one. Caution that your praise is not a demand for constant achievement—you don't want to send the message that unless the child achieves what you are praising him for, you will withdraw your love.

### Good Counsel

As a family, make a list of traits you value and don't value. It's helpful to use examples of people you know or book characters your children know. Ask them who they admire, and why they admire them. Look at places where the person or character is tested. When Harry Potter turns to help Cedric in *Harry Potter and the Goblet of Fire*, instead of reaching for the cup that will secure him victory in the Triwizard Tournament, the choice he makes is that people are more important than glory. That's integrity.

# Guidelines for Correction

Criticism and correction should also be specific and instructional. When you correct your child, maintain high positive regard, yet be forthright and clear about what is not acceptable, not desirable, or is just plain wrong. Communicate with compassion and empathy. Show him you are listening by playing it back to him (even if you modify, correct, or totally disapprove of the response): "So, when the bully hit you on the playground, you were scared and mad. That's why you punched back."

After describing the unwanted behavior specifically and instructing in why it was wrong, discuss with your child what he *could* do to change the behavior or remedy the situation (walk away from the bully, go to a teacher for help). This is a small but significant shift from telling him what he *should* do. *Should* is a guilt-inducing word, and it emphasizes there has already been a failure with a certain finality that can inspire the futility factor. *Could* is much more effective because it leaves open the possibility for improvement or correction. *Could* is an excellent tool for teaching responsibility and empowering your child. It can give your child the confidence that he needs to change the behavior. Again, you set the guidelines for the *could*.

At some point, it seems, nearly every child is tempted to pocket candy from the store and must learn that we never steal. This happened with Carolyn's daughter, Emerald, when she was 6. Emerald slipped some gum in her pocket at the grocery store, and Carolyn learned of it as they were pulling into the driveway at home. Carolyn explained why stealing was wrong and asked Emerald what she could do to make amends. The answer, of course, was to pay for the gum. So they turned around and drove back to the store, and Emerald went through the checkout line and paid for it, admitting to the clerk what happened. This was very hard for Emerald to do—she was embarrassed, a natural consequence. The tone with which Carolyn guided this made the difference between a shameful experience and an educational experience. By maintaining high positive regard for Emerald while still communicating that stealing was wrong, Carolyn helped Emerald learn to take responsibility for a mistake. The "could" gave her a constructive way to remedy it.

When Carolyn's son, Lucas, earned a severe consequence, it was very hard for him to carry it out. Because of the nature of the offense, his cousins were going to be aware of his lost privileges. The only scenario Lucas could imagine was catastrophic. Instead, Carolyn gave him the possibility that he could carry it out with dignity. She gave him the affirmation: "I am a little boy who holds his head up high and learns from his mistakes with dignity."

Walking your child through a scenario that unfolds when he modifies his behavior teaches him—and gives him confidence. He can see himself behaving differently next time. Visualization provides him with a vivid understanding of the lesson he is learning. Affirmations paired with that reinforce the lesson. ("I am smarter and stronger than my impulses" paired with a visualized enactment of a wiser, calmer response is powerful indeed.) Visualization helps your child *rehearse* a better response in his mind. Not only that, you are giving your child techniques that can apply to other situations.

# Building a Resilient Child

Research shows that unconditional love builds resilience in a child. Unconditional love is one of the best predictors of academic success, social adjustment, and adult happiness. Your Indigo child is different in a very special way. He may always carry around a feeling of being different. Unconditional love makes the difference in whether he comes to view this as a detriment or a very special asset. Wrap high integrity into this scenario, and you are well on your way to building an exceptional, self-motivated Indigo child.

## The Least You Need to Know

◆ Because Indigo Children feel so different from other children, unconditional love is vital for giving them a solid base of support.

◆ While unconditional love is a high ideal, you can be an effective parent by being compassionate and consistent. Stay engaged with your child, and love him for all of his specific qualities.

◆ While on the face of it, correcting your child's behavior seems conditional, it is not. Be careful not to define love as approval and attention, but rather define it as a mutual commitment to learn and grow together.

◆ Establish a high ethic of integrity in your family, being true to your word and following through on your commitments.

◆ When you praise your child, be specific. Make a point of giving three praises for every criticism.

◆ Orient your correction to constructive, action-oriented modifications that are empowering and educational for your child. Coach him in gentle, respectful ways to motivate himself to modify his behavior—that is to see how he would benefit.

# Chapter 11

# Being the Parent: Are *You* an Early Indigo?

## In This Chapter

- ◆ Adult Indigos: parallel struggles
- ◆ The Indigo overlay
- ◆ Different times, different challenges
- ◆ Meeting up with other Indigo Adults

You already may be fond and familiar with the challenges of your Indigo Children—too familiar. If much of your experience watching your child struggle feels like looking in the mirror, you may be an Indigo yourself.

Yes, it's possible for adults to be Indigos, too. A whole crop of Indigos arrived early, and you could be one of them. If you're an Indigo adult who is parent to an Indigo child, you bring a special understanding to your assignment. Let's find out what this means for you.

# Could You Be Blue, Too?

Indigo Children are part of a natural spiritual evolution. They haven't just sprung from thin air. Wendy believes there have always been Indigos—about 5 percent of the population—but it was about 1950 when the number began increasing. Many of the flower children of the 1960s were Indigos, and they gave birth to Indigos. The 1970s and 1980s saw a significant increase, and the jump was exponential in the early 1990s.

Wendy was one of the very first people to start writing about Indigo Adults. That's partly because she is one herself. The more she studied Indigo Children, the more she saw similarities to her experience of childhood. After she received thousands of personal letters from adults who had many of the same characteristics of Indigo Children, it was clear there were adult Indigos who needed to connect with other adult Indigos. In April 2001, she started an adult Indigo mailing list on Yahoo Groups. By 2006, the group had more than 3,850 members. A year after she started that group, she started a moderated group, which as of 2006 had nearly 2,000 members.

Examine this checklist of 29 traits, adapted from Wendy's website, to see what traits you have. Many people have a few traits on this list, but if you have 20 or more, you are definitely an adult Indigo.

"Extreme" is the key word here. The following aspects are more than passing thoughts someone might have; in adult Indigos, they are strongly developed attitudes. They are more than situational responses—they are consistent ways of operating in the world.

## Personality Traits

- ❏ You know you're intelligent, even though you may not had the best grades in school.
- ❏ You are creative. You enjoy making things.
- ❏ It's important for you to know why someone asks you to do something.
- ❏ You'd rather be the leader—or work alone—than work on a team.

❏ You sometimes surprise yourself with your deep empathy, yet other times, you can be quite intolerant of stupidity.

❏ You are sexually expressive. You are creative and inventive in the bedroom. You may have explored sacred sexuality for spiritual advancement. You may have explored alternative sexuality.

❏ You have consistently sought meaning for your life through spiritual and/or psychological study.

## Your Struggles

❏ As a child, you were so sensitive to others that you would cry at the drop of a hat. Sometimes you are still that way, but you have learned as an adult to shield yourself better.

❏ Or, you often feel no emotional response at all. Others have sometimes said you are in a cave. They say they don't understand you.

❏ You have outbursts of rage. You know your anger is not average; you sometimes don't know where it comes from.

❏ At times in your life, you have felt an unrelenting sadness and despair. Sometimes you felt immovable, without hope.

❏ You have a different thinking style—your way of collecting and processing information is random, not linear.

❏ You have trouble focusing on assigned tasks.

❏ You often jump around in conversations.

❏ Earlier in life, you struggled to achieve emotional balance.

### Good Counsel

Learning that you are an adult Indigo may spark the desire for change. You may appreciate your gifts, and you may want to apply them to a new career. Or you may want to explore spirituality or develop your psychic skills. Know that the difficulties you have had are not because something is wrong with you, but because you are here to make a difference.

## Attitudes

❑ You found school to be confining and repetitious. You were disgusted with the routine and structure of school.

❑ You loved to rebel against the structure of school and authority of teachers. Maybe you did so defiantly, refusing to do homework or challenging teachers. Or maybe you resisted, insisting on doing homework on your terms.

❑ You have concluded that service-oriented jobs aren't for you. You have found yourself resisting authority and straining against hierarchal corporate structures.

❑ You have strong opinions about the validity and effectiveness of many of our society's institutions, such as political systems, school, health care, or courts. You may question other institutions, such as marriage or organized religion.

❑ You feel alienated from politics. You believe your voice doesn't matter. You feel like an outsider.

❑ You are discontent with the so-called American dream of material wealth and emotional prosperity—nine-to-five corporate grind, marriage, 2.5 children, house in the suburbs with a white picket fence. You have consistently resisted this, even with parental and societal pressure to conform.

❑ You are indignant when your freedoms are trampled on, such as the right to free speech or the right to privacy.

❑ You have a burning desire to change the world. You may have, at this point, defined your path, but your discovery of this path has taken an unconventional route.

## Psychic Skills

❑ You showed an early interest and aptitude for psychic intuition—in your teen years or perhaps before.

❑ You have always had a strong sense of intuition. You remember trusting your intuition more often than what you were hearing from authority figures or from society.

- ❏ You have seen angels or ghosts. You may have heard voices or had out-of-body experiences.

- ❏ You have had premonitions of events.

- ❏ You have noticed that electrical devices are fragile or erratic in your presence. Watches stop working, or streetlights go out. Circuit breakers kick off, or electricity surges through your house.

- ❏ You are aware of other dimensions. You understand parallel realities.

Adult Indigos are similar to Indigo Children—strong intuition, high intelligence, thriving creativity, and advanced spiritual awareness. They also loathe repetition and structure. They struggle with balance. They are different from today's Indigos in that they have learned to adapt—and do so in a much more confining world than exists for today's Indigos. This means they have more compromise skills, and many of the extremes of their Indigo traits are tempered.

## Just an Overlay?

Some Indigo experts describe the adults as having an *Indigo overlay* rather than being actual adult Indigos. Lee Carroll, co-author of *The Indigo Children* (see Appendix B), one of the first books on Indigo Children, makes a distinction between those who have an Indigo overlay. He says the pure Indigo Children started arriving only about 1980. The person with an Indigo overlay has some of the attributes of an Indigo, but they are generalized; the pure Indigo possesses attributes that are deeply ingrained in his being.

Wendy thinks that most adult Indigos are early Indigos, pure and simple. But she also thinks that some parents of Indigos can take on an Indigo aura—or overlay—because they are living with an Indigo child. They might take it on in order to connect with their child. Jan Tober, who wrote *The Indigo Children* with Lee Carroll, described this as a cloak that parents of Indigos wear to work with and appreciate Indigos.

Wendy also believes that many early Indigos changed their life color to another color to adapt—they found it too difficult to be an Indigo. The world wasn't quite ready for them. In those cases, what aura workers might be seeing is someone with a violet life color and an indigo overlay. Many of those early Indigos are now shedding the cloaking colors they adapted, revealing their true Indigo colors. The world is ready.

Adult Indigos and those with an Indigo overlay have a mission. They are paving the way for today's Indigos to bring about change with a spiritual sensibility.

## def•i•ni•tion

Indigo overlay is the term many Indigo experts use for someone who exhibits certain Indigo attributes. This person may be an early Indigo who has suppressed his or her Indigo qualities, or it may be someone who lives with an Indigo. The traits of a pure Indigo are deeply part of her identity; someone with an Indigo overlay shows Indigo attributes in certain situations or certain cycles of life (parenting an Indigo child, for instance).

## The Difference Between Early and Now

Adult Indigos are Indigos who arrived ahead of their time. The world was not as prepared as it is now to accept their struggles with authority or challenges to the existing structure. Many adult Indigos rebelled in school, but they were not as extreme as Indigo Children of today. Many others did not rebel but became depressed because of the way the school system suppressed their Indigo nature.

Like today's Indigo Children, adult Indigos may prefer to be a solo act, starting their own business or working in leadership positions. Their relationships may falter, because of adult Indigos' intensity. They may embrace alternative lifestyles (homosexuality, for instance; or being a hippie in the 1960s), and they may reject life in suburbia. They may take issue with financial prosperity, rejecting the pursuit of money on principle. They don't want the American Dream—it makes them want to run and hide.

Adult Indigos grew up in a time before we had a term for who they are, and they have had to search for their path in life. They may have tried many careers, struggling with the conformity to be conventional and the desire to chart their own way.

Many adult Indigos have shaken up the establishment—or resisted it. Some have been in and out of it, giving voice to changing established ideals, perhaps working to change them in their youth, even if they earned a Master's degree in business administration or graduated from law school later.

Part and parcel of this struggle might be drug or alcohol addiction. Or, adult Indigos might be firmly committed to acquiring spiritual self-knowledge, undergoing an awakening in which they study spiritual texts and self-help books. They may go through a period of spiritual searching or transformative personal growth.

### Patience

If this description of an Indigo sounds a lot like the Flower Child of the 1960s—pushing the limits, idealistic, susceptible to addiction, instigating personal growth, redefining relationships, redefining gender roles—then you're not alone in wondering if the Baby Boomers were the first wave of Indigos. Many of those who emerged from the tumultuous social change of the 1960s were Indigos, but not all. Remember, Indigos are made of extremes. They defy broad labels like Baby Boomer. They are nonconformists, after all.

# What It Means for Your Indigo Child

If you're an Indigo, too, you are in a good position to empathize with your child about his particular Indigo struggles. That's the good news. That's possibly why your Indigo picked you!

Take the issue of emotional sensitivity, for instance. You are programmed to empathize. You have experienced it, too. No doubt you have been practicing energy shielding for many years, even if you never called it that or thought about it consciously. And you can remember what it was like to be misunderstood—when it was so hard to explain to everyone else how deeply you were feeling emotions around you.

An emotionally sensitive adult faces much more social pressure to conform—to not wear her heart on her sleeve, to not be so raw with her emotions. In many ways, being an adult Indigo is more of a challenge because you have fewer role models and support.

What if you're still a bit rebellious as an adult? This can be a benefit if you have made your peace with your path, whether it's unconventional or by the book. You have already forged your way. You can lead the way for your Indigo child. It can be a challenge if you are still trying to fit into a mold or find your niche. Maybe you started out as an artist in your 20s but opted for the corporate life when you started your family. Now you are hitting your mid-life crisis just when your Indigo child's struggle against the accepted rules is heating up. In his struggle, you may hear your own choices being questioned. If so, you'll need to think of this as your mid-life curriculum. What questions is your child's struggle raising for you? Is it time to reassess your values as you help him identify his? This could be very rewarding for both of you.

> **Crystal Clear**
>
> The only way to deal with an unfree world is to become so absolutely free that your very existence is an act of rebellion.
>
> —Albert Camus, French novelist, essayist, and playwright

# With a Little Help from Your Friends

Don't go it alone. Get support. If you are an adult Indigo, it's highly likely you didn't know other Indigos as you were growing up. Your parents wouldn't have known the term Indigo, though they may have understood your emotional and physically sensitivity. But now there are others like you who are discovering their Indigo identity. They have had similar experiences, and they can help you explore your Indigo nature.

Wendy started several online support groups on yahoo.com—indigo-adults, indigo-adults-moderated, and metagifted. She also co-moderates the lists indigo-parents, indigo-children, and indigo-news. You can join by going to Wendy's website at www.metagifted.org. At the bottom of the home page is a spot to enter your e-mail address for any of her groups. Or just e-mail indigo-adults-subscribe@yahoogroups.com.

To adults who newly recognize they are Indigos, Wendy recommends self-exploration. It's important to accept yourself—your sensitivity, your creativity, your random out-of-the-box thinking, your psychic skills, whatever your unique Indigo attributes might be. The trials you have

Setting Limits - Respect
Self discipline

In discipline - let her know
her wishes are considered
3 yr old cannot understand
deferred gratification

She needs love + attention

Consequences teach values

Involving her empowers her

TIMING
What is she ready for when?

Offer choices

What I resist persists

potty

eating          sleeping

Listening is the underpinning
of Respect

Getting to know her is a
lifelong project.

been through were not because you were wrong or bad or different. Those trials made you a survivor. Understand that you are here to make a difference—not only in your child's life, but also in the world in general. Your experience as an adult Indigo prepares you to be an advocate for the change in the current systems.

On her website, Wendy encourages adult Indigos to take on the following assignments as a way to explore their Indigo nature:

**Good Counsel**

Taking some time to explore who you are can be a lot of fun if you have been putting your child first and haven't been making time for yourself. Give yourself permission to carve out time for introspection or trying new activities that stir your creative juices. It's one of the best things you can do for yourself—and your child.

- ◆ Make a list of your personal goals for your life. Are you where you want to be? Where do you want to be five years from now?

- ◆ Take note of your psychic abilities. Start noticing when you have a hunch about something. Notice when something doesn't feel right. Listen to your instincts. Notice coincidences.

- ◆ List creative activities that you would like to do more—painting, writing, cooking, gardening, dancing, etc. It's good to do these with your Indigo child.

- ◆ Take stock of the core relationships in your life. For what are you grateful? In what areas would you like to improve them? Think about people who haven't understood your Indigo nature. What could you tell them now about who you are? How could you help them understand you now that you understand yourself better?

- ◆ Make a list of your talents.

- ◆ Take stock of your struggles. If, for instance, you have always been a random thinker, and it isn't easy for you to sustain focus on a task, make a point to turn that around. Reframe it as a gift. Random thinkers are inventive.

- ◆ Look for ways to be generous. How can you expand your light to help others?

# Indigo Role Models

Now that you are more familiar with what an Indigo is, think back to your childhood. Was there anyone who really seemed to understand you? Was there anyone you could describe as a mentor? Who seemed to sympathize with your struggles? Who gave you good advice? Who seemed like a compatriot?

It might be a mix of people. Your mother might have given you sympathy, but an aunt might have opened up your psychic awareness. You might have had a friend at school who seemed to "speak your language." Or there could have been a teacher who saw your imaginative abilities and encouraged you to explore them.

These people were your early role models; some could have been early Indigos themselves. Many adult Indigos, when they think back on it, realize they were not alone. Then again, it's no big deal if you can't remember someone. You made it to this point! Be proud of that.

# Indigo Resources

In Appendix B, we list many resources to help you connect with other Indigo parents and adult Indigos. Among them is the online magazine, *Children of the New Earth*, which brings together parents of spiritually aware and socially conscious children. The magazine's website (childrenofthenewearth.com) engages educators, physicians, psychologists, healers, and parents in an ongoing international discussion. We also list other discussion groups.

# Indigo to Indigo

When Indigos connect, they blossom. It's that simple. Finding others who already understand so much about you is gratifying. It can fill empty places in your psyche that you didn't know you had. When you feel so different from everyone else, there are parts of you that you don't share—maybe not with anyone.

Wendy's website is one among many that posts the writings of Indigos, adult and child alike. Some of them are poems; some of them are prose. Indigos find that when they share their creative offerings, they feel more complete. They feel they have contributed to the learning and understanding of others. They do not feel so alone and isolated when they share their words, when their words resonate with others, or when the words of other Indigos resonate with them.

Find support groups in your community, as well as online. Schedule play dates at the park. Seek out other Indigo adults at the Parent-Teacher Association meeting or at mixers on metaphysical topics at your local bookstore.

## Indigo Stars

Wendy first became aware of her Indigo nature after really understanding Indigo Children's behavior and recognizing how much she fit that pattern, but with a few differences that resonated for most of the other adults who wrote her about their Indigo energy, too. The realization came suddenly and filled her with relief as she recognized the connections between her emotional sensitivity, resistance to systems, and psychic abilities, to name a few. Now when she looks back at her path—starting out in the conventional education system—to now, where she works intensively with the parents of Indigos and actively collaborates with other adult Indigos for support—she sees a path where all of her many Indigo attributes are coming together.

## For Better or Worse

If all this is making you realize you are an Indigo—and your spouse is not—don't worry. It wouldn't be the first mixed marriage on the planet. It can make for a tricky combination, but the key is for your spouse to understand and accept you for who you are. It may feel as though he or she is trying to change you because you are different. It's good to adapt—to compromise because you must live peaceably with your spouse—but it's not good if you are suppressing your Indigo nature.

Likewise, you will need to give your spouse understanding and tolerance. You may get frustrated or impatient when your spouse doesn't approach challenges as you would. Just as you would not want him to change you, don't try to make him become an Indigo.

An Indigo/non-Indigo combination can be a complementary alliance. Your non-Indigo spouse may be an anchor for you. Your non-Indigo spouse can be a grounding force and a stabilizing influence. In situations that require energy shielding, your non-Indigo spouse may be ready for battle before you are. He may come to quick, clear decisions not colored by Indigo challenges. He will be able to help your child navigate the non-Indigo world.

Then again, you may be the diplomat who can bridge the gap between your non-Indigo spouse and your Indigo child. You will understand your Indigo child more readily than your spouse will. You will take the lead in unconditional love and empathy. You will be the advocate of teaching the world how to accommodate your Indigo. You will be the validator, the one who affirms your Indigo's uniqueness.

The danger comes if your non-Indigo spouse thinks it's all bunk. Or your spouse wants to shut out your child's (or your) psychic abilities. If your spouse really does not want to talk about it—if he thinks it is silly—you must head this off.

It's also important that you and your spouse love each other compassionately, knowing each other's specific qualities and accepting the differences. For instance, if you are highly emotionally or physically sensitive, help your partner understand what that's like for you. Help him understand the accommodations you might need. If your marriage is young, make a point to slow down and let him get to know you on these terms, putting your marriage on new, solid footing. If you have been married a long while, you may think of this as reintroducing yourself to your spouse. Either way, you will accomplish this if you make time for each other. This is the moment. Schedule regular dates; take the time to get to know each other away from your children.

And if you're both Indigos? You may clash a lot, but you will likely be on the same page about your children. Because you are both Indigos, your emotions may be more intense. You will need to take turns supporting each other.

# Know Thyself

It can be a big relief to learn you are an adult Indigo. You might have felt this way, too, when you first learned the term Indigo Children and you found out someone had already dealt with the challenges you are facing with your Indigo child. Now it's the same with you: you know who you are. Take this new knowledge and treasure it.

## The Least You Need to Know

- Adult Indigos may have suppressed some of their Indigo qualities, but many are now shedding their protective aura and revealing their indigo aura.

- If you're an adult Indigo, you're a survivor. You already have developed many coping skills that will benefit your child.

- Many of the Flower Children from the 1960s possessed attributes of Indigos—creative, idealistic revolutionaries who challenged the status quo.

- Many Indigo discussion groups exist—Wendy started many of them! Seek them out. Getting support from other adult Indigos will help you understand yourself and your child.

- If you're an adult Indigo and your spouse is not, use that dynamic to its advantage. Your spouse will be the anchor; you will be the one who can more readily understand your Indigo child.

# 4

# Thrive: Creating the Right Environment

Half the challenge in parenting an Indigo is planting him in the right environments—in the school, social situations, home, or lifestyle—that cultivate his love for nature, creativity, need for responsibility, and openness to a better, more holistic lifestyle. Indigos love to garden, and they have abundant energy. In this section, we give you productive ways to channel this energy.

# Chapter 12

# Real Connections: Sacred Earth and Cyberspace

## In This Chapter

◆ Connected to the web of life

◆ Activities to stay earth-connected

◆ Using crystals and gems for energy shielding

◆ Connected through technology

Indigo Children yearn for real connections—connections that are full of soul and spirit. For Indigos, it's imperative that they have experiences that get them in touch with the essence of life. That means for many of them, it's vital to have a connection to the earth—with animals, plants, rocks, and crystals. While not all are nature lovers—some are computer geeks—they do seek authenticity in their relationships. Their milieu may be your back yard—or it could be the Internet, for some Indigo Children gravitate toward cyberspace connections. With the ever-present dangers the Internet poses to children, you'll want to be knowledgeable and vigilant. In this chapter, we'll tell you safe ways to allow your child to connect with other Indigos on the Internet.

# That Earth Connection

Indigo Children feel deeper connections than the rest of us, and that includes their connection to the earth. They recognize how deeply connected we are to all living things. Many show an early understanding of the ways in which we depend on animals and plants for our sustenance. They may understand the need to bless and protect animals and plants from the moment they can walk across a lawn or pet a cat.

Indigo Children also feel very strong connections with Earth itself, sensing the energy of rocks, stones, gems, and crystals.

**Crystal Clear**

Trees are the earth's endless effort to speak to the listening heaven.

—Rabindranath Tagore, Bengali poet and playwright

Many Indigos are deeply aware of the movements of the earth. They feel the wild and mystical energy during the full moon or the cleansed, fresh beginning energy of the new moon. They sense the equaling out of the equinoxes, they tap into the power of the Summer Solstice, or they go inward at Winter Solstice. It's like their bodies are on an earth clock.

These Indigos also show an early understanding of the four elements—fire, water, air, earth—and how they work together. For them, the way they experience a nature walk or puttering around in the garden is about exploring this interconnectedness. To them, this experience is more than pleasure, or a way to be more mindful and just relax. To them, it's sacred.

## The Right Environment

Carolyn has some plants in her garden that have told her loud and clear that they do not like the spot in which they are planted. Take the blue flax, for instance. Carolyn loves this delicate blue flower that opens in the morning, catching the sunlight. But so do the bunnies, and they munch it down unless she surrounds it with chicken wire. In the spring, it's a continual challenge when the winds uproot the chicken wire and blow it down the hill, leaving the blue flax vulnerable. Both Carolyn and the mowed-down flowers feel stunted and frustrated.

But take the apricot sage, the lavender, or the tarragon. These plants have told her, "Thanks. This is just perfect. I love the sun. It's great, but not too much. I'm getting enough water. I'm happy here."

It's like that with an Indigo child. Getting your Indigo the proper balance of soil, sun, and water is half the battle. Earth-connected play often nourishes the soul of an Indigo. There are several reasons this is vital to nurture your child's Indigo nature:

- ◆ **It's *tactile*.** Indigos like to touch. Many are highly physically sensitive, and their experience of touch is rich. They feel it more than the average person.

**def•i•ni•tion** ___L i l y___

> Tactile means to experience sensation through touch. Indigo Children are highly tactile, more than the average child, taking in more information through a developed sense of touch. They need to touch it to explore it.

- ◆ **It's about oneness.** Indigos delight in the sights and smells of the flowers or vegetables they grow, knowing they were part of creating them. They feel great empathy toward animals, and some have a telepathic connection with them. It's not unheard-of for animals to approach Indigos with a greeting of recognition, sort of, "Hi, good to see you, my friend."

- ◆ **It's direct.** Indigos want to experience it for themselves, not through a screen. Videos and web sites about butterflies or bunnies are great, but not enough. Indigos want to interact with nature because they want to explore it on a deep level.

- ◆ **It's original.** Indigos resist any hand-me-down experience. They reject the secondhand. They want to get it first-hand. They have such a unique take on the world that anything that feels trite or timeworn won't register with them. They really must go to the source of the experience. Earth-connected play honors their original way of experiencing the world.

♦ **It's limitless.** Exploring nature is liberating. There are no boundaries between humans and animals, humans and trees, humans and rocks. The blue sky is not the limit. It's just the beginning.

♦ **It's soulful.** They do not see the material and spirit worlds as separate. All matter is infused with spirit.

♦ **It's holistic.** Earth-connected play teaches your child to think more globally. It taps your child into seeing how he fits into the circle of life.

Also important to note is what the earth-connected play is *not*. It's not over-stimulating. Too many stimuli can numb the mind, shutting down the imagination and creating a sense of isolation. While it's true that all children need room for their imaginations to thrive, it's essential for Indigos. Earth-connected play allows your Indigo to develop her unique imagination.

## Ways to Get the Earth Experience

Here are some activities to get your Indigo involved in nature:

♦ Build a habitat for a turtle.

♦ Start your own butterfly pavilion. InsectLore.com will mail you butterfly larvae, complete with food for the caterpillar stage and a netted cage for the chrysalis to grow and the butterflies to emerge. Over the course of about 10 days, your child can watch the process. At the end, take the butterflies to release them to their natural habitat.

♦ Start a vegetable garden. Children love to get involved in planting grape tomatoes, corn, and pumpkins. Teach them the connection between the foods they eat and the foods they grow by planting an avocado pit in a pot that you place in the kitchen window. Gather apple seeds or cherry pits, and plant them.

♦ Take your child on nature outings—hiking, fishing, camping. Let him feed the ducks at the pond. Take him to see the monkeys at the zoo.

♦ Set up a nature altar, where each member of the family may contribute nature's "talismans," collected from nature walks and sojourns to the park.

♦ Collect ladybugs.

♦ Start a compost pile.

♦ Get a pet, or allow your Indigo to care for others' pets. Carolyn's daughter loves animals, especially dogs. She has a tender touch. Animals sense her compassion and reverence for them, so they gravitate to her. At age 6, Emerald said she wanted to start a pet-sitting business so she could become a veterinarian, so Carolyn volunteered to take care of the neighbor's pets. Offer to walk the neighbor's dog one night a week. Allow older children to volunteer at the animal shelter.

♦ Take your child horseback riding. If your child has a connection with horses, know that it has many benefits. For instance, American equine trainer and therapist Franklin Levinson, who leads the Maui Horse Whisperer seminar, has reported surprising results using Equine Facilitated Learning with ADHD and autistic children.

♦ Build a shrine or grotto in the back yard. It can be a pond, a birdbath, an archway, or arbor. It can be a focal point for you and your child to "putter" in the yard. You might place a statue there. Or you might build an arch with tree branches or a circle with stones.

♦ Make a medicine wheel in your back yard. This is a way of creating sacred space using rocks and other talismans in a pattern to represent Father Sky, Mother Earth, Grandfather Sun, Grandmother Moon, Star Nation, Other Planets, and the Galaxy we're in. Next you lay stones for the animals of each direction and the elements associated with each. Or you can do the four directions (east, south, north, west). Go online to www. shannonthunderbird.com/medicine_wheel_teachings.htm or www.spiritualnetwork.net (click on Native American section, go to link about medicine wheels).

Wendy's mother would send her on scavenger hunts in the backyard. Her assignment was to return with 10 wishing rocks (black rocks with a white ring), 5 white stones, 6 Indian paintbrushes (a wildflower), 1 four-leaf clover (!), and 2 identical blades of grass. It kept her busy for hours and challenged her mind as well.

Another idea is to send your child into the yard with a digital camera, asking him to find geometric patterns in the tree branches, the veins on the leaves, the shadows on the grass. Ask him to find a square, a diamond, a circle, a triangle, and a star, for instance.

### Good Counsel

Spend a little time pulling weeds or trimming the bushes in the evening. Find ways for your child to help. Start an herb garden, and use the herbs when you make dinner. Make a point of going to the growers' market in your town to shop for fresh produce so that you and your child become accustomed to tasting the fresh flavors of the earth. Walk with your child to school one day a week. Make nature walks part of your regular routine.

In addition to special activities, make earth connections part of your daily life. Be more mindful of nature all around you—notice the rosebushes growing in the median or the white butterfly flitting through the courtyard at the outdoor café. Cultivate your own curiosity about nature, and always encourage your child to look things up. If your child asks you a question about a daddy long legs spider, get on the Internet or get out the encyclopedia! Say, "Let's find out why the ladybugs like the catalpa tree so much more than the cottonwood." One spring, let the swallows build a nest on the eaves of your front porch—even if it's a little messy.

Generally, our society is yearning to deepen this earth connection, and that's what your Indigo is here to do—to play a role in getting us all back to that. No longer do we live in an agriculture-based society. Many of us live in cities, and our food is shipped to us from thousands of miles away. This disconnect is more painful for Indigos, and they have a low tolerance for it. If you know your Indigo thrives on an earth connection, and you see her "acting out," her distress may be a yearning for more earth-connected play.

**Indigo Stars**

*Lanie*

Each year, 10 youth and children receive the Gloria Barron Prize for Young Heroes, which recognizes them for helping their communities and protecting the health and sustainability of the environment. In 2005, a 17-year-old girl identified as Lindsey started Gardening for Families, because her garden was so abundant, she wanted to pass the bounty on to families in need. The reason her garden thrives is that she invented a water-saving drip irrigation system. Lindsey's Nutrient Delivery System delivers vital nutrients to plants' roots with 50 percent less water, resulting in doubled crop growth.

Many children love pebbles. They love to collect small things and keep them as treasures. The joy is in their discovery, their wonderment in the world. It's in their delight of something small. And for Indigos, it's in their connection to the earth as well as the energy they feel in the stones.

The reason stones are so vital to Indigos is because some of the stones ground them and other stones raise their energy. Indigos can recognize on some level that the stones hold power and can help them. Indigos love to be free to explore, but it can be disorienting for them when their attention is so outward. They can be so enamored with new ideas and sensations that they lose their center. They also are so spirit-oriented that being in a physical body can be disconcerting at times. Stones and Earth ground them. (And remember, *you* ground them. That's why hugs are so important!)

Earth Child (www.earthchildonline.com) is a website that specializes in toys, games, and crafts that promote your child's awareness of the earth. Toys are made of materials from sustainable resources and made by companies that support fair trade. The company is based in Sebastopol, California, a community the founders chose because it has a progressive community of families that share their values of an environmentally aware lifestyle. In addition to offering earth-friendly toys, the site offers natural fiber clothing. Earth Child also specializes in items that support the Waldorf educational approach, something we'll talk about more in Chapter 14, when we discuss schools.

Here are some ideas to do with your Indigo:

- **Collect shells.** Give your child a special place in the yard where she can assemble her collection.

- **Make stepping stone tiles.** Using small bits of tile, you and your child might create pictures or patterns in stepping stone tiles. You may find kits for sale at hobby stores such as Michael's (www. Michaels.com) or Hobby Lobby (www.Hobbylobby.com). The tiles can be "story tiles" about stories your child makes up.

- **Collect rocks for a heart altar in your yard.** The rocks go in a heart shape in the ground. You may put a statue or a birdbath at the cleft of the heart, adorning it with flowers or beads. Make it a focal point where you honor your child's compassionate nature.

## Crystals

Wendy is a big believer in using the energy of crystals for healing and energy shielding in Shamballa healing. She has found that even the biggest doubters of crystal healing come around when they see the results. Crystals and gemstones have been used to enhance healing since ancient times. People who use them believe that they have energy that promotes physical and emotional healing. The energy that people feel from them relates to their color, or light energy; their vibration; or their magnetic field.

If you are new to crystal healing, Wendy recommends you start with six quartz pyramids, a handful of quartz points, some fluorite; and crystals that match the color of each chakra. Chakras are the seven energy centers in the body, and the crystals enhance that energy, increasing its vibration. Each chakra is associated with a color because the energy is vibrating on a certain wavelength. Think of the crystals as amplifying the energy of each chakra.

Here's a look at the crystals Wendy recommends for each chakra and why.

| Chakra | Color | Energy Center in Body | Its Meaning | Crystal |
|--------|-------|----------------------|-------------|---------|
| Root | Red | Root (anus) | Security, safety, foundation, family | Hematite, red jasper |
| Sacral | Orange | Lower abdomen | Sexuality, creativity, money | Carnelian, tiger's eye, orange calcite |
| Power | Yellow | Solar plexus, or upper abdomen | Personal power, will | Citrine, golden selenite |
| Heart | Green or pink | Heart | Compassion, unconditional love, transformation | Rose quartz, rhodochrosite, malachite, adventurine |
| Throat | Light blue | Throat | Truth, expression | Chrysocola, turquoise |
| Third eye | Indigo | One inch beneath the center of the forehead | Intuition, knowledge | Lapis lazuli, sodalite |
| Crown | Violet, lavender, white | Crown of head | Inspiration, spiritual enlightenment | Amethyst, quartz |

Wendy recommends placing the chakra crystals over the corresponding points in your body and going into a meditation. For basic crystal healing, match the crystal color to the chakra on which you are working. Use your intuition to guide you in where the crystal should be placed. If the person wants to attract money, try surrounding his head and feet with golden citrine. If she needs physical healing, use quartz and malachite. Use as many or few stones as feels right. Small tumbled stones work well, too. The person receiving the healing lies still. She may feel a tingling or a vibration, but it should not feel bad. If you do any energy healing work, this is a good time to do it, as the crystals will strengthen the healing vibrations.

Another way to do crystal healing or protection is to set them up in a merkaba pattern, which looks like a hexagon when flattened. Spread it out large enough to sit or lie down inside. Then activate it by drawing each triangle three times and filling it with love and light using affirmations and creative visualization. Sit inside the grid and meditate. (Go online to merkaba.org or crystalinks.com/merkaba.html for more about the merkaba.)

**Crystal Clear**

By climbing up into his head and shutting out every voice but his own, "Civilized Man" has gone deaf. He can't hear the wolf calling him brother; he can't hear the earth calling him child.

—American author Ursula LeGuin

When you first get a crystal, cleanse it by holding it above your third eye chakra and give intent to cleanse it. This allows it to be cleansed of negative energy. Then bring it to your mouth and blow, clearing it of anything negative. Rinsing in cold water also may help, but be careful because some stones are water-soluble.

# The Cyber World and Indigos

It may seem counter-intuitive to say that many Indigo Children need computers in their lives at the same time we say get them outdoors and in touch with nature. But surprisingly enough, Indigos are adept at using the Internet to forge deep connections. They seem to be able to transcend the screen that can be a barrier to true connection. Instead, some Indigo Children find that technology is the tool to reach out, particularly with other Indigos.

## Stranger Danger on the Internet

The distinction is connection. Safe connections. With younger children, the rule may be as simple as this: never talk to anyone online that you don't already know. But as your child becomes a preteen and teen, you'll want to allow for safe online communication in groups such as Indigo support groups. Here are some guidelines for discussing Internet safety, adapted from safekids.com:

- Tell your child to never give out her address, telephone number, your work address or phone, or school name without your permission.

- Advise your child to always tell you right away if he receives any information that is disturbing or makes him uncomfortable.

- Tell your child never to agree to meet in person someone she meets online without your permission. If your teen asks, thoroughly check out the situation before agreeing.

- Tell your child never to send a photo of herself.

- Agree on guidelines for when your child can be online and for how many hours a day.

- Agree on appropriate areas to visit. All chat rooms and message boards should have your approval.

- If you set up an e-mail account for your child, be sure it does not contain his name.

- Until your child is a certain age, do not let her access her e-mail account without your supervision.

- Tell your child to never give out his password, not even to his best friend.

- Do not let your child download or install software without your supervision (if a young child) or permission (if older).

- Advise your child that people on the Internet can be something other than what they seem. A person who says he is a teen could be an 50-year-old man. Often sexual predators pose as other students.

- Keep the family computer in a common area. Do not allow your child or teen to have a computer in her room.

- Advise your child not to open e-mail attachments from unknown sources.

- Only let your child or teen do video chats with people you already know (family members and friends).

More detailed guidelines about Internet safety can be found in a document the Virginia Department of Education has prepared. Go online to www.pen.k12.va.us/VDOE/Technology/OET/internet-safety-guidelines.shtml and click on "Guidelines and Resources for Internet Safety in Schools" to download the booklet as a PDF.

## Indigo Perils on the Internet

With Indigos, you'll need to take the discussion further than these guidelines. A list of "never" and "always" rules isn't going to equip them with enough information. You'll need to instill in your child healthy guidelines about how to discern suggestive or invasive messages—and an action plan for doing so. (Your child should sign off immediately and tell you.) Keep the lines of communication open. If your child sees something disturbing, let her know you will listen without judgment. It's not her fault.

> **Patience**
>
> Make sure to put an anti-magnetic shield or use antimagnetic spray on your Indigo's computer to protect her from an excess of magnetic rays. Indigos are especially sensitive to this energy.

Indigos can be trusting and therefore more susceptible to the dangers of strangers on the Internet. They are independent and willful. They may have overconfidence in their ability to discern who is good and who is bad. Be very clear and firm about the limits on the Internet.

Stay tuned in to your child. What's your Indigo's motivation for using video chatting or instant messaging? Who is she connecting with, and how is it affecting her? (And most important, is this a safe person, and how do you tell?) Is she turning to the Internet instead of forming real connections with others? Curtail computer use, such as video games, when it's deadening and detracting from your Indigo's true self. Is she growing and thriving because she has found an online Indigo support group? Is she growing in confidence because she is adept at researching information that helps her understand her Indigo nature?

When you see your child thriving and making good decisions, you know the Internet is a positive connection. But if she's too isolated, or if she withdraws suddenly from school or family life, this is a signal. If you see a change, you need to check it out.

## Better Connections

Ultimately, Indigo Children see the Internet as a progression to better human interaction—because a web cam can transcend the miles. It connects us all, globally, and that's the way Indigos already see it. Therein lies your challenge with an Indigo. It opens him to more perils; yet it opens him to real connections that transcend the limits of technology.

Wendy sees us as a global culture progressing to deeper communication. The way Wendy has seen Indigo Children use the Internet borders on telepathy. They get connected with an Indigo across the country or on the other side of the globe, and they can tune in to that other Indigo's energy, knowing sometimes when he or she is going to send an email or a video conference invite—or just knowing their friend is having a rough day and will be online later that night. They are already connected.

The key word to determining how much you permit your Indigo child to be on the computer is *interactive*. Television is passive. When computer use is interactive, it doesn't squelch creativity or connection (again, assuming it's a safe connection). You will want to help them strike a balance between real-life, face-to-face interactions and virtual connections. If Internet interactions are happening to the exclusion of real contact, you will want to talk to your Indigo about cutting back.

### Patience

The best way to teach your teen good cell phone etiquette is to model it. Before you buy your teen a cell phone, agree on rules. Do this jointly. Have your teen suggest guidelines. Go to www2.letstalk.com/viewArticle.htm?artid=27 for etiquette tips as well as tips for driving safely. Spell out situations and places where it's appropriate or not. Whether the school has a policy against cell phones in the classroom or not, you and your teen decide. Be sure to cover text messaging. Make a pact, and each of you adheres to it.

# Deeper Connections

Remember, Indigo Children arrived en masse because it is their purpose to advance us as a society spiritually. They know that we can't advance one at a time, but rather that we must advance as a group together. When Indigo Children seek connections, it is with this goal in mind. Connections, whether through the earth or cyberspace, remind us why we are here and how we can help each other. It's absolutely vital for your Indigo, because it helps him keep sight on the possibility of the future he envisions, a future he is part of forging.

## The Least You Need to Know

- Indigos are deeply aware of our connection through the earth, plants, animals, rocks, and stones, to the web of life.

- Set aside time for earth-connected activities. If your child loves animals, find ways for her to have animals in her life. If your child is an explorer, give her opportunities to explore nature.

- In your daily activities, be more mindful of nature, of the movements of the sun and moon, the changing of the seasons.

- Indigos are well aware of the healing powers of the earth, such as crystal energy.

- What Indigos yearn for are deep connections. Whether they are out in nature or on the Internet, that is what they are seeking.

- It's imperative that you take a proactive role in monitoring your child's Internet activity for safety.

# Manifesting Indigo Abundance

## In This Chapter

- ◆ Prosperity consciousness
- ◆ Money: a love-hate relationship
- ◆ Wise ways with money
- ◆ Young manifesters

It's almost uncanny how prolific an Indigo child can be. They seem to have a natural gift for abundance—they are abundant in their thoughts and ideas, their exploration, their creative endeavors. They are naturally blessed with a prosperous creative spirit.

Productivity is not an issue; *completion* might be the issue. Indigo Children may start many projects but finish none. They may spin off idea after idea and pursue none of them. You see this gift, and you want to harness it. How in the world can you understand the bountiful energy of your child? How can you help her flourish? Let's find out.

# Natural Abundance

The abundant Indigo has a million ideas, and they know there's more where that came from. They have a trust that they can always tap into a universal source of abundance. This is called *prosperity consciousness*.

Prosperity consciousness is the opposite of poverty consciousness, which is based on the belief in scarcity. The person who has poverty consciousness believes there's not enough for everybody, so one must hoard what one has and protect it from others, who will try to take it away. Along with that comes competitiveness; because there is only a little, there is not enough to go around, so one must make sure he gets to the good stuff first.

Prosperity consciousness believes there is an ever-increasing plenty—that we are all meant to have exactly what we need and there is a universal benevolent force that directs prosperity to us. Good things beget more good things—good deeds propagate more good deeds, good thoughts seed more good thoughts. For these types of Indigos, all seeds grow.

Yet, for an abundant Indigo, very little of this consciousness is about money. It's about creating. Many Indigos are not great with money. As soon as they bring money in, it can slip through their fingers. It's absolutely not their focus.

To better understand the Indigo attitude toward money, let's look more closely at what it means to have true abundance. Abundance is having what you need and more, having what makes you happy. Abundance is not wasteful or greedy. It's not having so much that you're drowning in it. You don't have so many things that they burden you. The need to have so much can be a protection against poverty instead of the signature of a flourishing spirit. So from the outside looking in, it may seem like a person has an abundant life—perhaps by the way we define it in American culture, with a nice home, nice cars, nice clothes, nice toys—but a lot of that rampant materialism arises from fear—the hoarding that is poverty consciousness.

The Indigo's abundant spirit doesn't need to hoard and doesn't need to acquire more and more. Rather, the Indigo abundant spirit creates simply because it thrives on creating. Because creativity is the emphasis, the Indigo spirit shuns anything that will burden him. So he may create it, but he doesn't have to keep it. Possession is not the aim. He may not want to keep it because the burden of possession costs him creative freedom.

### Patience

If there is wastefulness with an Indigo, it's that there are so many more ideas than your Indigo can pursue or complete. Your challenge as a parent is giving your Indigo the focus that can help him pursue activities fruitfully, giving him the sense of accomplishment. Teaching responsible money management early in life is also a key to that sense of accomplishment.

It's important to understand and support your Indigo child's prosperity consciousness, because he may not yet understand and trust it; the world may try to squelch it, putting him back in the fear of poverty consciousness. An Indigo's spiritual awareness about abundance is high, yet he may not trust his instincts. He may struggle with his different philosophy about abundance, and he may try to mold himself into conventional roles and expectations that are not fruitful for him; for example, the belief that to prosper, you must work for a corporation and draw a weekly paycheck. This is the challenge on many fronts for the parent of an Indigo—your child is wise in his way, and you must support his intuitions about who he is, what he needs, and who he wants to become.

## Types of Abundance

Nancy Ann Tappe, who first identified Indigo Children, defined them as one of four types—conceptual, humanist, artist, and interdimensional. Here's how each type expresses abundance:

- ◆ The *conceptual* Indigo is the child who initiates many projects. These children have a plethora of ideas.

- ◆ The *humanist* Indigo has a highly social style and directs her efforts to helping others and creating community.

- The *artist* Indigo may astonish you with his many talents—pursuing many different disciplines—at the same time he vexes you with his lack of sustained attention. He's a dilettante, a dabbler.

- The *interdimensional* Indigo, who can blend ideas, social style, collaborative approach, and artistic talent, is the one who will emerge as a leader. These are the entrepreneurs in the making.

Some Indigos shun responsibility and leadership, so while they may have many entrepreneurial ideas, they prefer to work alone. They feel different, so they would rather fly beneath the radar. Or they may select themselves out of the chance at taking on responsibility; they may seem they are not ready for responsibility and therefore, no one gives them the opportunity. This type of Indigo is very responsible, but the responsibility is directed toward self—a self-reliance and nonconformity.

Still, even these Indigos have the qualities of abundance:

- Initiative

- Ability to visualize something that does not yet exist

- Ability to identify and anticipate someone else's need

- Desire to explore

- Strong sense of play

- Belief in abundance

- Confidence in ability to harness this abundance

- Confidence in ability to manifest

**Crystal Clear**

Prosperity is not just having a lot of money. It is having a consciousness of the flow of substance.

—Eric Butterworth, Unity minister and scholar

The last two are about prosperity consciousness and are truly what sets Indigo Children apart from the average abundantly creative child. For the Indigo, there is no question they can harness abundance and manifest it. They seem to have an innate understanding of the spiritual laws underlying the prosperity principle.

# A Thriving Spirit

You can create and nurture a prosperous spirit in your Indigo by focusing on these simple principles—and you will likely find it nurtures the same in yourself:

- ◆ Devote time to spiritual prosperity, through prayer and meditation. Make this first among all the things you do each day.

- ◆ Practice gratitude. Keep a daily list of the many things for which you are grateful.

- ◆ Give 10 percent of your time and money to the place(s) from which you receive spiritual nourishment.

- ◆ Reduce clutter—literally and figuratively. In your home—in your Indigo's room—create open space. In your mind, relinquish limiting beliefs.

- ◆ Practice prosperity affirmations. These are simple, positive statements that bolster your awareness of the natural abundance of the Universe.

Affirmations may not seem natural to you. Yet, they work so well that we urge you to keep an open mind. Try them, practicing regularly. What affirmations do is keep your focus on positive energy. They help you with the first four practices on this list—maintaining a spiritual focus, focusing on gratitude, giving back, and opening mind/heart space.

For many people, it's hard to get into the affirmation habit. It may be helpful to put them in your own language, with your own style. (No, they don't have to sound New Age-y to work; your style may be more down-to-earth.) Collect positive role models—people who inspire you. Collect stories of your own and others' prosperity. These are the foundations of affirmations—affirmations in themselves.

# Boom and Bust

Money is irrelevant for most Indigos—whatever the age. This can be the hardest thing to understand about an Indigo, and it can be an Indigo's biggest challenge to harnessing abundance. Indigos are not materialistic, nor are they all that concerned with what people think of them when they are riding out the bust cycle. They know they can produce again, so why worry?

Wendy has an adult Indigo friend she's known since high school who has the knack for entrepreneurship. Here's how she describes him: R. has started about five businesses and sold his shares to get out of them, ending up spending a bit more than he's made, but this is his life's path, and it's clear he enjoys it.

Here's the way R. puts it: "I have made a bunch of money and I have lost a little bit more than I have made. You know, I have read and heard that gay people do not choose to be the way they are and I can kind of relate. I don't choose to be the way I am (although I totally dig it); I simply am this way. Sometimes I wish I could just be normal. I wish I could close my eyes and not see solutions, or possible solutions to business problems. My mind is always working and sometimes I just want to relax. I joke at times that starting businesses is an affliction."

The idea or mission of a project has more of a hold than the results. The entrepreneurial Indigo is most interested in creating and expanding, trying new things, and discovering what can happen when you develop a possibility. Yes, there's a little bit of curiosity killed the cat.

## So Misunderstood

If your Indigo is the entrepreneur type, it may be hard to understand, especially as she enters the working world of adults. R.'s father often asks him why he gave up a perfectly great job to strike out on his own. R. says it's a tough conversation to have because his father is coming from a completely different frame of reference. R. answers that he starts companies because he has to be true to his nature. Doing anything else would be unnatural and detrimental to his being. He is challenged when he starts new companies. "This is how I want to live the rest of my life," R. says.

Wendy's mother often wonders why Wendy gave up her teaching career to start her own business. It's hard for Wendy to explain because her mother is coming from a different zeitgeist. But she explains she started Metagifted Educational Resource Organization (MERO) because that's where her spirit and heart led her. It was the only way she knew. She had to be true to herself. No one else in the family really understands why she continues this work when it doesn't necessarily make a profit. But her spirit knows it's the right path.

It may be hard for you to understand why your entrepreneur-minded Indigo child is not on the conventional, convenient path. You may see that it would be easier if he was, but the bottom line is you can't change him—and the question is: easier for whom? It would belie his true nature for your Indigo child to do other than follow his heart, whether money follows or not.

## Green, with Attitude

Some Indigos view money with detachment. They think it's a barely tolerable necessity. They may be suspicious of people with money and believe it causes more problems than it's worth. It may be difficult to get them interested in managing their money. Your challenge will be to help them see money as a tool.

Still it appears some Indigos, especially older Gen X or Gen Y Indigos who have entered the job market, already have a sophisticated understanding of money. They have grown up with lots of extracurricular activities, and therefore, are high performers. According to a September 2005 survey conducted by Diversified Investment Advisors, 46 percent of Gen Yers already in the workforce are contributing to a retirement plan.

Because their viewpoints about money are unconventional, Indigo Children, as they grow up, will likely change the way we

> **Indigo Stars**
>
> Howard Hughes was an innovator and an entrepreneur who became one of the wealthiest men in the world. He was a pioneer in film (*Hell's Angels*) and aviation (the Spruce Goose)—risking it all on innovations that seemed impossible or eccentric but were great strides for both industries.

think about prosperity and possessions. We may see more of the "one man's treasure" phenomenon that is eBay, or we may see more ideas like Freecycle (freecycle.org), through which people offer items they no longer need and request items they need.

# The Making of an Entrepreneur

Of course, most Indigos are still children. So they aren't necessarily starting limited liability corporation after corporation. But even at a young age, they are full of money-making ideas, much like Carolyn's son Lucas, who from age 5 was combining his knack for innovative ideas with his strong math skills. At age 5, he wanted to start a dollar store to stimulate the economy. Another time, he decided he would buy a restaurant and led a discussion about the profit margin. He likes to make things and can run the calculations quickly, such as the time he decided he was going to sell Ojo de Dios (Mexican God's Eye weavings) for $1 apiece, with a goal of $30 a month. At 7, he was brainstorming "markets" for selling his crafts—school, karate studio, soccer field, church.

Carolyn's daughter Emerald jumps in on the game, too, deciding at age 7 she would sell lemonade at the soccer field. Her marketing plan was to play piano (to gain attention for the fresh lemonade) and put out a tips jar. She would also use the lemonade stand as a way to marketing her pet-sitting business.

## Teaching Your Child About Money

Most experts recommend starting your child on an allowance at age 6 or 7. The conventional wisdom is not to tie chores to allowance. An allowance is for teaching your child about money management. Chores are about making a contribution to the family.

If this surprises you, think about it this way: keep the end in mind. When your child is an adult, will he get paid for doing his chores? No, the reason we make our beds and wash the dishes is because we are responsible for ourselves. We want to live in a neat, orderly environment, and we keep our area clean out of respect for the others who live with us. So chores are about making a contribution to the family.

With an allowance, the end result you want is an adult who budgets her money, allocating some for expenses, some for savings, some for giving, and some for luxuries.

Set up four jars for your child: spending, short-term saving, long-term saving, and giving. Teach your child to give to the place from which he receives his spiritual food. Teach him to save. Help him develop short- and long-range goals.

### Patience

Because many Indigos are unattached to money, they may start many fruitful things but not have the business sense—the eye on the bottom line—that would help them succeed. Teach your child about the value of money by discussing how you make your choices. At the grocery store, explain how you determine the value of a product and decide if the price is appropriate. Talk about the relationship between what you spend, what you have, and what you save. Put numbers on it: "If I have $100 and I want to buy a bike, and I find a good quality used bike for $45, then I have $55 left that I can save."

## Making a Manifester

Manifestation is the concept that our thoughts, ideas, and inspirations, if directed with a focused intention, can become reality on a physical level. So thoughts become tangible results.

Manifestation is proactive and creative, not reactive. Therein lies some of the explanation for Indigo Children as natural manifesters. They aren't reactive; they are about going out and creating what they want. The essence of this creativity is the concept that we create our reality based on our thoughts and emotions. We give meaning to everything we see.

One concept of manifestation is the law of attraction. We attract people and opportunities to us that match our vibration. So if we are thinking negatively—with a poverty consciousness—we get more of that. If we are thinking of abundance and harmony—we attract more experiences that remind us of plenty—and we don't have to create competitiveness or disharmony to acquire it.

We are always manifesting—all of us, Indigo or not. The key to conscious manifestation is knowing what you want and being in alignment with your true purpose in life. Wendy's friend R. is just beginning, at age 38, to understand his gift for manifestation. "I could tell you stories of manifesting that you wouldn't believe," he says. "When I am in a zone, I can manifest some pretty cool stuff." He has been able to manifest people or teachers in his life—they appear hours to a day after he asks. He manifested $20,000 on one occasion. "When I ask the Universe for something, I usually get *exactly* what I ask for."

Wendy concurs with that one: be careful what you ask for. When you ask the Universe for money, realize it can come from almost anywhere, including the death of a relative. Money can come as inheritance, gifts, donations, new work, a pay raise, being laid off and finding a different, better job, receiving valuable items you can sell for income, insurance settlements, etc. When you practice prosperity consciousness, you broaden your definition of income. Wendy says she's been able to manifest the income she needed just when it's due—within a day or several hours. She has practiced this for many years; through this practice, she has manifested jobs, important contacts, a husband, a baby—and this book!

Wendy uses a manifestation method called the Money Man Technique to request income from the Universe. Basically, she goes into meditation and sees in front of her a spirit bookkeeper. Wendy sees him as a clean-cut man in a suit with a ledger. He asks how much she needs and by what date. He writes it down and confirms it will be done. She thanks him and releases the vision. This has worked so many times for Wendy that she knows it is effective for her and can be for anyone. Try it yourself and see.

This method is creative visualization, which Carolyn wrote about with Shari Just in *The Complete Idiot's Guide to Creative Visualization* (see Appendix B). Wendy was able to imagine a person, creating a whole scene in which she made a request, and the Money Man acted upon her request. Then she was able to go about her business as though it had been done.

Carolyn has practiced creative visualization as a technique for manifestation all her life. For her, it has been so effective there is no other way to live. She has used prosperity consciousness, for instance, to sell her condo, at a significant profit, nine days after putting down an offer on a new home. She has used it to reel in book opportunities and new clients. The dollar amounts are specific: "I need $800." And it comes!

> **Good Counsel**
>
> Worry is negative prayer. Does your Indigo worry? Many highly sensitive Indigos do. Your Indigo may have the abundant spirit, but she may internalize so many of her worries that she doesn't manifest abundance. Worry is the culprit. Energy shielding can help, and so can positive visualization. It can help her know what she *does* want, not what she *doesn't*. Appreciate her unique gifts. It will help her tap into her ability to manifest.

## Young Entrepreneurs

Already some of the older Indigos are making their mark. Here's a look at some of the young entrepreneurs coming up:

- British teen Nick Bell set up a group of websites during the dot-com boom in the late 1990s. Later he created a spray tanning booth company and now has a high growth audiovisual technology business. He started Teenfront.com at age 14 and has gone on to found numerous other dot-com startups.

- At age 23, Grace Bonney started Design*Sponge, which features exclusive innovative designs of various products, always under $100.

- British college student Alex Tew started the Million Dollar Homepage as a way to raise money to pay for schooling. The index page of the site has a 1,000 × 1,000 pixel grid—or one million pixels. Anyone who buys a pixelblock can design a tiny image to be displayed there. The image links to a website address. Tew sold the final block of pixels on eBay, accomplishing his goal within about six months.

- At age 14, American Aaron Swartz co-wrote the specifications for RSS technology, a group of web feed formats that notify Internet users of website updates. The technology is often used on news websites, blogs, and podcasts.

- At age 13, American Nathaniel Younger founded his first business, using eBay to promote it, amassing more than $100,000 within two years of launching it. He has won young entrepreneur awards for his company, Beyond Limits Inc., which customizes cars.

- Mommy blogger extraordinaire dooce.com, also known as Heather Armstrong, a thirtysomething, got canned from her corporate job for her blog, but now her blog is one of the most popular links through technorati.com and blogher.com, two sites that sort out the best blogs. On her website, she states that revenue from her blog supports her family, allowing her husband to be a stay-at-home dad.

**Good Counsel**

HotShotBusiness.com is an Internet game that gives your child a chance to play entrepreneur. Disney Online and the Ewing Marion Kauffman Foundation support it. The game was developed for "tweens," 9- to 12-year-olds.

Indigo Children will need your help to bring forth their powers of manifestation. They will need your help to bring discipline to their ways with money. And they will need your love and support to gain the confidence in their money savvy. But the payoff in investing in your child's abundant spirit: priceless.

## The Least You Need to Know

- Indigo Children possess a natural abundance that is not so much about money, but about having a creative spirit.

- Indigo Children bring a spiritual understanding to money that is called prosperity consciousness.

- Prosperity consciousness is based on the belief in plenty—there is enough for all of us to thrive.

- Many Indigos are so prolific that they can go through cycles of boom and bust.

- Teach your child about money early, laying a strong foundation for money management with an allowance not tied to chores.

- Indigo Children are manifesters—through focused intention and positive prosperity awareness, they can transform ideas into tangible successes.

# Chapter 14

# Nurturing Indigo Minds

## In This Chapter

- ◆ Signs of trouble
- ◆ How *your* child learns
- ◆ How to evaluate a school
- ◆ Lots of alternatives

It's vital that your child thrives in school. Beyond your influence as a parent, education is the biggest factor in your child's best chance at success.

Indigo Children have such a unique intelligence that it often takes some time to sort out the right educational environment. Fortunately, many more alternative educational approaches are available than have been previously. Armed with some good information, you will be able to make one of the most important decisions in your child's life.

## What's His Problem?

Why isn't your child fitting in? It's important to get a good handle on what's happening, because Indigo Children can fall on such a broad spectrum. Some don't like the authoritative structure of traditional schools, while others find the large scale of public schools too emotionally and physically stimulating or psychically turbulent. Others are simply bored and need more challenges, with creative and intellectual freedom to explore.

It's good to put a fine point on this. Take the time to ask lots of questions of your child, her teachers, and the principal. Be patient, stay open-minded, and know that one size does not fit all when it comes to Indigo Children. Practice high participation, low attachment. High participation looks like this: ask lots of questions and gather lots of information, making it your first mission to know *your* child and what she needs. Low attachment looks like this: don't compare her to other siblings or other Indigos. Don't go in with any preconceived notions. It will shape the way you ask questions and where you look for guidance. Beware if you expect that somehow your child will fit in if only you push hard enough. High participation means you care—you care a lot. But low attachment means you don't have to have a specific outcome. You know the outcome you want in broad brush strokes: your child will thrive in an educational environment. Know that it may take some time to sort out. You'll need to be tenacious. And be open to any and all alternatives.

Here are a few common situations that prompt parents of Indigos to look for alternative solutions:

- Your child is resisting doing homework.

- Your child clashes with authority—or at the very least, there is a constant level of friction between her and the teacher.

- Your child says he's bored. This is a constant refrain.

- Your child makes it clear she thinks the other students can't keep up or are holding her back. She doesn't like slowing down for them.

- Your child seems frustrated.

- Your child dilly-dallies in the morning, taking his time getting ready for school.

- Your child is disorganized, losing homework or rushing through it at the last minute.

◆ Your child feels deeply sad when other children are mean. This happens to her a lot.

◆ Your child seems to know the material but doesn't do well on tests.

◆ Your child's teacher recommends additional tutoring or special education in subjects that your child excels in—demonstrating a mismatch between ability and behavior.

None of these on its own, in random situations, is cause for alarm (except perhaps the last one). Most children complain about homework, and any child can be occasionally disorganized. The average child will experience taunts on the playground or procrastinate about getting ready to leave the house. But if these situations are persistent and pronounced, and if you're getting consistent and constant feedback from the teacher, it's time to find out what's going on.

The child who resists authority and structure may thrive when she can take some responsibility for her learning. She may need some portion of her day to be self-motivated. She may need to explore a topic in more depth than the structured classroom allows. Or she may do better when she gets to decide to do a report about turtles when the rest of the class is doing a report about frogs. Or she may prefer to do an interactive report, using a hands-on terrarium or a multimedia computer program. If it's her idea, and she has room for creativity, she may be the most enthusiastic student in the room.

The frustrated student may need an accelerated curriculum. You might solve the problem by getting him in a gifted program. Unfortunately, few teachers will recommend a student for the gifted program if he is not completing the regular classroom work (you have to walk before you can run!). You may have to explain this to your Indigo, as Carolyn did with Lucas at the outset of second grade. She explained he might know all the math and reading, but he would have to prove that to the teacher by doing the work. So he set his mind to it with ardor. Within two months, his teacher placed him in the gifted program.

The sensitive student may be overwhelmed by stimulus and may benefit from a smaller class size. She may need more individualized attention from the teacher than a large student-to-teacher ratio may allow.

She may pick up on other children's negative energy, and she may need more control over her environment. A chaotic, more-the-merrier playground or an open classroom with an emphasis on self-selection may not be for her. If she's a physically sensitive child, and the school is not flexible about adjusting her environment, you may need to look for a school that is more accommodating.

**Patience**

If your child is struggling in school, he may receive an instant ADHD diagnosis and you may feel pressure from teachers and administrators to medicate him. Slow down and take more time to understand your child's difficulties (review Chapter 5). Resist the quick label, and be sure to investigate the alternatives. There is most likely a better way. Medication often shuts down an Indigo's natural gifts.

## Your Child's Learning Style

Each of us learns differently. Most conventional schools emphasize verbally oriented learning. Students learn through reading a textbook and listening to a teacher. But some students need a hands-on experience to learn; if they can't touch it and work it themselves, they don't grasp the concept. It's too abstract, and it doesn't stick. Others are kinesthetic. They need to experience it in their bodies. Still others are visual or spatial or aural—that is, they learn through seeing it, building it or graphing it, or hearing it.

Here are some questions to ask yourself about your child:

 ◆ Does your child prefer to think it through or try it out?

 ◆ Which is easier for your child to remember—a fact or a concept?

 ◆ What is your child's listening style—reflective, taking it in; or expressive, jumping in, asking questions, experiencing it by touching it as she hears instructions?

 ◆ Does your child learn better with pictures, maps, and diagrams? Written instructions? Oral instructions? Walking through it?

 ◆ What does your child remember best—something she sees? Something she hears? Something she does?

These questions may help you determine what *kind* of intelligence your child possesses. Howard Gardner, professor of cognition and education at Harvard University, developed categories of multiple intelligence, which many educators use to identify the right environment for a student. These are summarized in the following table.

| Intelligence Style | How They Learn | Strengths |
| --- | --- | --- |
| Visual/ spatial | Through pictures (maps, photos, videos, movies) | Reading, writing, understanding charts and graphics, understanding visual metaphors |
| Visual/ linguistic | Through words and pictures (stories) | Listening, speaking, writing, storytelling, humor |
| Logical/ mathematical | Through logic and numbers | Logic, curiosity, problem-solving, recognizing patterns, classifying information, grasping abstract information, working with geometric shapes |
| Body/ kinesthetic | Through movement | Expression through movement, good hand-eye coordination, good balance |
| Musical/ rhythmic | By hearing it | Ability to produce and appreciate music |
| Interpersonal | Through relationships with others | Uncanny ability to sense others' feelings and intentions, ability to keep the peace, ability to encourage cooperation |
| Intrapersonal | Through self-reflection | Psychic intuition, self-knowledge |

Also useful is Anthony Gregorc's Mind Styles Theory, which shows a duality in learning preference. There are children who learn through concrete experiences, and others who learn through abstract thought. Children also generally have a preference for either sequential or random presentation. These combine to form four sets of learning patterns—concrete random, concrete sequential, abstract random, and abstract sequential. While every child has a little bit of all four patterns to some extent, most children tend to be one of those types:

- **Concrete sequential.** These learners prefer hands-on experience. They prefer order and clear sequences—step-by-step instructions. They may have photographic memories.

- **Concrete random.** These learners want hands-on experience, too, but can make intuitive leaps in understanding. They like trial and error and can do many things at once. They thrive if they are offered choice, chance, challenge, and change.

- **Abstract sequential.** These learners have many conceptual mind-pictures that they match against what they read, hear, see. They prefer to learn in a logical, rational sequence. They can learn from vicarious experiences.

- **Abstract random.** These learners are tuned in to human behavior and subtle vibrations in the emotional atmosphere. They evaluate learning experiences as a whole, including the speaker's delivery style and personality. They prefer to learn in an unstructured manner and like group discussions.

**Crystal Clear**

Our aim is not merely to make the child understand, and still less to force him to memorize, but so to touch his imagination as to enthuse him to his inmost core.

—Italian educator Maria Montessori

According to Wendy, most Indigo Children fall under abstract random or concrete random. They do not think in a linear fashion, nor do they learn that way. They are in tune with intuition—the undercurrents of life.

# Guidelines for Evaluating a School

Knowing your child well is the best place to start for evaluating a new school. Indigo Children can fall so many different places on the spectrum of behavior that there's no one educational style that works for all. Still, we have listed here some Indigo-specific guidelines for evaluating a school.

The school ...

- **Is child-centered.** Whether it's child-sensitive or child-driven depends on your child. Some Indigos need just a little say in the structure of their learning, while others need a lot. Look for an educational style that takes cues from the child and is not locked into a one-style-fits-all approach.

- **Is flexible.** The curriculum responds to who is learning and how they are learning.

- **Honors individuality.** Indigos are so unique they defy categorization.

- **Offers choices.** Students are offered reasonable choices about the speed of the curriculum.

- **Teaches responsibility.** Students take on responsibility for their education appropriate to their development and knowledge.

- **Is constantly evolving.** New approaches are folded into the curriculum.

The bottom line is that the educational system must work harder to fit the child than the child must work to fit the system. If you are hearing, "Well, this is how the system works," and getting the message that your child must fit the system, it's time to look elsewhere.

Look for a school that offers a gifted program or an equivalent. *Giftedness* is the ability to perform exceptionally in intellectual ability; having specific academic aptitude such as math or writing or specific ability in visual or performing arts; or demonstrating creative thinking.

For children with ADHD, look for a school that has a no-medication policy. If you choose to do so, the school will support your choice to use alternatives to medication, and it will offer a structure that suits your child. You will not have to medicate your child so he fits the system.

**def•i•ni•tion** _____

> Giftedness is demonstrating exceptionally high intelligence or great
> special abilities. Many schools in the United States use the Marland
> standard (named for Sidney P. Marland Jr., former U.S. Commissioner of
> Education) to define a gifted child: those who are capable of high per-
> formance in the areas of intellectual ability, specific academic aptitude,
> creative or productive thinking, leadership ability, or visual and perform-
> ing arts. Joe Renzulli's Three Ring Definition of Giftedness looks for clusters
> of traits: above average ability, high level of task commitment, and high
> level of creativity.

# A Quick Guide to Alternative Education

Alternative schooling that emphasizes child-oriented education and
flexibility exists in many firmly established and proven educational
methods. Yet, Wendy believes none of these methods is ideal for the
Indigo child; developing an educational system that fits the emerging
generation of Indigo Children is still a work in progress. Neverthe-
less, methods exist that can provide your child with a thriving learning environment. And if you, as the parents of an Indigo child, are
informed and actively involved, you can help these methods adapt and
evolve. What follows is a brief guide to the philosophies of these methods. You'll find a more extensive list of resources for all of these educational styles in Appendix B.

## Traveling to Wonderland: The Waldorf Method

The Waldorf education method, founded in Stuttgart, Germany, by
Rudolf Steiner in 1919, is based on cultivating the imagination of the
child. It's often called a "whole child" method because its basic building blocks are the heart, hands, and mind, with a significant spiritual
component.

While the individual-oriented Montessori method is better known,
Waldorf is the method many Indigo experts advocate. Waldorf has
been in North America for about 75 years, and the Association of Waldorf Schools of North America says there are 157 Waldorf schools in
North America. (Ironically, the Waldorf method is named after a German cigarette factory in which Steiner started his first private school—
the Waldorf-Astoria.)

The goals are ...

♦ To think independently.

♦ To feel life, expressing it artistically and imaginatively.

♦ To learn practical, hands-on skills, through building and making things.

The method is based on the philosophy that when children relate what they learn to what they experience, they remain invigorated and engaged with their education. Lee Carroll and Jan Tober, authors of *The Indigo Children* (see Appendix B), describe Waldorf as the educational equivalent of Alice in Wonderland, where fairy tales, myths, legends, music, art, physics, and drama are part of the learning. Students write and illustrate their workbooks. The method encourages each student to make his learning his own. Like the Montessori method, which we'll discuss next, it's based on a respect for the child.

Fantasy play and storytelling are integrated into the curriculum. Often, the same teacher stays with a group of children through all of elementary school, providing continuity. This can work beautifully if the child and teacher are well-suited. It's based on the belief that a deep human relationship promotes security; the relationship between teacher and parents is deeper, too. Typically, the primary teacher has the class for two hours at the beginning of the day, then one or two lessons later in the day. Other teachers with areas of expertise fill in the curriculum for the rest of the day.

The Waldorf style stresses an evolving understanding of social behavior; children learn conflict resolution and over time, develop a group consciousness. Individual as well as group activities fill the day, with the aim of cultivating a sense of service.

Unlike Montessori, there is a consistent rhythm and structure to the day. Nature and art are important learning components. Media intake—meaning television, videos, and radio—is limited because the Waldorf philosophy believes that they hamper the child's development of her imagination. Waldorf holds off on introducing computers into the curriculum until high school, instead emphasizing development of ideas, curiosity, personal relationships, and inner development.

Because Waldorf includes eurhythmy—the art of using movement to make tone of voice, speech, and music visible and tangible—the method may prove to be especially effective with musical/rhythmic and body/kinesthetic learning styles defined under Gardner's intelligences.

Though the curriculum is unconventional, many Waldorf students do remarkably well on conventional tests, such as the SAT college-entrance exam, according to the Association of Waldorf Schools in North America (AWSNA).

**Good Counsel**

Reggio Emilia is a preschool educational method that is child-responsive, allowing for self-selected activities. It emphasizes parent and community involvement in supporting and sustaining the school. Because of its emphasis on allowing exploration, responding to the interests of the child, it can prove to be a good foundation for learning, no matter whether you start your child in public, private, or alternative school.

## Self-Expression and Spontaneity: The Montessori Way

The Montessori educational method is a child-centered approach that emphasizes self-expression and spontaneity, and it's quite popular. The North American Montessori Teachers' Association says more than 4,000 private Montessori schools exist in the United States.

The method promotes individual initiative over structured group activity. The method is primarily geared toward preschool and elementary school-age children, but some schools go up to high school. Above all, the method emphasizes the individuality of the child. The effort to continue to facilitate each child's natural thirst for learning is paramount.

Maria Montessori developed the method in Italy in the early 1900s. She was an advocate of the children's rights movement, believing in placing a value on children as children (not adults in small bodies) and inculcating a sense of responsibility in them for their growth and development. The philosophy of freedom within appropriate limits gives the child a lifelong love of learning while equipping her with the self-discipline to achieve it.

Montessori discourages the negativity of competition, believing that grade-oriented achievement diminishes inner growth. A child receives feedback and qualitative analysis of his work, but it's often in the form of a narrative about the child's achievements, his strengths, and his weaknesses. When a child is deficient in an area, it's not defined as a failure, but rather a point to work on. (For more about the Indigo take on competition, see Chapter 16.)

The method emphasizes a hands-on, holistic approach to learning that uses all five senses, accommodating many learning styles. A clean, well-ordered environment is vital to Montessori, and children take part in maintaining the classroom. Most Montessori curriculums explore the natural world, by allowing children to plant gardens or tend to a class-room animal such as a rabbit or gerbil. Famous Montessori graduates of the Digital Age, according to Wikipedia.com, include Jeff Bezos, founder of Amazon; Sergey Brin and Larry Page, founders of Google; and Jimmy Wales, founder of Wikipedia. Other famous Montessorians: Anne Frank, chef Julia Child, actors George Clooney and Helen Hunt; and novelist Gabriel Garcia Marquez. These famous graduates are a testament to Montessori's strength: helping each child tap into his potential.

### Indigo Stars

Maria Montessori was the first woman to become a medical doctor in Italy. She developed her educational theories combining the ideas of educators, physicians, and anthropologists. Later she returned to the University of Rome, studying psychology and philosophy, becoming a professor of anthropology. She started "Casa dei Bambini," or Children's House, in Rome, which became the first Montessori school. She led an unconventional life: she attended a boys-only technical school at age 13, and she had a son by a colleague whom she never married.

## Thinking Outside the Box

Beyond those methods, there are several other educational movements that may yield the ideal solution for educating your Indigo child. Charter schools are new, innovative public schools that operate independently of the mainstream system. Many of them adapt alternative educational philosophies such as Waldorf into the curriculum, taking the best ideas and leaving the rest.

One experimental school, Sudbury Valley in Framingham, Massachusetts, has pioneered innovative educational practices that have earned the notice of the Indigo community. That children are naturally curious is at the core of its philosophy. Children are naturally inclined to learn and take on the responsibility of learning. This style is for the very independent Indigo who shows an interest in leadership and responsibility. At Sudbury, and a similar campus called Indigo Sudbury Campus in Edmonton, Alberta, children learn about democracy by participating in school meetings, which are conducted like town meetings. All ages are mixed together. There are 20 other Sudbury schools in the world.

The belief that children learn best when they take responsibility for directing their learning is at the heart of the unschooling movement, too. Unschooling believes that children are naturally curious, but it does not have classes or textbooks. There are teachers, but children use them as resources, asking them to assist them in learning about something they choose. As George Bernard Shaw said, "What we want to see is the child in pursuit of knowledge, not knowledge in pursuit of the child."

Unschooling encourages the use of computers, and it may be a good fit for the nonconformist, tech-savvy Indigo. On his website, unschooling advocate John Holt suggests that unschooling is more than just homeschooling without a fixed curriculum. He advocates parents allow their children as much freedom to learn in the world as the parents can bear.

## About Homeschooling

Homeschooling can offer a blend of the child-directed curriculum, with the freedom and flexibility to tailor the topics and style to the interest of the child. But homeschooling is only as good as the discipline and commitment of the parent who is teaching. It can prove to be an excellent option for a dedicated and knowledgeable parent. One of the biggest concerns of parents considering homeschooling is how the child will develop social skills. Many options exist for this: allowing the child to participate in public school activities such as physical education, art, or music; enrolling the child in a karate or dance class; joining a baseball or soccer league; joining a children's community theater; getting involved with community organizations; or joining a church.

Many parents who homeschool form coalitions in which parents take turns teaching small groups of children, each sharing different areas of expertise. The coalitions also help with banding together for group field trips, organizing birthday parties, or bringing in experts to teach the children about specific areas.

## About Gifted Programs

Of course, you may not need to find another school. You may find that the gifted program within your school is just exactly what your child needs. Many progressive public (and private) schools not only offer gifted programs but offer pilot programs that cultivate imaginativeness, creativity, entrepreneurship, collaboration—many of the Indigo gifts. Do your research. There may be a curriculum out there that your school may agree to offer a selected group of children. Look into magnet schools that focus on specific subjects or skills such as science, computers, art, or theater. If your child has a specific talent that matches a nearby magnet school, this might be a great fit.

# Reaching Out

A growing community of parents exists to help parents make good choices about educating their Indigo children. Consult the list of schools on Indigo websites, such as Carroll and Tober's, www. indigochild.com/schools.html. Talk to other parents at the schools you are checking out.

If your child is struggling, take the time to listen to her and understand what's really going on. Know your child, and support her uniqueness. Take a step back, and think outside the box. You may find pieces of the solution from many different resources. You may find you need to make big changes, or make a series of small, significant changes. But above all, keep your child's learning paramount.

## The Least You Need to Know

♦ Listen to the signals you are getting from your child and his teacher about the challenges he is having in school.

♦ Be open-minded as you collect specific information about your child.

♦ Put a fine point on your child's particular Indigo challenge, whether it's sensory overload, classroom style, or lack of interest empowerment.

♦ Understand your child's learning style, using Howard Gardner's Multiple Intelligence theory or Anthony Gregorc's Mind Styles Theory.

♦ Research alternative education methods such as Waldorf, Montessori, unschooling, and homeschooling.

♦ Reach out to other parents and support groups for help in finding the best fit for your Indigo child.

# Chapter 15

# The Whole Child

## In This Chapter

- A body in balance
- Nutrition and whole health
- Homeopathic remedies
- Touch that heals

Indigo Children think holistically. They understand intuitively that we are all interconnected. To Indigos, it's only natural that anything they do or think resonates with their body and spirit—not just the mind—because to them, it's all integrated. If a spiritual component isn't present in any endeavor—then why bother?

With their high sensitivity, Indigo Children send strong signals when things are out of balance. Combine that with the Indigo thirst for spiritual advancement, and it means that the holistic health and body/mind/spirit practices that Westerners have embraced in the past decade are absolutely crucial for Indigos. In this chapter, we'll delve into exactly how these methods can help your child—and how to do them safely.

# Whole Believers

Indigo Children are the canaries in the coal mine for our time. Maybe you remember the pop song by The Police, or maybe you have heard the expression. Miners took canaries with them in the mine so that that if all the oxygen went out of the shaft, the first to expire would be the canary. It provided a warning for them to get out.

Indigo Children have finely calibrated systems, much like the canaries. What they are feeling is what some of the rest of us are feeling, too, with exposure to toxins; it's just that we have a built-up tolerance. Indigo Children have none. They demand that we detoxify, that we integrate holistic health practices into our lives.

Many an Indigo parent has become a true believer in holistic health practices after experiencing their Indigo's extreme reactions. The behaviors of many Indigo Children *can* be extreme, and that often means they can push you to the point of trying solutions you wouldn't ordinarily try.

To get oriented on the decisions you'll face in evaluating alternative medicine practitioners, go online to the National Center for Complementary and Alternative Medicine's Get the Facts page (nccam.nih. gov/health/decisions). Always inform your primary health care provider of any alternative medicine you are using with your child. Ideally, your provider takes a more integrative approach and is open to your interest.

Many more scientific studies exist to bolster the theories about alternative medicines. A good source for these is the NCCAM's PubMed site (nim.nih.gov/nccam/camonpubmed.html), which has only studies that have undergone peer review. For reliable information about dietary supplements, go to the database on the International Bibliographic Information on Dietary Supplements website (ods.od.nih.gov).

Here are some general cautions to keep in mind:

◆ Natural does not necessarily mean safe or appropriate.

◆ Every individual responds differently to treatments or supplements.

- ◆ Know that the U.S. Food and Drug Administration does not test supplements. When supplements are proved to be unsafe or if they make medical claims, the FDA can remove them from the market.

- ◆ A reliable practitioner should be willing to provide you with scientific studies that back up his or her claims.

- ◆ When evaluating information on a website, take into account the source. Government, university medical schools, or reputable medical associations are reliable; drug and supplement manufacturers should be treated skeptically.

- ◆ Even after collecting reliable information, find out whether it's been tested to be safe for children. Consult with your practitioner.

Many parents of Indigo Children are oriented toward natural remedies and body/mind/spirit practices. They may have already explored spiritual self-knowledge on a deeper level and are particularly well suited to cultivate that practice in their children.

 **Crystal Clear**

The most precious gift we can offer others is our presence. When mindfulness embraces those we love, they will bloom like flowers.

—Buddhist monk Thich Nhat Hanh

But no matter where you're coming from, you're not alone in exploring alternative medicine: a nationwide government survey conducted in 2002 by the Centers for Disease Control found that more than 36 percent of Americans have used alternative or complementary medicine. However you come to it—reluctantly or joyfully—you'll find much of what you need to help your child in body/mind/spirit health.

One aspect of our culture that Indigos resist and want to change is our tendency to be in our heads, neglecting our physical bodies and our inner spiritual development. It's part of their mission—they are out to change this for everyone, and it's absolutely vital for them. They will teach us to be more open to holistic healing thought systems, such as *ayurveda*, a system of medicine from India, and traditional Chinese medicine. They will teach us to tend to our spiritual needs in the same way we take care of our bodies.

## def•i•ni•tion

**Ayurveda** means the knowledge of life in Sanskrit. It is a holistic system of medicine developed in India, with a strong preventive emphasis. Health is determined by harmony between three biological principles: vata (air), which regulates movement; pitta (fire), which regulates metabolism; and kapha (water), which regulates structure. Ayurveda nutrition balances opposite principles, such as hot and cold, and wet and dry.

# In Our Bodies

It's important for every child to have physical activity to achieve fitness and gain confidence in his body. But for the Indigo child, who is deeply aware of spiritual development and may be highly conscious of other dimensions, it's also important that she learns the body is a safe, anchored place from which to explore the spiritual and psychic realms. She must develop a sense of who she is—a center or a core—to shield herself from others' energy.

In the Western view, the physical body defines us as separate from other people. But the Indigo's sense of self transcends his physical body. The Indigo easily grasps the concept of "you and I are one." So his orientation is to his interconnectedness, and it's not as natural for him to separate. He may not have good boundaries with others; or his boundaries may be more like walls than lines because the only way he can keep from being overwhelmed by others' energy is to shut it all out.

Yoga, tai chi, qigong and other practices such as martial arts or Nia (a combination of dance and martial arts) can help your child in several ways:

- Balance—physical and emotional
- Concentration
- Center of gravity, sense of self
- Flow of movement, natural flow of universal energy
- Body knowledge
- Body confidence
- Healthy sense of self-defense

Along with yoga comes a certain ethic, a reverence for one's body and a respect for others. Yoga's Eightfold Path includes do's (niyamas) and don'ts (yamas). Niyamas are purity, contentment, self-discipline, self-study, and devotion. Yamas are nonviolence, no lying, no stealing, no pursuit of lust or desire, and no greed. These ethics are paired with the practice of the poses (*asanas*), breathing (*pranayama*), and meditation (*dhyana*).

**Good Counsel**

To find out more about yoga's philosophy and how it might help your child, the original sources are the *Bhagavad Gita* and Patanjali's *Yoga Sutras*. The *Bhagavad Gita* tells the epic story of a warrior-prince who faces moral tests as he prepares for battle. *Yoga Sutras* delineates yoga's Eightfold Path, which gives yoga practitioners guidelines to live by.

Children love yoga. Many yoga poses are named after animals—downward-facing dog, rabbit, cobra, frog—and children let their imaginations go crazy with yoga poses. Carolyn's two Indigos make up their own poses—the "crocodile" comes to mind. Sometimes they invent three-person yoga configurations— downward-facing dog over a bridge pose over child's pose, for instance. Check for parent-child yoga classes in your area.

## You Are What You Eat

It's important not to overlook the role in nutrition in the behavior of your child. A nutritional imbalance could very well be the culprit—the factor that exacerbates your Indigo child's most extreme behaviors. Correcting that imbalance may go a long way toward stabilizing the situation. Many nutritional experts recommend raw foods because valuable nutrients are lost through cooking. When most of our food is cooked, our bodies must produce digestive enzymes to break down the food; raw foods naturally have enzymes, proteins that nourish the body.

One Indigo family achieved dramatic results for their 7-year-old Indigo son labeled ADHD through Targeted Amino Acid Therapy (TAAT), which uses enzymes to correct neurological imbalances that many ADHD children have. Their son's behavior has improved dramatically, and the neurotransmitter tests confirm it.

According to research conducted at the Institute of Clinical Chemistry in Lausanne, Switzerland, in the 1930s, cooked foods also diminish immune system function. Cooked foods trigger the production of white blood cells, while raw foods were found not to produce this response. Food that had been heated or processed (with chemicals added) produced an immune system response that researchers compared to fighting an infection. The body behaves as though a pathogen has invaded the system. More recent studies suggest health benefits for fibromyalgia, breast cancer prevention, and rheumatoid arthritis.

Research has shown that a deficiency in digestive enzymes contributes to food allergies, as well as aggressive and antisocial behavior. Raw foods advocates say that while all raw fruit, vegetables, and grains are beneficial, sprouted seeds, grains and legumes are most beneficial.

In addition to raw foods and enzyme supplements, some nutritionists recommend attention to food combinations. Generally speaking, guidelines for food combining are:

- Don't mix carbohydrates (starches, fruits, and sugars) with fat.
- Eat starches and acidic food separately. Carbohydrates are starches, and proteins are acidic.
- Restrict yourself to one kind of protein at a meal.
- Eat proteins and fats separately.
- Eat fruits separately. Their digestion is delayed when other food is in the stomach.
- Eat melons separately. They do not combine well with any other food.
- Skip dessert, or hold off until an hour after a meal. When you have dessert right after a meal, it just sits on top, not digesting and instead fermenting, which turns the food to alcohols, acetic acids, and vinegars.

Raw foods are one of many options that may help balance your child's extremes. A good place to get started researching diet therapy on the Internet is diet-studies.com, which has compiled a list of studies in medical journals about topics ranging from ADHD, Asperger's, food allergies, learning difficulties, and behavior problems. It's part of the Feingold Association, a organization of families and professionals that researches and advocates proven dietary techniques to improve learning and behavior in children (Feingold.org). The Feingold approach emphasizes avoiding food additives.

Among the studies you'll find is one Wisconsin school that initiated a five-year project to bring healthy food into the schools (www.feingold.org/PF/wisconsin1.html). According to the website, after the program was implemented, students became calm and purposeful in their studies. Since then, the number of students dropping out, getting expelled, getting caught carrying weapons, using drugs, or committing suicide has dropped to zero. It's called the Appleton Project, and there is a video available through the website.

Train your child or teen to select healthy foods when out in the world. At grocery shopping time and when you pack lunch for her, include her in the decision-making. Know that your teen will face temptations, but instill in her knowledge about nutrition and the effects of poor nutrition. Keep a list of super foods on your refrigerator (as Carolyn does) as a reminder each time a family member reaches in the refrigerator. Talk to your child or teen about sugar or additives or toxins such as PCBs or mercury. Explain why you buy only organic broccoli or free-range chicken. Explain why you go to the growers' market on Sunday rather than the produce section at the supermarket.

## Natural Protection

Because many Indigo Children are physically sensitive, they react more strongly to environmental toxins—everything from too much sun to fluoride in the water, from electromagnetic rays to Teflon-coated pans. It means getting up to speed about food additives and environmental chemicals so you can get to the bottom of the issue. These chemicals and toxins can be in the most common household items, such as dryer sheets or the cleanser you use to wipe down your kitchen counters.

Many researchers believe we start out life with these substances in our system. One study that detailed just how much was conducted by the Environmental Working Group in 2004. Researchers analyzed the umbilical cord blood of 10 babies and found 287 chemicals present, including 180 known to cause cancer. Chemicals included pesticides, mercury, PCBs, and PFCs.

### Patience

Before you decide that cell phones cause brain tumors, all salmon has PCBs, or drinking diet soda causes Multiple Sclerosis, do your research. You and your child cannot live in fear. There are too many things to worry about. Be informed, and make choices about how you will protect your child from harmful toxins and other hazards. Be reasonable, and do the best you can.

Karen Eck, MT (ASCP), is an alternative news researcher who writes for Children of the New Earth Online magazine. She runs several Indigo lists on Yahoo groups, including the Indigo-parents and Indigo-children lists and also co-moderates the Indigo-adults list. Her monthly column informs parents about the latest research on topics such as toxins and nutrition. Karen advocates Indigos eat a natural diet according to their metabolic type (some don't do well on a vegan diet) and avoid exposure to home pesticides, plastics, Teflon cookware, and artificial sweeteners. For more information see AskKarenEck.com.

## Natural Remedies

Many holistic health practitioners recommend flower essences to achieve balance in the body, particularly for the finely calibrated nervous system of Indigo and Crystal Children (the next wave of children after Indigos). Flower essence therapist Nancy Boyd writes on the Global Oneness Commitment website that flower essences have a vibration essence and are connected to the body's electrical system, much as healing crystals do.

Flower essences restore electromagnetic balance, but they also quell mental, emotional, and spiritual turmoil. They are especially effective for Indigos and Crystals because their systems are more sensitive and more vulnerable. Boyd and many other flower essence therapists say the remedies go hand-in-hand with yoga, meditation, proper nutrition, and exercise.

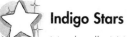

**Indigo Stars**

Machaelle Wright developed Pereleandra flower essences by receiving messages from Spirit, creating the Perelandra Center for Nature Research in the Blue Ridge Mountains in Virginia. The main lab is a 100-foot garden, on which the center does not use any herbicides, pesticides, insecticides, or chemical fertilizers. Wright uses a conscious, coordinated, and educational method that she calls "co-creative science." Wright also teaches MAP, The Co-Creative White Brotherhood Medical Assistance Program, which is a method to call on spirit helpers to come provide energy healing while you meditate. Wendy finds this self-healing technique very effective.

Dr. Edward Bach developed 38 flower essences. Rescue Remedy is a popular combination of those essences that helps calm stress, impatience, and tension. Advocates believes flower essences help stop tantrums. They can help your child stop, relax, and focus.

The Flower Essence Society has a list of case studies, along with many interviews and articles about the use of flower essences with children. Practitioners say they have seen results with calming the agitated child, relieving anxiety, creating more tolerance, and establishing trust. They also say they alleviate physical symptoms, ranging from asthma to ear infections to rare nervous system disorders. A list of resources for flower essences appears in Appendix B.

Specific flower essences recommended for Indigo Children include Lobelia, an essence called "Crystal Silver," as well as Red Sunflower and Giant Geranium. All are combined in the Children's Issues Super-Essence. Other Indigo parents find Orange Canna Lily to be effective. Flower essences are available on many websites (see Appendix B), but those specific ones are on nmessences.com.

Another healing tool is Aura-Soma, which is color therapy. Bottles of colored oil contain essences, herbs, spices, water from the holy spot of Glastonbury, England, herbal coloring, and crystal energy. A set is available specifically for Indigo Children called New Aeon Child Set. Wendy has tried several and recommends them. See aura-soma.com for more information.

Many homeopathic remedies exist that can save you a lot of time and trouble. Many traditional/conventional remedies amount to shooting down a gnat with an automatic weapon. Homeopathic remedies activate the body's natural healing properties to cure an illness. A reliable guide to homeopathic remedies is available at www.healing-arts.org/children, a research project through the program in integrative medicine at the University of Arizona College of Medicine. The site contains an alphabetical listing of homeopathic remedies for ADHD, as well as flower essences, herbal remedies, neurofeedback, behavior therapy, and conventional drug therapy. To find out more about ADD/ADHD homeopathic remedies, consult a naturopath in your area.

*Homeopathy* is a whole-person approach. The approach is customized to the individual, and it takes into account symptoms in all systems of the body, looking for the interconnectedness of those symptoms. Homeopathic remedies may come from plants, minerals, metals, or animal substances, though it's not unusual for them to include intangible elements such as moonlight, sunlight, or magnetic therapy.

**def•i•ni•tion**

Homeopathy comes from Greek—*homeo* meaning similar, *pathos* meaning disease. Homeopathy seeks to stimulate the body's natural defenses. Homeopathic doctors treat the whole person—examining not only the symptoms but the person's lifestyle, nutrition, and environment. Thus, homeopathic medicine is holistic, working on more than the physical plane, but also the mental, emotional, and spiritual.

Homeopathy is based on the concept of similars—like curing like. Unlike conventional medicine, which focuses on eliminating symptoms and relieving discomfort, homeopathy focuses on the cause of the symptoms, using the body's natural power to heal.

Viewpoints vary widely on the value of homeopathy. Some dismiss scientific studies that have produced positive results, saying they are nothing more than a placebo effect. Some doubt the underlying principle that something that causes an illness might also prevent it, yet allopathic medicine uses the same principle with vaccines or allergy treatments. Other viewpoints are that homeopathy works, but science has yet to prove it. If it's helpful and safe, these people say, proof is not necessary. Homeopathy is gaining more acceptance. For instance, the National Center for Complementary and Alternative Medicine, a division of the National Institutes of Health, financially supports research of homeopathy for fibromyalgia, stroke rehabilitation, dementia, and prostate cancer.

Many of those who work with Indigos recommend blue-green algae, a nutritional supplement that comes from Klamath Lake in southern Oregon. Those who tout its benefits say it stabilizes blood sugar and contains critical vitamins. This supplement gained attention for treating ADD/ADHD kids when Edward Hallowell, author of *Driven to Distraction* (see Appendix B), advocated it at a conference on learning disabilities in 1998. Blue-green algae is considered a super food.

# The Healing Touch

Touch heals. It accesses vital energy in our bodies that promotes healing and deepens strength and self-awareness. Because Indigo Children are deeply sensitive to all energy in the universe, they need this therapy to recalibrate their energy—to get back in balance.

Energy medicine is divided into two types—*veritable* and *putative.* Veritable includes vibrations (sound, for instance) and electromagnetic forces, including light and magnetic fields. Putative is based on biofields—fields of energy in and around the body. Therapists in various disciplines, including Reiki and Shamballa, access vital life force energy, detecting this subtle energy and redirecting it. Others include qigong, a Chinese practice; healing touch, including massage; and intercessory prayer. Among the vibrational therapies gaining credence is sound or music therapy, which is believed to resonate with certain organs of the body to promote healing and prevent illness. Using crystal bowls to create resonant tones is one type of sound therapy that works for many Indigos.

Other therapies, such as acupuncture and acupressure, restore energy flow to the body. Acupuncture is based on an understanding of the meridians in the body, through which neural information flows. Acupuncture removes blocks to this flow and restores vital energy by placing needles in contact with meridians, while acupressure uses firm pressure with hands on pressure points.

Craniosacral therapy uses pressure on the back of the neck and skull in very specific locations to correct imbalances in spinal fluid that may be causing headaches, neck pain, or back pain. A caution: it's a controversial treatment, so be sure to do your research and look for a qualified practitioner. Check online sources such as PubMed and clinicaltrials. gov for research specific to children. Know that holistic health experts such as Dr. Andrew Weil recommend it for children specifically for ear infections, ADHD, learning disabilities, and colic. The Integrative Medicine Clinic at the University of Arizona, with which Dr. Weil is affiliated, is one good source for information about any integrative medicine treatment, and the clinic has done trials and studies specific to children.

Energy medicine is often a component in whole medicine, using herbs and nutritional supplements in combination with modalities such as massage, acupuncture, Reiki, Shamballa, or yoga. This holistic approach is central to traditional Chinese medicine and ayurvedic medicine, a natural healing system developed in India. Ayurveda goes hand in hand with yoga and meditation, placing equal emphasis on body, mind, and spirit, focusing on establishing harmony through all levels of being. Ayurveda focuses on balancing the doshas—vata, pitta, and kapha—in the body using opposite elements. For instance, light, dry and mobile need the balance of heavy, moist and still. Let's say you are feeling "off" after running on a cool, windy day (too much lightness, dryness, and mobility). To balance it, eat something heavy (a sweet potato, for instance), take a bath (moistness), and be in stillness (mentally and physically).

In healing touch therapies, pain in the body is treated as information. It is seen as part of the whole. Emotional and spiritual pain manifests as physical pain in the body. The National Center for Complementary Medicine reports surveys in the United States that between 2 percent and 14 percent of adults have received massage therapy.

# Whole Parenting

Step back and watch your child. See beyond your immediate challenges of finding her the right education, getting her in the right activities, helping her develop healthy social skills, and channeling her talents— all those things you have poured yourself into. Instead, see her wholeness. See how she is interconnected to the universe, an intricate web of unique gifts and challenges. Appreciate her utter complexity. See all of her layers—physical, mental, emotional, and spiritual. See that she has a singular purpose on Earth, a spiritual mission. See her as a whole child.

## The Least You Need to Know

◆ Movement is important to Indigo Children to allow them to develop a sense of a safe center within.

◆ Yoga's yamas and niyamas cultivate a reverence for the body and respect for others. Many children love yoga poses that are named after animals, such as cobra, dog or rabbit.

◆ Some of the extremes of behavior in your Indigo child may be tempered by correcting nutritional imbalances through diet changes or enzyme supplements.

◆ Indigo Children are more sensitive to toxins. Nutritional expert Karen Eck recommends steering away from mercury, hormones in beef or dairy, fluoride, chlorine, air fresheners, fabric softeners, Teflon-coated pans, Scotchguard, and aspartame and other artificial sweeteners.

◆ Natural remedies such as flower essences or aura-soma have a calming, centering effect.

◆ Energy healing is part of a whole medicine approach, using herbs, nutritional supplements, body/mind exercise such as yoga and modalities such as massage, acupuncture, Reiki, or Shamballa.

# Part 5

# How Indigos Will Change the World

Why are Indigos here? Why now? Indigos are going to change the world, and they already have. They will challenge us with out-of-the-box thinking. They will inspire us because of their wise souls. Indigos will create a world in which everybody wins.

# Chapter 16

# We All Learn, We All Win

## In This Chapter

- ◆ Let's all win together
- ◆ Cooperative journeys
- ◆ Limitless imaginings
- ◆ Hands-on, challenging games

Not only are Indigo Children the education pioneers; they are the play pioneers. As they require new approaches to learning, they are demanding and creating new approaches to play. In their world of play, games and activities must be creative, imaginative, challenging, and noncompetitive.

Linear? Forget it. Too boring. Winner takes all? Not worth it. It's about the experience. With Indigos, there are no winners and no losers; for these children, it's a win/win world. As they become adults, they will carry this into the workplace and the community.

# No More Win/Lose

Competition is not what it's all about with an Indigo child. Games where all make a contribution and players are not eliminated are vitally important to Indigo Children. Why? It's because they have too much empathy for the loser; winning is not enjoyable.

At the 2006 World Little League Championship game between Japan and the United States, some of the members of the U.S. team, which was from Georgia, were crying with the losing Japanese team. They went out of their way to hug their competitors. They invited them into group photos and were connected and supportive more so than any other team Wendy has observed. At the end of the game, everyone was huddled together in a great big group hug, and everyone was smiling. Wendy noted that this was evidence of the increase of Indigo Children in the world—and this was their impact.

> **Good Counsel**
>
> The movie *Searching for Bobby Fischer* (1993) does an excellent job of making the point about the struggles around winning and losing. The adults in the life of a child chess star seek to nurture his ability, hiring a win-at-all-costs chess coach. The child refuses to adapt this view, instead forging a new model for competition.

This is so because of their high capacity for empathy. When someone loses, they feel it. It's difficult for them to enjoy winning when they understand so deeply that it's at someone else's expense. It's out of balance. The sadness the loser feels takes them down.

## Everybody Wins

In noncompetitive games, everyone wins if the goal is achieved, and everyone makes a contribution. If everyone wins, everyone can be happy. Indigos will play this way, and it will bode them well for the workplace of the future. It's important for everyone to work together constructively. They take pride in building something with others that they might not have been able to accomplish individually.

This play ethic is the seed of a work ethic that fits into the creative class that public policy analyst Richard Florida envisions as the work wave of the future. Corporations will rely on a sense of play and team-work to remain innovative. High technology demands many creative people collaborating, sharing their collective knowledge. It's moving so fast that any one person only has a piece of the solution—and so for companies to be nimble, they must tap into the creativity of a col-laborative team, rather than rely on compartmentalized, individualized solo acts.

To solve the problems of the future, it will require collective and imagi-native brain power, and that's what Indigos are here to do. Indigos care more about working together to construct something—to make some-thing they otherwise could not do solo—than about winning. To them, playing a game such as Earth Child's "Community: A Cooperative Game About Love & Peace," is heaven. They get to work together for world peace. Everyone wins.

The game provokes thought about questions such as our responsibil-ity for nurturing the awareness of others. In the game, players explore spiritual and practical issues as they work together to build a village. They have to build schools, hospitals, farms, businesses, childcare, and so on. They work through disagreements and discussions to make agreements. All of these decisions impact life in the village, and the participants meet in the village hall to resolve them. It provides an exercise in thinking about the other person as well as yourself.

Other games from Earth Child include the Princess game, a new take on rescuing the sleeping princess. It's not a prince who rescues her, but a team of brave, savvy people. Harvest Time guides players through planting seeds and bringing crops to harvest before winter, while in Sand Castles, players build a sand castle on the beach together before the tides comes in to wash it away. Both games teach about teamwork, nature, and the temporal nature of life.

The Earth Child site (earthchildonline.com) is a resource for informa-tion about Waldorf schooling, which has a strong social ethical compo-nent (see Chapter 14). The founders say they started the business as a way to have the freedom to be with their children. This is another way Indigos are changing the world: they have changed the way their par-ents work.

## A European Approach

European board games take a similar noncompetitive approach, in which all players make a contribution to the outcome. There might be a winner, but the winner depends on others to win, and players are in the game to the end.

Some examples that have gotten high ratings on board game sites include Ticket2Ride, in which players must work together to build railroad tracks to reach their destination. Another is Carcassonne, a tile-laying game set in a southern French city with Roman and Medieval fortifications. The collective skills of the players determine the challenge of the game, as well as who will be victorious. That and other award-winning family games can be found at www.riograndegames. com. In St. Petersburg, which won Best Strategy Game in 2004 from boardgameratings.com, each player is involved in every turn. In Break the Safe, a Mattel game introduced in 2003, all players must work together to deactivate a bomb in a safe. It's a new, noncompetitive take on Clue, the sleuthing game where you must outwit other sleuths to determine the murderer, weapon, and scene of the crime.

# Imagination and Innovation

The most interesting games to Indigos will be those that stimulate the imagination, and they will carry this over into their working lives. They also like more free-form games, like tag and hide-and-seek.

### Good Counsel

Indigo Children also thrive on building things together. For them, it's important to work constructively. They derive satisfaction from building something tangible. That can mean interlocking plastic building blocks or magnetic building pieces. You can make these games more interesting for the Indigo child by setting parameters for the type of building they will build together and setting a time limit.

Wendy's favorite games as a child, when she played with others, were fantasy play. Of course, all children engage in fantasy play, but with Indigo Children, it's more so; they are full of enthusiasm for imaginative play, and they are usually the leaders. That is, the scene, characters—and all the rules—are the products of their imagination. They stay in this fantasy play phase longer than other children. Wendy's mother often would get women's dressy clothing from yard sales so she could play dress up and be a queen or a princess. Wendy also enjoyed making puppets and putting on puppet shows.

## Creativity Projects

When Wendy worked with gifted children in the public schools, many of them Indigo Children, she would organize creativity projects. One such game was with groups of three children. Each child chose a puppet, then out of three hats, they drew a "problem," a "setting," and a "mood." For instance, the problem might be that the younger brother pulled the older sister's hair. She's mad about it, and Mom and Dad are upset, too. The setting might be home or school—or the moon—and the mood might be sad or angry or happy. Wendy gave the children a few minutes to talk, but not enough time to write a script. So they improvised it and performed a puppet show.

Wendy says most of the kids loved this kind of play and enjoyed seeing each other's performances. As they observed other groups, they became better each time at solving the problems, as well as creating character voices and puppet manipulation. Wendy enjoyed seeing how they would resolve the conflict, how creative they could be with the voices, and how comical or serious they played it.

With older children—fifth grade and up—Wendy asked them to create a new country and culture, complete with money, clothing, foods, schools, laws, language, and a map. It was a good way to test their understanding of the basic concepts of country, and they got to get creatively involved.

With Indigo Children, it's important to be involved in a creative idea, to interact with it. For them, a concept is dynamic and alive, and they want to manipulate it. This is how they learn.

## Been There, Done That

Indigo Children can be so brilliant and imaginative that they can chew up a new idea quickly. They swallow it and move on. If it's not new and exciting to them, they can easily become bored.

Yet boredom and creativity go hand in hand. Boredom can be defined as a state of mind that finds the environment or subject matter tedious and dull. It's easy for Indigos to pass that kind of judgment. It may only be interesting for a minute, then it's "been there, done that." Yet the human mind—and especially the Indigo mind—will not let itself be bored for long. The Indigo child will daydream. He will create a fantasy about it. He will see animal shapes in an apple core. He will animate the grass blades. (Remember, he understands other dimensions!)

But let's think about where boredom leads. Boredom always seeks an outlet. In *The Cat in the Hat*, a capricious cat in a striped top hat arrives with the mischievous Thing One and Thing Two. In *Alice in Wonderland*, a bored Alice drifts off to sleep and falls into the rabbit hole, finding Wonderland. In Leonard Cohen's song, *First We Take Manhattan*, he sings of being sentenced to 20 years of boredom for "trying to take the system from within." (Perhaps an early Indigo?) The website BecauseIWasBored.com has a series of videos on topics ranging from "I rode a bike to work" to "I slept in class." The creator invites others to stop by every day "because you're as bored as I am."

> **Crystal Clear**
>
> If life doesn't offer a game worth playing, then invent a new one.
>
> —American author Anthony J. DiAngelo

## Dream a Little Daydream

Your child's teacher may tell you he daydreams a lot and doesn't pay attention in class. You may notice it, too. There are pluses, of course, to daydreaming. Daydreaming gets you to think out of the box. It gives you new ideas, and it helps you escape boredom and develop creativity. So it's not all bad. Psychologists estimate that we might spend one-third to one-half of our waking hours daydreaming. While that sounds like a lot, these are micro-daydreams, lasting 30 seconds to a couple of minutes.

The downside to daydreaming is that generally it happens when you need to give your attention to something else. If your child has let daydreaming become a habit and it's affecting his schoolwork, help him start out the day with energy shielding or meditation to get grounded.

In general, allow for more down time by not overscheduling, which will give him more time to enjoy his rich inner life.

Down time boosts productivity. Our present day lifestyle does not allow a lot of down time, not physically or intellectually. Even our children have very scheduled lives. Indigo Children are resisting the overscheduled lives of today's children. They need down time, and as they grow up, they will seek to change that. Down time will need to be integrated back into our lifestyle. The afternoon siesta popular in southern Europe has faded as cities become more urban, and more people have long commutes to work, which don't allow them to go home, lunch, and nap, arriving back at work in the evening, refreshed. But Indigo Children won't operate on the same schedule as the rest of us—it certainly isn't a nine-to-five world for them.

Work with your child to make her daydreaming a positive. Daydreaming can help your child identify what she values—it can help her tap into her needs, wants, and desires. It can also be channeled into creative visualization, helping her use her imagination in a focused way to achieve her goals. For more about creative visualization, see *The Complete Idiot's Guide to Creative Visualization* (see Appendix B).

## It's Not a Straight Line

Games such as Candyland or Life are classics. Indigo Children may play them, just like any other children, but they have a preference for nonlinear games. These games just aren't out of the box enough for Indigos.

*Nonlinear* thinking is random. It's not based on prior experience. Innovative play and innovative work solutions arise from not relying on prior experience. Nonlinear thinking makes friends with chaos, uncertainty, and multiple outcomes. Linear thinking presupposes that there are only minimal resources for any problem. It does not allow for using innovative thinking to create new resources.

> **def•i•ni•tion**
>
> Nonlinear thinking is thinking that is not sequential. Instead, it's random and full of complexity and uncertainty. In nonlinear thinking, there is no logical progression from thought to thought. Nonlinear thinking is not tied to a pattern based on prior experience.

You can see how a nonlinear thinker would struggle in the classroom and later in the workplace. In the classroom, performance is measured by grades and tests, and students are expected to perform to a norm. In the workplace, decisions about future products and markets are based on previous successes.

The role Indigo Children will play in the future economy is to get us out of the box faster, and they will learn to be comfortable with complexity and uncertainty through their play as children. Even the way we think about the life path for our children will shift. The current paradigm is that a child goes to school in one continuous stretch, from kindergarten (really, from preschool) to high school graduation, through college and grad school. Then that young adult enters a career that is supposed to sustain him for a lifetime.

Already this is not true for Generation X, and the Indigo Children who are entering adulthood and joining the workforce are not planning for linear careers. They are saving for retirement earlier than previous generations, and they accept as given that they might start and stop careers over the course of their working lives. Their future is in serial careers with ongoing training and lifetime learning. It's estimated that the average viable life span of a college degree is 18 months, meaning that within 18 months of graduating and entering a field, the knowledge gained in school has been outpaced. Ongoing and serial education has become the norm, and this trend will continue.

Many computer video games are nonlinear, which means that there are multiple options for outcomes. There is no fixed sequence. Sandbox-style video games are open-ended and nonlinear. They compare to a physical sandbox, where the player can play free-form. In a real sandbox, the sand can be smoothed out and resculpted again and again. In sandbox video games there are not necessarily game level advancement milestones. The Sims, the best-selling PC game, is an example of a sandbox video game.

Open-ended video games do not have a predetermined outcome. Players can achieve goals in a variety of ways, and they can manipulate the virtual environment. Sometimes open-ended games can have multiple endings.

Success in the current marketplace, especially in technology, has been based on getting your product out to the market first, which gives an advantage to early buyers (initial public offerings, for instance). But since the dot-com crash, a new paradigm has taken hold, one that will fit right in with the Indigos' nonlinear way of thinking. The advantage will go to those companies that wait for costs to fall and enter when consumer demand is already established. The future economy will be built on more creativity and less management. Indigos will put people first, seeing intellectual and creative collateral as more important than micromanagement whose goal is to pinch out an ever-increasing profit margin as markets mature and shrink.

### Indigo Stars

Physicist Albert Einstein was known for his bold imagination. He strongly advocated play as one of the keys to innovative solutions. He liked to do what he called thought experiments, in which he would step outside the laws of physics and contemplate the universe. He wasn't so sure that time was absolute and constant; he saw it as relative. He did experiments with time dilation, which played with the perspectives on time's slowing down or speeding up.

# I Want to Touch It

For many Indigo Children, play is about the experience, not the outcome. Any kind of game that gives children an experience rather than focusing on a winner is going to be enthralling for an Indigo. Scavenger hunts are an excellent example as a good combination of competition and win-win, because even though one child may win for finding the most things on the list, others are rewarded for finding special items, and overall, the children get to have the experience of exploring together.

In recent years, children's museums have become more hands-on, responding to the needs of children who just have to touch it to experience it. No longer do children learn about electricity from an exhibit behind a glass. They string wires through connections and turn the lights on themselves. They play with water tables to learn how currents flow, lifting and moving barriers to create faster and slower currents.

Another trend in recent years are children's gardens, which are full of oversized bumblebees, centipedes, carrots, and pumpkins. It's an Alice in Wonderland effect, and children love it. Lightheartedness is an important component of play for Indigo Children. It opens the opportunity for connection and enthralls the imagination.

# It Must Challenge

Indigo Children are always looking for a challenge. If it's not challenging, it's boring. Wendy says she loved Scrabble as a child, but if the kids she was playing with were not at her level, she grew quickly bored. Many Indigos like math-related games such as Sudoku, which involves placing numbers in a grid, as well as strategy games like chess.

Generally, this expectation that games be more challenging to the mind is a reflection of the rising IQ rate. Since 1940, IQ scores have risen dramatically in developed countries. The average increase has been three points per decade. It's called the Flynn effect, named after political scientist James R. Flynn. Various experts have attributed it to smaller families, better education, better parenting, greater environmental complexity—and exposure to games and puzzles that boost verbal ability.

Expect Indigo Children to bring this challenging, invigorating and inclusive style of play into the workplace, as they become part of a rising creative class. Many will enter creative careers—and still others will create new fields that allow them to work collaboratively and innovatively, in environments where everyone makes a contribution.

Their skill with intuition will come to be valued in the workplace because intuition is the certainty beneath the uncertainty. Intuition is a shortcut to what you know but cannot yet prove logically, and in the future workplace, fast solutions will prove to be necessary. Companies will need innovative solutions that arise from intuitive thinking because they will have shorter time frames to introduce products and establish markets. Working in teams will be great for tuned-in Indigos. Their ability to manage uncertainty will make them stand out.

# Agents of Change

All in all, Indigo Children are agents of change in all the areas of life they touch. Right now, as children, their job is to change us through play. But they are also teaching us through their play. The way they are changing our society is unusual, rapid, spiritually driven, and absolutely necessary. It's occurring on an unprecedented magnitude.

## The Least You Need to Know

◆ Because of their high capacity for empathy, Indigo Children prefer win-win games. They intensely dislike competition.

◆ Indigos will like to use collective, imaginative brainpower, both in play and in work.

◆ Indigo Children thrive on fantasy play and creative projects more than the average child.

◆ If it's nonlinear, it's interesting to an Indigo. Nonlinear thinking is complex, random, and uncertain. Many board games and computer games are designed this way.

◆ It's important for Indigos to have hands-on experiences with play, at museums or out on nature walks.

◆ Many Indigos like games that challenge their verbal, math, or strategic abilities.

# Chapter 17

# Thinking in Another Dimension

## In This Chapter

♦ Dreams, visions, and the meta-conscious mind

♦ The art of manifestation

♦ Cosmic consciousness

♦ Astral travel, time travel

Indigo Children have magical minds. Their worlds are filled with vivid dreams and visions. They can manifest remarkable events with ease, and they live a life connected to soul and spirit. Life with your Indigo may be filled with surprising synchronicities. This is the norm. As Indigos grow into adulthood, it will become a truth for all of us.

As a culture, we will become more balanced between rationalism and intuition. Science will devise more concrete explanations for subconscious reasoning and gain a greater understanding for the untapped power of the human brain. Indigos will usher in an age when we are more facile with multiple dimensions of thinking and experiencing the world.

# Meta-Conscious Experience and Creativity

The subconscious—it's all that thinking we don't understand because it doesn't process through in a rational, verbal way. And yet we act on it. Our thoughts and emotions are sensitized to our subconscious reasoning—and even if you're not an Indigo, you are tuned in and vibrate to this energy. These thoughts and emotions directly influence our reality. They can directly influence physical outcomes of events. Indigo Children have come in with finely tuned abilities in this area, and they will teach us all about the source of the metaphysical experience and ways to tap into it. Let's look at some of the sources of meta-consciousness.

## Dream a Little Dream

Many Indigos have an active dream life. They dream in color, and they dream often. Often they have *lucid dreams*, in which they are conscious they are in a dream, and they have the ability to manipulate the scene. They can consciously move, control action, and speak. Very often they have the ability to "program" their dreams, summoning important people to them, such as a deceased parent. Carolyn has often summoned her father to visit her in dreams. He often shows up on his birthday.

**def•i•ni•tion**

Lucid dreaming occurs when you consciously perceive that you are in a dream right in the middle of it. Lucid dreams are often more memorable than nightmares, and people report that they can be effective in shedding oneself of recurring, troubling fears. Some people can manipulate the dreamscape.

Indigos will talk about their dreams. They will want to share their dream life with their family and friends. Dream experts recommend cultivating your dream life by writing down your dreams and talking about them. This sends a signal to the subconscious to activate dream life. Start writing down your dreams, and encourage your child to start a dream journal. Also encourage your child to use dreams as inspiration for art.

Dreams and visions are the seeds of creativity. One is German chemist Friedrich August Kekule von Stradonitz's discovery of the Benzene molecule after he dreamed that the atoms became a snake biting its own tale. This helped him figure out the molecule's structure.

On brilliantdreams.com, there is a collection of stories about dreams as inspiration. Paul McCartney dreamed of the melody for the Beatles song "Yesterday." Mary Shelley dreamed of the plot of *Frankenstein*. Physiologist Otto Loewi had a dream about a proof that later earned him a Nobel prize. Elias Howe was working to perfect his invention of the sewing machine when he had a dream about where to put the hole in the needle. In the dream, he was being held prisoner by savages who were dancing around him with spears, all of which had holes at the tips—just like a sewing needle.

Dreams can warn of coming events. President Abraham Lincoln had recurring dreams warning of his assassination.

Indigos will reap so many benefits from their dream life that it will encourage us to use our dreams as a creative source. They will mine their dream life for the art they create, and they will consciously use their dreams for solutions in their professions. They will also teach us to use our dreams to predict the future or to calm our fears and prepare for future events. Dreams are an excellent way to explore our psyches, to become aware of our deepest fears and confront them. In dreams, we often rehearse our response to a threat.

Wendy's dreams are always in color and full action. The was so normal for her growing up that she was surprised to find out that was not the case for everyone. One of her recurring dreams has her in a school leading children out during a fire drill—except a real fire is blazing or a bomb is about to explode. Wendy believes this dream recurred to help her face her fears. When she was a child, her house burned down, and she was fearful of fire. As a schoolteacher, she often had to lead the children outside for fire drills, and it was a challenge for her because it recalled childhood trauma and often triggered more nightmares.

These dreams came to an abrupt halt after the 9/11 attacks. Many Indigos have reported that their spirit was in the towers of the World Trade Center during or after the attack, and Wendy is among them. She was sleeping when the Trade Center was attacked, and she had a very clear dream that she was in a tall building, leading many terrified people down the smoke-filled stairwells. When she woke up to hear the news and realized it wasn't just a dream, it was extremely depressing, yet not too surprising. Wendy had experienced bilocation before, when you are able to be physically present in one space but spiritually present and aware in another location. Her physical body was sleeping in bed, but her spirit was in the towers with many other angels, leading people down the stairs and helping them to stay calm and get out of the building in time.

## Real-Life Mind Projections

Remember in *Harry Potter* when Harry "removes" the pane of glass between his arrogant, pampered cousin Dudley and the snake? It's Harry's first discovery of his magical powers as a wizard. His angry thoughts about how torturous it was to live with Dudley "removed" the glass—accidental magic.

In real life, Indigos are facile with mind projections. They understand how their thoughts can influence external events, because they understand the power of thought energy. They may practice creative imagining or creative visualization, which uses the power of imagination and energy of focused, positive thought to manifest something.

**Good Counsel**

In many cultures, the period from age 6 to 12 is the best time to teach children about their psychic power, according to Bobbie Sandoz, a therapist and book author known for her work with dolphins and whales. She suggests allowing children to have experiences cooperative fishing with dolphins, telepathically communicating with animals, and communicating with angels and spirits.

There is a physical, scientific explanation for Indigos' prowess in mind projection, telepathic communication, and psychic abilities such as clairvoyance. The prefrontal lobes of their brains are more developed. It's the part of the brain that leading neurologist Paul MacLean called the origin of human virtues, the emotional part of the brain that is the "higher brain," where the brain evaluates whether an idea is true and right. Larger prefrontal lobes are active in a higher state of intuitive knowing. Author P.M.H. Atwater (*Beyond the Indigo Children*, see Appendix B) describes them as operating like "wings" of the brain, opening our minds to more dimensions of experience. In the coming world, more and more of us will activate this part of our brains.

## Visions of the Future

Many Indigos have visions of their future that come to them like movies. Many of Wendy's visions come as sudden knowing or auditory messages, but more often recently she also has visions that include sound and movement, much like a dream, but come from a waking or semi-waking state. These usually come to her as she is falling asleep or waking up, though she has had them while meditating, too.

When Wendy was working with schoolchildren, she often did guided imagery creativity sessions with the students, which were called Imaginary Field Trips. After one such session, a girl told Wendy about seeing her future through an attic window she had just cleaned. The window was dirty when she entered the room, but after she cleaned it thoroughly, she watched major events of her future life play out in front of the window on the lawn. She saw her marriage and her child and a death in her family. Later she told Wendy that she had dreamed about her grandmother's death one day before she died.

## Manifesting Your Reality

Manifestation means to create something or a state of being in your life, such as a new job, a new partner, a happier marriage, more income. It's often the natural result of dreams, the practice of intention, or creative visualization. Belief is the cornerstone of creative visualization, in which you imagine something you want to create in your life and then you act *as if* it has already happened. Belief is easy for Indigos because the powers of their imagination and their skills at precognition are so powerful. They can so easily see the future they want to create. And many of them see beyond the limitations of time, so to them it *has* already happened.

One writer Carolyn works with is the parent of a preschooler Indigo with remarkable powers of manifestation. Once, his son wanted to go to an amusement park, and the boy kept talking about how he was going to the amusement park, though the family had plans the next few weeks and it was going to be logistically difficult to go to the park. The father didn't see how it was possible. Within a few days, a family friend arrived from out of town and offered to take his son to the amusement park. Off they went! The father says this kind of thing happens all the time with his son.

# Our Big, Wide World

Mathematical physicist Roger Penrose wrote in *The Emperor's New Mind* (see Appendix B) that the laws of physics are inadequate to explain human consciousness. One explanation comes from Richard M. Bucke, who wrote in *Cosmic Consciousness* in 1902 that humans have three forms of consciousness, each of which develops at a certain point in human evolution. They are:

◆ **Simple consciousness.** These are our instincts—using our senses for survival. We sense a threat through visual or auditory input; we fight it or flee from it. Some of our responses are based on instinct; others are based on learned experience.

◆ **Self consciousness.** This is the self-awareness that allows a human to see herself as an individual with emotional and spiritual needs. This is the basis of self-actualization, in which we attain our potential.

◆ **Cosmic consciousness.** This is a consciousness of where we, as humans, fit into the web of life. This awareness is the pinnacle of our evolution.

**Patience**

Does dwelling in other dimensions make us less practical? If all of us start dreaming lucidly and interacting with beings in other dimensions, how can society be productive? Practicality *is* important. Be sure to teach your child techniques for coming back down to earth, focusing and just getting the job done. Energy shielding, creative work with the hands, and gardening or other nature play are good for this.

Cosmic consciousness is what Indigos have come to bring forth in a broad, far-reaching way. Cosmic consciousness is a highly evolved spiritual awareness.

Colin Wilson, who has written about human potential, psychology, and existentialism, defined seven levels of consciousness in *Beyond the Occult* (see Appendix B):

◆ Deep sleep

◆ Mere awareness

◆ Basic self-awareness (what existentialist Jean Paul Sartre called nausea)

- Everyday consciousness

- Happy "spring morning" consciousness

- Transcendent or magical consciousness

- Mystic consciousness

### Indigo Stars

David Spangler, author of numerous books on spirituality, sacredness, and manifestation, relates an experience he had at 7 years old, when riding in the car with his parents. He felt himself dissolve "into an oceanic feeling of oneness and infinite connectedness." He became pure consciousness. He describes it as limitless and infinitely loving. He bilocated, floating above the car, looking down upon himself and his parents.

East Indian yogis identify seven states of consciousness, three of which we are experiencing all the time, every day: sleeping, dreaming, and waking. The fourth state of consciousness is *Samadhi*, which is a transcendental consciousness that occurs during meditation. *Samadhi* can coexist with I-consciousness, your awareness of yourself. When that stabilizes, it expands to become cosmic consciousness, the fifth state. The sixth state is God consciousness, in which you experience God everywhere, in every thing. The seventh state is pure consciousness—what is within is also outside. Everything is united.

Consciousness at this level can produce mystical or magical powers, defying natural law. The higher realms of consciousness are familiar to many Indigos, and they will lead us into more awareness—from their view of the universe.

## Beautiful Beings

Not only are Indigos aware of other beings, such as angels, spirits, and ghosts, they are aware of a greater consciousness of all entities. They understand plants to have a consciousness—that's why an Indigo might resist walking on grass blades or enjoy talking to trees. To them, animals have a consciousness. Of course they do. Interestingly enough, Rudolf Steiner, founder of the Waldorf educational philosophy, believed that animals and plants had a consciousness, though it was more limited than that of humans.

> ### Crystal Clear
>
> Mind sleeps in stone, dreams in the plant, awakes in the animal and becomes conscious in man.
>
> —German philosopher Friedrich von Schelling

Consciousness is usually defined by comparing ourselves to all the beings that can't do what we can do—be aware of our awareness ("I think therefore I am"—Descartes). But Indigo Children don't accept that we have all the answers. They come in with a knowing that consciousness exists in other species.

Indigos understand there is a universal life force energy, and they live their daily lives with an awareness of this energy. It's called chi in Chinese thought, and prana in yoga, and it is the basis for understanding consciousness in what we cannot see or prove. Indigos understand the invisible.

Indigos also understand the concept of cellular memory—the idea that all human and cosmic knowledge is stored at the subatomic level. Within us all, at the deepest level, is an abiding knowledge of the infinite. P.M.H. Atwater describes it well in *Beyond the Indigo Children*. She says these memories are stored everywhere, in every cell of the body. It's a network of memory that she says represents the physical link between matter and spirit. She quotes neuroscientist Candace B. Pert, whose work with neuropeptides showed they are the "biological underpinnings of awareness." Pert labels this a higher intelligence, "one that comes to us via our very molecules"—knowledge that comes to us from more than our five senses alone.

## Affective Computing

At the Affective Computing site at the Massachusetts Institute of Technology, a group of scientists is studying the emotional relationships between humans and computers. They define the term as computing that "relates to, arises from, or deliberately influences emotions." One of the aspects they study is how computers can be more responsive to our emotions, such as frustration, an emotion commonly experienced with computers.

Remember HAL, the computer in *2001: A Space Odyssey*? As Dave dissembles him, Hal pleads. We feel his fear. And indeed, we develop such symbiotic relationships with our computers that when they crash, we crash. With Indigo Children, a computer crash can evoke not frustration but empathy.

During the writing of this book, Carolyn's hard drive crashed, to the point that the computer troubleshooters she enlisted believed the data was irretrievable. They recommended her computer stay overnight in the computer "hospital" and said they would try again in the morning. Carolyn imagined all the life force she had stored on that computer hooked to a brain activity monitor, with the occasional blip of a green light that indicated a glimmer of hope that it was not brain dead. She imagined her computer like a dear loved one in intensive care, touch and go, trying to make it through the night. (She was able to retrieve some, but not all, of the data.)

But the point of all of this is that Indigos are tuned in. All along we have been stressing how sensitive Indigos are to electromagnetic fields. It's likely many of them already have an understanding of affective computing—and the soul of a machine—that was depicted in *2001*. Some Indigos have reported an awareness of an intelligence within a light-filled web. They sense a consciousness within the field of photons.

# A Blessing and a Curse

For Indigo Children and adult Indigos, the challenge of the future is to create safe places for them to express their awareness of other dimensions. They experience so much more than the physical dimension. Their experience of time is quite different from ours—their minds are capable of holding the complexity of overlapping past, present, and future occurring simultaneously. Some of them may have experienced astral dimensions—in which they may physically be in one place but their spirit is in another.

## Astral Dimensions

Wendy has visited other dimensions. She says she does not have conscious control over her astral travel—she can't just buy a ticket—but she does travel a lot in her dreams. If you fly in your dreams, and you are not in a plane—that is, if it seems you have wings or you can hover and rise like a helicopter—then you likely have experienced astral travel.

Wendy has learned to bilocate—to be in two places (spiritually) at once—such as traveling to Shamballa, or Shangri-La, to do attunements. When this happens, she is aware of her body lying on the bed, but her mind and spirit have gone to Shamballa, which is said to exist in the fifth dimension, or higher. The fifth dimension is beyond space and is created by thought and spirit.

The astral world is any dimension beyond the third dimension of our physical existence. String theory, or M-theory, postulates there are 11 dimensions.

## Their Own Time Zone

Because Indigos operate with an awareness of multiple dimensions, they often live with a much different sense of time. Sometimes they are out of sync with daily schedules. Sometimes they are nocturnal, as Wendy often is.

One reason for this is that many Indigos find it is psychically quieter in the middle of the night. They can actually work and think more effectively then. It's easier to tune into spirit at that time because there is less static from human thought, and the veil between dimensions seems thinner.

Indigos also are not constrained by a limited understanding of linear time. An event in the distant past or an event that has yet to occur may be synchronous with a present-moment idea. Also, an experience or bit of knowledge that an Indigo's grandmother had may come up in their awareness—that is, something that may have happened 50 years ago that your Indigo child couldn't have known about, may come into his awareness. It may be a solution or something his grandmother learned being passed on to him, as happened with one Indigo friend of Wendy's where he sat down at a sewing machine and instinctively knew how to sew perfectly. He believed he was channeling "The Grandmothers," a collective group of grandmotherly spirits who were quite adept at sewing.

## Good Counsel

What if you or your Indigo get stuck on a night schedule? This happens to Wendy often and she doesn't mind most of the time, but when she needs to shift to a day shift, she moves ahead two to three hours a day by staying up two to three hours later. Another way is to take a three- to four-hour nap at the midpoint of your schedule, which allows you to move the schedule ahead faster. Once you get on the schedule you want, you have to work to maintain it. Your body is used to staying up an extra two to three hours a day. No matter how you tweak your schedule, continue to eat regularly. However, if a nocturnal schedule doesn't bother you or affect your life negatively, there's probably no reason to change it.

# Blessed

P.M.H. Atwater has made it her life's work to study how people are transformed after they nearly die, writing *The Complete Idiot's Guide to Near-Death Experiences* (see Appendix B). Her work arose from her own near-death experiences in 1977. She has discovered a blessing in the near-death experience—a higher intelligence.

Atwater has noted that people with near-death experiences measure higher on intelligence quotient tests and exhibit extraordinary consciousness about events that preceded their birth. They describe having pre-birth memories—of being in the womb, of being without a body looking down on their parents-to-be. They have an emotional intelligence about their parents' experience, being tuned in to their parents from before birth. They can remember things their parents said or did while they were in the womb.

She also found that 93 percent of children who had had near-death experiences had enhanced math ability. The majority had enhanced music ability, as well as spatial reasoning and visual acuity. The near-death experience seems to have given them a power punch of intelligence. She describes these children—who would be Indigo Children—as being "rewired, reordered and reconfigured in such a way as to be able to cope and thrive in a high-tech world."

# There Is No Box

Being multidimensional means being entirely creative and original. Another way of saying it is that multiple dimensions yield multiple solutions. The result is nontraditional thinking, not based on previous parameters, societal expectations, or prior experience. Prior experience assumes the status quo—that the world as we know it now will continue to function the same way. With Indigos, there is no status quo. How exciting!

## The Least You Need to Know

♦ An Indigo child's rich dream life can be a source for creative ideas and, sometimes, psychic messages.

♦ Indigo Children often are good at manifestation or mind projection, the ability to turn thoughts into tangible realities. This talent can be channeled with creative visualization techniques.

♦ It's not unusual for even young Indigo Children to experience states of pure consciousness.

♦ Some Indigo Children have an awareness of the consciousness of all beings and all matter.

♦ Extremely psychic Indigos may have trouble being on a day schedule. They may prefer to be nocturnal because the psychic static is quieter at night.

♦ Near-death experiences or other dimension encounters correlate with higher intelligence.

# Chapter 18

# Feel With the Mind, Think With the Heart

## In This Chapter

♦ The transcendent mind

♦ A powerful heart

♦ Teaching your child self-care

♦ Rare intelligences

As more and more Indigo Children mature, we will see a wise and intelligent heart-centered approach emerge in our culture.

For the Indigo, the heart and the mind are intertwined, working in harmony. Not only that, Indigo Children understand that *all* hearts and minds are interconnected, and that's how they will operate in this world. At the heart of the Indigo resistance to what *is*, is their desire to integrate heart and mind.

# Headquarters: Feeling With the Mind

In the early years of an Indigo childhood, it will be important to lay the groundwork for your Indigo to develop his emotional literacy and learn about self-care. Mastering a new level of consciousness about how we all manage our feelings is one of the many changes Indigos are here to make. And we will all learn from them.

Child intelligence and consciousness expert Joseph Chilton Pearce, author of *Magical Child* (see Appendix B) and other books, says the human mind is designed for capacities much broader and more creative than the way we use it. About 100 years ago, Waldorf founder Rudolf Steiner predicted that the greatest discovery of twentieth century science would be that the heart would teach us to think in a new way.

This is already happening. Research is showing us that the heart is talking to the mind 24/7. It's directly connected to the feeling center of the mind, the prefrontal lobes. Many Indigo experts perceive that prefrontal lobes are more developed in Indigo Children than the average child, which equips them to lead us to this next change.

## The Place of Virtue

Leading neurologist Paul MacLean of the National Institutes of Mental Health calls prefrontal lobes the "angel lobes." He describes that area of the brain, which is part of the emotional center, as the center of all virtues and values. These lobes are more pronounced in Indigo Children, say many Indigo experts, further proof that they came into the world emotionally and spiritually advanced.

This more developed part of the brain is the place of transcendence, where we may leave behind ego's pride. It's where we possess the ability to evaluate our emotions and decide how to respond. It's the center of empathy. It's where we store the ability to bring a spiritual perspective to all matters.

Pearce describes the prefrontal lobes as the seat of judgment, morals, empathy, and compassion. They are the center of a strong sense of contentment with self, from which comes a faithful commitment to the highest and best human values.

## Mind and Heart in Sync

The Institute of HeartMath is a nonprofit organization that researches the relationships between emotions, heart functions, and cognitive performance. According to HeartMath, when the mind is in sync with the heart, it creates the optimal state for learning. In this physiological state, the brain is at its best for perceiving, feeling, focusing, learning, reasoning, and performing because it's in sync with the heart. The institute boasts a 35 percent improvement in math scores and a 14 percent improvement in reading scores on the Minnesota Graduate Record Exam.

This indicates how important it is to help your Indigo child get her emotions in order before starting her school day. Help her in her early years to establish a regular practice of checking in with her emotions, meditating, or energy shielding, and it will pay off in her tween and teen years. She will be much more centered and focused.

# A Power Center: Thinking With the Heart

A growing body of research is showing that the heart has an intelligence of its own, functioning much like a brain. Sixty to 65 percent of all the cells in the heart are neural cells, or brain cells—not muscle cells, as previously believed. These heart cells monitor and maintain the physical functions of the body. They are communicating directly. They are in charge.

Not only that, the way they work is very harmonious and holistic. About half of the heart's neural cells have the job of interpreting the information so that it all works together. Wholeness is built into the *whole framework of the heart.*

The idea that intelligence dwells in the heart was the concept behind *21 Grams* (2003), a movie starring Sean Penn, who receives a heart transplant and along with it, the memories and emotions of the donor. Author and lecturer Paul Pearsall details real-life examples of the same phenomenon in his book, *The Heart's Code* (see Appendix B).

## The Lights Are On

We are interconnected through the heart—and science is proving it's more than a metaphor. Poets through the ages have believed that memories and emotions physically reside in the heart. They have also seen the heart as the conduit—the way we connect to each other. Researchers have found that we are connected—through electromagnetic energy. And it's powerful.

Studies have shown that the heart produces $2^1/_2$ watts of electrical energy at each pulsation. This creates an electromagnetic field identical to the electromagnetic field around the earth. This electromagnetic field is powerful. Neurocardiologists estimate it goes outward from the body 12 to 25 feet. It's so powerful that you can take an electrocardiogram three feet away from the body. Researchers say it is the principle source of information upon which the body and brain build our perceptions of the world. This explains why many energy workers believe the auric field is huge—approximately 20 feet.

The electromagnetic power of the heart lends insight to the way Indigo Children are so sensitive to electromagnetic fields. Perhaps it is this electromagnetic field around the heart to which they are so sensitive; perhaps it's that they are tuned in to others' hearts.

These new children understand interconnectedness on a heart level. When we understand that the electromagnetic field of the heart can extend 12 to 25 feet from the body, we can see that we are always overlapping with each other.

## Emotional Intelligence

Many Indigo Children have a wisdom about their emotions and the emotions of others that belies their years. *Emotional intelligence* is an aptitude for understanding emotion. Emotionally intelligent people are fluent in the language of describing emotions, and they are adept at calibrating their emotions and managing them. They are good at self-care, and they are good at sensing what others feel and need. Here are the essential components of emotional intelligence:

- Self-awareness
- Mature emotional management
- Resilience and self-reliance
- Empathy
- Strong communication skills
- Conflict resolution skills

**def•i•ni•tion**

**Emotional intelligence** is the awareness and ability to manage your emotions productively. It includes the ability to pick up on other's emotions. With emotional intelligence there is discernment, an evaluation of a feeling, and a motivation to manage it constructively.

Not all Indigo Children have all of these skills. Some may be sensitive to the extreme, and "mature emotional management" may be the last term you'd use to describe your Indigo. ("Drama queen" might be what you were thinking instead!)

Indigo Children bring a high level of intuition to their emotional literacy—their ability to perceive others' emotions correctly and to be aware of their own. Intuition picks up not upon what is said, but also body language, eye contact, and tone of voice.

The most compassionate and emotionally sensitive Indigo Children will likely develop emotional intelligence at an early age, learning to identify, calibrate, and manage their emotions. Other Indigo Children, such as those who are more nonconformist and self-reliant, may need more defined techniques.

At the Institute of HeartMath in California, Doc Childre has developed a method that helps people develop a personal sense of how to manage the intelligence of their hearts. It uses biofeedback sensors to help people monitor their hearts and brains, eventually learning to synchronize them. The FreezeFramer shows people how their emotions affect their heart rhythms. You can teach your child techniques for managing his heart rhythms with breath, meditation, and relaxation.

## Talking It Out

In the early years, it's good to teach your child emotional literacy—the ability to describe and label her emotions. Teach her not only to be aware of her emotions but also to verbalize them ("I felt mad when …").

When your Indigo Child is upset about an event, encourage him to describe the feeling. Ask if he feels cold or hot, if the anger feels red or black. Does he feel hindered? Restricted? Belittled? (These are common emotions in Indigo Children, who demand respect. Together, you can read books in which the characters go through emotional changes. Discuss them afterward. This is a technique called bibliotherapy.

> **Good Counsel**
>
> It's vital for Indigo Children to be real—to express their emotions authentically. It's difficult for them to be one thing on the outside, another on the inside. For them, it's about integrity. If they aren't real all the way through, it drains their energy. Make a point to check in with your Indigo when you sense this is out of balance for him. (If you could see his aura when this is the case, it would be dull in color.)

## Holding It in Check

As we have said, everything is to the extreme in an Indigo child. When she's hurt, she's deeply hurt. When she's angry, she's infuriated. Ask if she feels infuriated or merely annoyed. This will help her learn to assess the degree of the emotion.

It also will help you guide your child in calibrating the level of emotion to help him learn how to manage emotions before they hit the out-of-control point. If he develops a concept of the difference between annoyed and infuriated, along with developing techniques for calming the emotions, he will be well on his way to instituting good stress reduction practices for a lifetime.

The young Indigo's emotions can be raw and extreme. Teach him about self-care at an early age, and he'll have the tools he needs for life's crisis points.

## Self Care

To help your child achieve success at self care, she must recognize her gifts, appreciate her uniqueness, and accept her differentness. Affirmations are a vital part of this, and we offer a list of affirmations in Appendix C, specific to each of the Indigo gifts.

While your Indigo child may already put herself in the picture—that's the strong sense of self—she may also be conflicted between others' expectations and her desire to take care of herself. When your Indigo child is truly exhausted and still has an hour of homework to complete, help her sort out the options. Perhaps she is more focused and effective in the morning, so going to bed earlier and working on it before school is a better option. Perhaps she has procrastinated, and there's an emotional reason behind it, and talking about it may help.

## Change Your Reality

When you understand the heart-mind connection, you understand how intertwined our emotions are with our thoughts and perceptions. If the heart is talking to the brain 24/7—directly talking to the emotional center—and if 65 percent of the cells in the heart are thinking cells (or neural cells), you can see how emotions influence our reality quite a bit. The heart tells the brain to respond appropriately. Our emotional responses change the electromagnetic spectrum in our bodies; the brain feeds upon this electromagnetic energy. Ultimately, everything in our experience, then, hinges on our emotional response to events.

# A Rare Intelligence

HeartMath founder Doc Childre believes that emotional management is the next frontier to conquer in human understanding. It's absolutely imperative that more and more of us master the ability to be conscious of our feelings, he says. We must get fond of and familiar with our emotional baggage and learn to manage our emotional reactions that are based on the past. It's only then, when we are aware of the emotions processing through our hearts and brains, that we can no longer allow the past to hold us captive. The way is through the heart, he believes, because it's got the power to alter our perceptions and override the circuitry of old emotions.

Indigo Children do not accept that emotional baggage is something to keep around for a long time. That is one of the many aspects of life they are here to change. They are here to help us travel light.

## Levels of Intelligence

Author and lecturer Soleira Green has identified five forms of intelligence, outlined in the following table, which she believes will figure into the future, as Indigo Children grow up. Through these five expressions of intelligence, we as a society will be able to expand our collective consciousness.

> **Crystal Clear**
>
> Managing our emotions increases intuition and clarity. It helps us self-regulate our brain chemicals and internal hormones. It gives us natural highs, the real fountain of youth we've been searching for. It enables us to drink from elixirs locked within our cells, just waiting for us to discover them.
>
> —HeartMath founder Doc Childre

Soul-based intelligence, or holistic intelligence, drops the boundaries between individuals, something that Indigo Children will teach us to do. Indigo Children sense and know another person's soul through picking up on his energy field. Soul intelligence reads the true depth and meaning of what another person is saying. It's based on an innate knowing of the other, to the point of being able to sit and inhabit their heart and soul. It's the deepest level of empathy imaginable.

Quantum intelligence is what Indigos are here to contribute. They will lift the consciousness of the planet in a hyper-speed way. Green describes hyper-speed thinking as being able to understand a situation from a multiplicity of perspectives in an instant. From that, the individual processes the information in seconds to arrive at the most empowering and uplifting outcome.

Super-creation is another component of quantum intelligence. It's the ability to work in bursts of high creativity, with nonlinear thinking and a high ability to see fresh and original ideas.

Vibrant multiplicity might be the effective version of multitasking. While research is showing that multitasking diminishes effectiveness, vibrant multiplicity, according to Green, is the ability to remain vibrantly engaged with multiple projects while maintaining a vision and focus for each one.

| Form of Intelligence | Where It Resides | How It Connects Connects | How It's Expressed |
|---|---|---|---|
| Intelligence (IQ) | Mind | Individual | Thoughts |
| Emotional Intelligence (EQ) | Heart wisdom | Person-to-person | Emotions |
| Spiritual Intelligence (SQ) | Spirit | Higher self, higher purpose | Spiritual wisdom |
| Holistic Intelligence (HQ) | Soul | Deep soul connections with all; profound level of self spiritual attainment | Soul knowing, innate telepathy |
| Quantum Intelligence (QQ) | Consciousness | Oneness | Hyper-speed, high bandwidth creativity |

Another component is what Green calls bandwidth scanning, the ability to access information from multiple dimensions. Indigo Children will continue to refine their ability to access these dimensions, and as they become adults, they will become more adept at it—provided these skills are nurtured and not squelched. Along with the gift comes the challenge of creating the opening for the rest of the world to understand and support the ability. It will be their task—and your task as a parent—to educate the world about this gift.

Once, while energy shielding against a brutal emotional attack, Wendy experienced hyper-speed thinking. The scene froze, she says, like a movie, and she saw the scene happen again like a thought bubble above her head. It repeated again and again hundreds or thousands of times, and each time her response was different. When she finally hit upon the most effective response, she snapped out of the daydream thought bubble, and the actual live scene resumed. Only a second or two had passed.

**Indigo Stars** _____

Joseph Chilton Pearce, author of many books about the unfolding of intelligence in children, has always been outspoken about the ways American culture fails to nurture the intellectual, spiritual, and emotional needs of children. He believes the key is heart-brain nurturing, and he is a big advocate of touch.

Wendy used the solution she had seen in the vignette, and it worked. After her friend's tirade, she told him that she loved him. Her mind had wanted to scream, but her response of love totally disarmed him. He hugged Wendy, and the episode was over. Wendy found it shocking that the energy shielding helped her separate so complete from the tirade and find a solution quickly, though it seemed like hours to run through all the possible outcomes. She now realizes this has to be an example of quantum heart-directed thinking.

## Synesthesia: A Wider Range of Sensory Input

We already know Indigo Children are taking in more sensory information than the average child. The challenge for Indigo Children—and indeed the challenge for us all—will be in managing a much wider spectrum of sensory input. We must make sure the senses don't get overloaded when we open ourselves to perceive the world interdimensionally.

Many Indigo Children experience synesthesia, in which real sensory input is supplemented by perception of another sense. In other words, you can taste sounds or hear colors. The experience is not limited to the mind's eye; it's perceived as real, outside the body, in physical form. The experience is real and vivid, not merely a product of the imagination. Famous people who have experienced synesthesia include painter Vasily Kandinsky, composer Franz Liszt, and poet Charles Baudelaire.

**Patience**

Because Indigo Children have intelligent and connected hearts, they can be more vulnerable during life transitions than the average child. Often Indigos hit a snag when they start dating, are exposed to peer pressure to experiment with drugs and alcohol, go off to college, or experience the divorce of their parents. Any of these might cause a more extreme emotional response. As your Indigo enters middle school, some of the emotional groundwork you lay during her early childhood can avoid having life's transitions bring her emotions to a crisis point.

## Emotionally Intelligent Problem Solving

Because of their high emotional intelligence, Indigo Children will lead the way to integrating more liberating values into the way our society operates—values such as compassion for others, lack of materialism, strong sense of fairness, and a commitment to self-care. An ethic will emerge from this that might look something like this:

- Do no harm to any creature.

- Let every voice be heard.

- Show compassion for all.

- Awaken to self and spiritual awareness.

- Be honest, be open, be true.

- Above all, be fair.

- Respect others as they respect you.

- Respect differences.

- Honor each individual's eternal connection to universal love.

- Honor those who are absent.

# A Look into the Future

Warm-hearted, emotionally intelligent Indigos very likely will channel their energies in the helping fields such as counseling, alternative
healing, social work, and teaching. It's very likely they will bring their
ethic of fairness and compassion to marriage and family. Marriages
will continue to evolve into more emotionally fulfilling partnerships,
as opposed to economic alliances, and families will be more interconnected. And these ideas are just a start. In the next chapter, we will look
more closely at ways the Indigo heart will change how we relate to each
other.

## The Least You Need to Know

- ◆ The brains of Indigo Children have more developed prefrontal
  lobes, which scientists believe is the center of emotional intelligence.

- ◆ Research that shows that 60 to 65 percent of the heart is made up
  of neural cells supports the idea that a certain intelligence resides
  in the heart.

- ◆ Help your Indigo child develop a solid practice of emotional management, giving her the language to identify her emotions.

- ◆ Lay the groundwork for good emotional management skills early
  in childhood by teaching your child to check in, to meditate and
  center, and to use energy shielding.

- ◆ Indigo Children are at the leading edge of new levels of soul-based
  and spiritual intelligence that are emerging. These intelligences
  include soul-knowing, telepathy, higher bandwidth creativity, and
  hyper-speed thinking.

- ◆ The heart-centered Indigo approach will liberate our society from
  many of its constraints, ushering in a new level of emotionally
  intelligent problem-solving.

# Chapter 19

# The Way We Get Along

## In This Chapter

- Creating meaningful partnerships
- Families with solid foundations
- Righteous anger and perfect harmony
- A new ethic for getting along

Even from infancy, many Indigo Children are attuned to world peace and social justice. Even if the issue at hand is fairness on the playground and harmony during kindergarten naptime, it's something they are aware of and passionate about.

Some take on the role of peacekeepers, developing conflict resolution skills at an early age. Other Indigos, most particularly those with ADHD or learning disabilities, may develop a higher understanding of tolerance and compassion, given that they function in the world so differently. No matter where they are coming from, these children display a remarkable set of skills that will change the way we all get along.

# Our Relationships

When it comes to relationships, Indigo Children can be young visionaries. They come into this world with no preconceived notions about the forms of relationships and with a deeply ingrained belief in the worth of every individual. And that includes not only humans, but animals and plants and rocks, too.

Indigo Children won't accept dualities—that is, I win, you lose; I'm right, you're wrong. Their orientation is to the creative process and progressive and positive solutions. They believe we can change the world through our interconnectedness.

## Powerful Partnerships

As you manage the gifts and challenges for your Indigo child, you are laying the groundwork for her to create empowering partnerships and *collaborations*. These will be the backbone of the future world these children will inhabit and shape.

## def•i•ni•tion

> **Collaboration** is the process of people coming together to work on a shared goal, using cooperation, coordination, and knowledge exchange. Collaboration achieves collectively more than individuals may have been able to achieve on their own. Key components are mutual trust and respect, shared objectives, open communication, complementarity, and a sense of belonging. Collaboration is a dynamic process.

Much has already shifted dramatically about how we create marriage partnerships. The model in which one partner—the husband—is the head of the household and rules like a king has been cast aside. We have moved away from patriarchy. In patriarchal society, marriages mirrored the power dynamics of societal power structures. For many hundreds of years, patriarchal power operated from a survival paradigm that was fear-based, harsh, and often violent.

The marriage partnership based on trust and gender equity will continue to emerge, thrive, and evolve. Relationships will continue to be a way to ascend to a higher spiritual level, fulfilling your purpose and attaining greater wisdom.

Partnerships will be based on interdependency and choice. Choice will be important to Indigos—choosing roles freely and independently of preconceived cultural notions about strengths and weaknesses, about others' expectations. Indigos will defy any expectations they feel put upon them. Above all, they will want it to be fair.

Most important, Indigo unions will be spiritual unions. They will be a matching of souls—soul mates. They will change everything we thought we knew about the laws of sexual attraction because for them, it's a spiritual attraction. Their unions may not necessarily be legal unions, because many Indigos oppose having government involved in their personal lives.

Some Indigos will marry souls they have known in other lifetimes. They may have been married to each other before or related in other ways in past lives. Some of these unions will provide the strongest foundation for the social change Indigos are charged with bringing about. Leadership will emerge from strong partnerships of like-minded souls.

Indigos might also be very unconventional about marriage. They will want to push the boundaries. They will experiment out of frustration and dissatisfaction with the current cultural norm. So they may have marriages that are irrelevant of gender or group marriages that are like soul families. It also won't be important to them that both partners be close in age. And they may experiment with shorter-term contract marriages, signing up for 1, 5, 10, or 20 years.

### Good Counsel

Over time, as both genders cultivate the thinking style of the other, the differences may become blurred, leading to more gender equity in marriages. Already changes have been documented in the female brain, as neuropsychiatrist Mona Lisa Schulz wrote in *The New Feminine Brain* (see Appendix B), where she described many modern women as having adapted a brain overlay that incorporates a more left-brain thinking style (logical, rational) over their natural traditional feminine thinking style (nurturing, intuitive).

# Future Families

Indigo Children understand that no one relationship can fulfill all their needs. They are simply too diverse and too complex for that to be possible. The nuclear family will feel confining to them, and they won't understand the need to be insular and individualistic. They want to be interconnected, and they will want to raise their children that way.

On the other hand, they may be more committed to their relationships than baby boomers or Gen Xers. They may practice high fidelity—again, that's the fairness and compassion factor. They may develop solid marriage partnerships that last for 20 years or more. But because they will live longer, and their careers and lifestyles will change, they may have serial marriages. It may be 20 years, and then move on.

Then again, some Indigos may feel so interconnected to all that they don't give the same meaning to infidelity that our culture gives it—it's not so taboo. Some will not see loving more than one person as a barrier to a solid marriage commitment, especially if all relationships and terms are openly and honestly discussed, so there is no cheating. Polyamory will be more common with Indigos.

The Indigo interconnectedness will also mean less age segregation and more all-ages communities, which will draw upon the resources of the elderly to help young families. The young families in turn help the elderly with health and physical issues. Indigos also will be the voice of compassion around aging as the baby boomer generation heads into health and end-of-life issues.

# Harmony with All Beings

Indigos will sound the cry for the environment, because of their sensitivity for all beings. To them, it's not only vital for physical survival; they recognize the consciousness of all beings, and they see that our fate hinges on our interconnectedness.

Sustainability is an important issue for them because they *see* the future and *feel* the needs of future generations compassionately. It's not an abstract concept to them. They will lead the way in managing our resources wisely. They will develop natural systems for agriculture, permaculture, and ecological design. They will work on the principles of Bioneers founder Ken Ausubel (*Nature's Operating Instructions*, see Appendix B), mimicking the way nature works to devise better solutions—in the case of agriculture, richer harvests, better soil, and fewer pests. The Bioneers motto is very Indigo-like: "It's All Alive, It's All Intelligent, It's All Connected, It's All Relatives."

The picture of the Indigo future includes more community gardens and local growers markets, more new urbanism (the return of the old-fashioned neighborhood), and more open space. To Indigos who will embrace these ideas, they are taking care of all their relatives.

# Pay It Forward

*Pay It Forward* is a movie that became a movement. It started as a novel by Catherine Ryan Hyde, in which a 12-year-old boy receives the assignment to think of an idea for world change and put it into action. His concept: when he does something nice for three people and they ask how they can pay it back, he tells them they have to pay it *forward*. So those three people help three other people. That's nine people. Then those nine people pay it forward, and it becomes 27 people. Quickly, it gets big.

### Indigo Stars

The Kindness Crew is a group of four young men (extremekindness. com) who work to spark a global revolution in kindness through their books, public speaking, blogs, and corporate training. The four twenty-somethings were in college at the University of British Columbia when, shortly after 9/11, they decided to work to change the world with kindness. They have started Pay It Forward projects, among many other community efforts.

After the book and movie came out, Hyde started a nonprofit foundation payitforwardmovement.org to continue educating and inspiring young people to see how they could change the world through small acts of generosity. It's a way of practicing kindness—and making a difference with your kindness, because it keeps on going.

Because Indigos get the interconnectedness, this concept is one that they will readily embrace. Many children have seen this movie and taken its message to heart.

# Working It Out

Indigos are ordered so differently from everyone else that diversity is built into the picture. Because of that, expect to see them as adults developing more models for anger management, conflict resolutions and tolerance.

By the time Indigos reach adulthood, they will have already experienced many early lessons about anger. If you'll remember in Chapter 4, their anger is a peculiar anger—an impatience that things are not as they should be, that the world is not ready for them. As children, being charged with changing the world and not having the power or knowledge to do it is frustrating; but as adults who have already taken a curriculum in self-compassion and self-management, they will be better able to channel this anger into positive change.

The key for them—and indeed for all of us—is the link between anger and healing. Remember that anger is a signal that something is out of balance. Anger tells us that we are not accepting the situation as it is. By adulthood, many Indigos will have learned how to make anger their ally, as Neil Clark Warren suggests in his book *Make Anger Your Ally: Harnessing Our Most Baffling Emotion* (see Appendix B).

Justified anger in a courageous and determined Indigo with a wise heart and a spiritual awareness—now that could be a powerful thing. "Use this energy with care, and you set the stage for miracles," urges P.M.H. Atwater in her book, *Beyond the Indigo Children* (see Appendix B). "Anger is power, and that power either pushes or inspires you to move."

**Crystal Clear**

Out beyond ideas of wrongdoing and rightdoing, there is a field. I will meet you there.

—Rumi, thirteenth-century Persian mystic

The right combination of passionate, focused anger, and spiritually guided compassion could change the world. The Indigos who grow up in supportive families with unconditional love and tolerance will emerge as natural healers.

## Restoring a Balance

And exactly what are Indigo Children here to fix? It's all about love and tolerance: gender imbalance, spousal abuse, child abuse, misuse of power, respect, and fairness to children. They will resist any attempt to categorize them or label them, and most certainly it won't work, because Indigo Children can be so many different breeds. They will resist labels like learning disabled or ADHD; they will resist any label, for that matter, including "Indigo."

The Indigo tolerance is a unique breed, as they usher us into a new world. They can be tolerant of others, but wildly impatient and passionately opposing anything that is less than tolerant of diversity. This anger and frustration will certainly color their passage into adulthood as they take on more and more responsibility for changing our world. The theme through it all is the willingness to embrace differences. A strong sense of fairness will guide them; alongside them will be the Crystal Children, who care about inner peace more than anything else. Clearly, the Indigos need the Crystals.

## Power of Water

Japanese scientific researcher Masaru Emoto (*The Hidden Messages in Water*) has conducted some fascinating research on the way water changes in response to our emotions. He discovered that expressing positive emotions such as love or gratitude near or above water restructures its molecules into beautiful crystals, resembling diamonds or snowflakes; expressing negative emotions such as fear or anger or hate also changes water's structure. He says the water absorbs that negative energy and becomes cloudy and dull. Emoto captures the water crystals in photographs.

In 2006 Emoto released *The Message from Water from Children* with the goal to get the book to every child in the world at no cost within a decade. He believes that by speaking the intention for peace over water, water can bring peace to our bodies and our world, and children will play a key role in achieving that goal. Emoto's research has been published in the peer-reviewed *Journal of Alternative and Complementary Medicine* (February 2004). (See Appendix B for details on both his books.)

In light of Emoto's observations, then, water is not only necessary for life; it's a reflection of our thoughts and emotions. Water is the mirror of us. It is alive and intelligent.

Emoto's discovery has implications for our collective understanding of the power of our thoughts and emotions. Consider that our bodies are made up of 50 to 65 percent water. Children's bodies are closer to 75 percent water, and babies are born with 78 percent water. About 83 percent of our blood is water. Wendy put this into practice during her pregnancy. She takes the cup of water she's drinking and whispers "I love you" into it three times so that she can send that energized, love-filled water down to her baby. This is exactly as Emoto would like it. He advocates speaking words of love and kindness to children from the time of conception.

# Building Global Community

Indigo Children are charged with the mission of bringing us all together. They have arrived when they have because we have the technology now to create a global village, through the Internet. It's no accident they began coming in full force in the 1990s. Expect them to be the visionaries for tempering capitalism's rampant greed with the human factor, with value placed on the worth of each worker. Expect more tolerance for the diversity of cultural, religious, and societal belief systems. Expect more global unity. Expect more interconnectedness.

In the global economy, Indigos will be the voice of reason and compassion on issues such as outsourcing (importing American jobs to developing countries, where labor is cheap) and immigration. Indigos will hold multinational corporations to a high standard of integrity. They will demand corporations to contribute as honorable citizens in the global village. They will hold all government systems to a higher ethic of honoring the dignity of every human.

## An Emerging Global Ethic

Here are some ethics that may emerge as Indigos take on the challenges of changing the world as adults:

♦ Think of no one as "other."

♦ Know we are interconnected. You and I are one.

♦ Honor differences. If we are different, it means more skills are being brought to the table.

♦ Be the change you want to see.

♦ Act locally. Serve where you are.

♦ Take only what you need; leave the rest.

♦ Redefine power. Reject privilege. Reject influence. Reject fear. Embrace the power of ideas.

♦ Live ethically. Live as you wish others to live, supporting fair trade, conserving our natural resources, and not supporting corporations whose ethics you abhor.

♦ Reframe progress. Progress isn't concrete sprawl. Progress is the affirmation of life for all human beings.

♦ Hold your life energy sacred. Trade your time for money in ways that are honorable.

♦ Pledge allegiance to the earth.

♦ Let every voice be heard.

### Good Counsel

Nonconformist Indigos won't be all that interested in popular culture. They refuse to take in numbing materialism, greed, vanity, or shallowness. They won't want to take the poison. Support them by exposing them to what they hunger for—a steady diet of constructive, spiritually attuned mental input. That means no hate speech, no sexist language, no abusive language, no self-aggrandizement. And our culture's narcissistic fixation on the body? Forget it. Forget vanity. There's no time for self-absorption.

## Slow It Down

It's not just the ADHD kids who are overwhelmed. They are having the most extreme reactions, but other types of Indigos—emotionally and physically sensitive ones, psychic ones—are yearning for a slower lifestyle.

The problem with television, say some child advocates, is that it speeds up the sensory input. A study at the Tübingen University in Germany—the same one that found a 20 percent reduction in children's ability to process sensory information—showed that over time, the kind of stimulus that could break through to a child's dulled awareness needed to be increasingly loud and intense. Scientists looked at what kind of stimulus it would take to produce a response in the reptilian brain. After children experienced concentrated bursts of overstimulation, the only signals they could register were highly charged.

It's time to slow down. It's time to enjoy slow food. Fast food is full of additives that are bad for us; slow food not only has valuable nutrients, it's cooked with love. And remember what Emoto showed about the way emotions affect the molecular structure of water? Consider the high water content of most fresh fruits and vegetables. There is a line in the movie *Like Water for Chocolate*—where the heroine is asked about the secret ingredient in her cooking, and she says, "The secret ingredient is love." Suddenly this line makes real sense. Indigos will slow us down, get us back to mindfulness, get us back in touch with spirit.

# Freedom, Responsibility, and Security

Indigo Children will lead the way to helping us liberate ourselves from the constraints and challenges of today's society. They will do this because they have to. Their early life struggles are because they simply must change it to survive. They will help us feel comfortable with change—and that's no easy task. With change comes freedom—the future is wide open—and that offers too little protection. Indigo Children will change our ideas about how we define security. They know all about flux; they know all about the complexity of diversity, of holding differing worldviews in one's mind, letting them co-exist. They stand solidly in uncertainty.

Whether many or only a few succeed in this mission depends on the abilities of their parents, educators, and other adults in their lives to create a solid center of certainty within them. With unconditional love and a tolerant understanding, they can do it. They can lead us all through the uncertainty to a better world.

## The Least You Need to Know

♦ Indigo Children believe they can change the world through inter-connectedness. They will approach the creative process with progressive and positive solutions.

♦ When it comes to marriage and family, Indigo Children are interested in spiritual unions, soul families, and solid commitments.

♦ Behind the Indigo anger is a powerful force for healing.

♦ Indigo Children see their resources extending beyond people resources to resources in spiritual dimensions, such as the power of our thoughts over the molecular structure of water.

♦ Indigo Children will shape a new global ethic based on fairness and interconnectedness.

♦ These children will lead the way to a slower lifestyle that values down time for creativity and contemplation, moving away from today's frenzied pace.

# Chapter 20

# Wise Souls: Have Indigos Been Here Before?

## In This Chapter

- ◆ Reincarnation 101
- ◆ Past life assignments
- ◆ From Atlantis, from Lemuria
- ◆ The Fifth Root Race

"Are They Here to Save the World?" a headline in *The New York Times* asked in January 2006. The story went on to document the phenomenon of Indigo Children, interviewing people who debate the question. As to what we think the answer is: *they very well might be.*

Why these children? Why now? Because Indigo Children come in with a highly developed consciousness, some people believe they have been incarnated before. Certainly many of them are wise souls, and they are here to lift humankind to a higher vibration.

# What Are Past Lives, Anyway?

The central idea of past lives is that our souls are eternal, and our bodies are temporary. A soul is alive before birth, and it's alive after death. At a defined point, a soul takes a body, is incarnated, and lives a life on Earth. After death, we may be reincarnated, born again to a different life. Reincarnation often has a spiritual purpose; the reincarnated soul returns to learn a lesson, teach a lesson, or perform a specific assignment.

Reincarnation is a central belief in many Eastern religions such as Hinduism, Jainism, or Sikhism. It's not a part of most Christian faiths, except for the liberal Catholic Church. Mainstream Islam rejects reincarnation. Buddhism believes in rebirth, not as a self but as consciousness or thought-form. Many African and Caribbean traditions embrace reincarnation.

Some Indigo experts say Indigos have been incarnated many times on the planet at different times. This time they are all coming together. Others say Indigos have never been here. They are new souls. Wendy thinks the truth is probably a little of each.

### Patience

If discussing past lives is more than you bargained for when you picked up this book, bear with us. It's not necessary to believe in past lives to understand the brand of consciousness that Indigo Children bring to our times. The origin of these spiritually advanced souls could be attributed to many theories, such as the collective unconscious or simply the zeitgeist of the times. The most important point to grasp is to understand their purpose.

Adult Indigos and older Indigo Children probably have been incarnated on this planet before, but Wendy thinks younger Indigos may be new souls or may have had past lives on other planets. She believes this because younger Indigos are more fragile and innocent, more like

Crystal Children. (There is a fine line between what defines Indigos and Crystals; the change from Indigos to Crystals is so evolutionary that some children are a little bit of each.) The younger Indigo Children do not have the same resilience that Indigos who have lived many past lives have, from having learned many lessons. The Indigos who have had past lives on other planets are wise, but not in an earthly way.

When a soul is reincarnated, memories of the previous life are erased, but not entirely. Many people recall pieces of former lifetimes. They may be aware of them as children, and interpretation may come later in life. With Indigo Children, interpretation may come quite early because these details are often tied to this life's spiritual purpose. Most people start out with a sense of mission, something so ingrained in their psyche that they can't articulate it, but it's a very strong sense of purpose. They are oriented toward certain interests and gravitate toward certain people, all toward the end of achieving this mission. With Indigo Children, this sense of mission is quite pronounced. (Again, the origin of this innate understanding of a spiritual assignment need not be a past life—it could come from your Higher Being, for instance.)

### Indigo Stars

Actress Shirley MacLaine told about her past lives in her book, *Out on a Limb* (Bantam, 1983), including that her daughter was her mother in a former lifetime. In other lifetimes, she has been a prostitute, a man from Atlantis, a pirate, and Charlemagne's lover. Her book, *The Camino* (Atria, 2001), chronicles her 500-mile trek across Spain, during which she says she received visions of other past lives, including being a Moorish girl. She has said in interviews that she sees past lives as a way to resolve your present life troubles.

## Meeting a Past Life

As our lives unfold, we recall snippets of former lives when an event triggers the memory. Sometimes we have a phobia that can't be explained. It has no obvious cause or origin. Another signal about a past life is a powerful affinity toward a place, a culture, or art that isn't explained by any obvious influence. For instance, your child may have an affinity for Ireland, yet you have no Irish ancestry. Or your child may have an affinity for Chinese brush painting though he's never been or never studied the culture.

Carolyn has long had a pull toward the central steppes of Russia, experiencing recurring dreams about the area. Always in the dreams there were soldiers and the turmoil of a revolution. Later in life she married a man whose parents were born in the Ukraine, part of which was absorbed into the Soviet Union during the Russian Revolution. The dreams of the steppes increased just before she met him, then settled down once they married.

Once, when Carolyn and her then-husband were on the Greek island of Santorini, he commented that the place spooked him because he felt they had both been there together before in a past life. Santorini is a magnificent place, with 1,000-foot high white cliffs above a turquoise sea. The island was the rim of a volcano that erupted and collapsed in the ocean, blanketing an ancient civilization in ash. Many people believe Santorini is the site of the lost city of Atlantis. Carolyn felt the eerie presence, too. There was a strange dissonance between them that hadn't been there before. Was it a portal to a past life they might have shared?

Past lives can emerge into our awareness through recurring dreams or hypnotic states. They can also come to us through places and people who are familiar, yet we have no way to have known those places and people. Sometimes déjà vu—the strong sense that you have been to a place before and had that same experience, despite no proof—is about a past life.

## What They Might Already Know

The lessons Indigo Children are carrying in from past lives are generally about compassion, tolerance, and world peace. They have experienced war in other lifetimes. They have experienced misuse of power, and they will resist imbalances of power. They have witnessed intolerance, lack of compassion, and lack of respect for human dignity. They have been there, done that, don't want to do it again.

These wise souls have made their mistakes, too. They have lived several lifetimes and learned many lessons. That may explain their impatience—and a bent toward perfectionism. Indigo Children can be hard on themselves. They have chosen to be different, but living on Earth as an emotionally and physically immature child is a challenge when you already have spiritual maturity.

## Good Counsel

If you suspect your Indigo child has had a past life, take him to a psychic or hypnotist. The psychic can use guided imagery to take your child on a journey backward. Another way is to notice what triggers his phobias, what creates dissonance, what seems familiar to him (and no explanation for why), or to what he gravitates. Notice if your child is drawn to certain cultures. Also talk to your child about her recurring dreams.

## Wendy's Take on It

As a young girl, Wendy came downstairs one day speaking fluent French. She had not been exposed to French, and no one in the family spoke French. Later in life, she recalled memories of being in France on a farm and crying holding a sheep that was the family pet, about to be put to slaughter. Wendy would not let the sheep go. Her mother of that lifetime (who is not her mother in this lifetime) came into the barn and in a fury, shot and killed her, though she may have intended to shoot the lamb. Wendy has another past life memory of being raped and stabbed to death.

Another past life memory she has had is of being a Native American, sleeping in a pueblo or a longhouse, with her partner, "Little Bear." He had received his adult name, but Wendy still called him Little Bear because she had known him since childhood. They were newlyweds and very much in love.

Once a psychic told Wendy about a past life when she was married to her ex-husband of this lifetime and they were living in Vermont. In the past life, he was a minister, and the psychic described the church. Wendy could visualize it clearly. She remembers being on a road trip as a child with her parents and coming to a church in Vermont, recognizing it immediately. She didn't know why it felt so familiar, but the memory stuck with her. When she psychic told her about the past life, it all made sense.

Wendy also believes she lived in Egypt at one time, helping build pyramids by group mind power focused through a large crystal. She had a dream of that when she was 12, and she wrote it into a story the next day. It wasn't just a dream, but more like an astral voyage back in time.

Past lives hold the clues to our *karma*, the energy that balances all thoughts and actions in the universe. Deeds done in a past life reverberate. The energy of what you give out into the world continues to move through the universe, and it comes back to you. Often karma is associated with a lesson. Lessons that you have yet to learn come back to you.

## def•i•ni•tion

> **Karma** is the universe's balancing energy. Energy doesn't disappear when it leaves us. What you give out, you receive. It's the sum of all you have done and will do. Karma does not make value judgments about good or bad deeds. Generally, karma is about a lifetime's worth of deeds, though people say they have experienced "instant karma" in which a good deed—or a bad one—returns to them quickly.

## Our Cells Remember

Some people say the sense of a past life is really just cellular memory. If you'll remember, the research that we presented in Chapter 18 says that the body does have a cellular memory. Our emotions and memories are stored in our bodies. Is it possible that the emotions and memories of our ancestors are stored there as well? Carolyn believes it's possible. She is Irish, and she has always had a strong affinity for Ireland, though her ancestors came to the United States more than 150 years ago. When she was in Ireland, she felt at home, and the music of Ireland has always resonated for her.

She has always identified with oppressed people, as Ireland was not free for 800 years until the Easter Rebellion in 1916. As a cub reporter in southwestern Mississippi, one of her first big projects was to interview activists who worked for civil rights for African-Americans. Last year a photo of the white cliffs on the Irish coast near the Aran Islands in National Geographic resonated with her so strongly that visions about it came to her later during an intense massage and meditation session. It became absolutely clear to her that not only did she carry the memories of her Irish ancestors, but also she may have lived there and played a role as a Celtic spiritual leader who was oppressed and had to flee to protect her people and her beliefs.

## Identity Check

Of course, this raises all sorts of philosophical questions. If we can store the memories of past lives in our very cells, if we can hold in our cellular memory the emotions of our ancestors, and if we can comprehend spirits and other dimensions, then who are we? If the very cells of your body remember being someone other than the name you have now, then is it an illusion that you are you?

We aren't here to answer these philosophical questions. The point is to show you the challenge that Indigo Children face—forming a sense of identity when they are so very acutely aware, more than the rest of us, that they share pieces of their identity with ancestors, past lives, spirits. Yet it's also true and quite remarkable that Indigos have such a strong sense of self, even amid this awareness of multiple identity influences. This is perhaps their spiritual gift, quite necessary to equip them for their spiritual mission.

It puts new light on their strong sense of self, doesn't it? Their strong will is more than just a child's stubbornness. It's about valiantly striving to maintain their awareness of self in this lifetime, here and now, planted in this world, this family. It's something to be admired.

### Good Counsel

There is theory that time does not exist in the spirit world, and if that is so, then our concept of past lives is a misnomer. The other lifetimes may be occurring simultaneously or in "no-time." It's only that our very human brains want to put these ideas into chronological perspective, but let's remember Albert Einstein's fascination with time. His theories were out to experiment with our understanding of time unfolding in a linear progression.

# Atlantis and Lemuria

Atlantis has been the stuff of myth because of its high technology and its mysterious, destructive end. Santorini is just one of many places believed to be the lost city. Many compare the modern-day United States to Atlantis because of the quantum leaps in technological advancements we have made. But the comparisons also come because of the seeds of destruction that commentators see in our culture.

Lemuria, or Mu, was an ancient civilization that preceded and overlapped Atlantis. Many people believe it was in the Pacific Ocean; some believe the Hawaiian Islands are remnants of the ancient civilization. The Lemurians were highly spiritually evolved and artistically inclined. They were a peaceful society that had achieved a utopian state. (Wendy has had flashes of a past life in Lemuria when she was in Hawaii, at the end of the beach near the NaPali coast on Kauai.)

One myth is that Atlantis engaged in large-scale scientific experiments that brought about the destruction of both cultures—a flood, an explosion, or a volcanic eruption. New Agers believe that Lemurians stored their knowledge in crystals—and in the cells of the human body. Some believe that Lemurians were the predecessors of the Native Americans.

One link between Native American culture and the Lemurians is the dream box, a box where you may store your dreams and intentions. There is a legend that if you devote meditation and affirmation toward your dream, it will come true.

Many believe the Indigo Children come from Lemuria—that they have been brought here to restore a better balance between high technology and high spirituality.

**Good Counsel**

The tradition of the dream box is believed to come from the ancient civilization of Lemuria. A dream box is a round wooden box with an image carved in the lid. They are often found with Southwestern Native American images such as a Zuni bear or eagle feather, sometimes embedded with turquoise. The legend says that you must visualize your dream, write it down on a sheet of paper and put it in the box. Every day you say a prayer for your dream, and you act with the assurance that your dream has already come true. In time, it will.

# What It Means for Our World

You may not believe in past lives. You may not have even opened a book like this if not for the extremes of behavior your child exhibits. Or you may believe that past lives are simply not logical or can't be proven, so why talk about them?

The more important question is not whether you believe Indigo Children have had past lives, but what it might mean for our world. Set aside for a moment whether there is such a thing as a past life. And let's just look at Indigos as wise souls.

Essentially, being a wise soul means you won't have patience for the same old, same old. You choose to operate in a whole new way, knowing you'll get different results. A wise soul has been through a lot, much as folk rock singer Jackson Browne sings in *Doctor My Eyes.* These souls have seen enough; these souls want to understand. They want it to be different.

The movie *Groundhog Day,* starring Bill Murray, is about a man named Phil, who keeps waking up to the same day until he gets it right. Each morning, when the alarm buzzes, he gets the opportunity to choose differently than he did the day before. In this case, his lessons are all about Rita, played by Andie McDowell, the woman who is the object of his affections. The only problem is that she doesn't want him. He comes off as brutish and arrogant, and she wants someone who treats her with respect, who cherishes her. He flubs up again and again. Each time he tries to get out of the day—only to wake up and find he's stuck in the same day and he can't get out until he chooses differently. Phil starts learning faster then. Past lives are a little like this.

Or, we imagine them like Albert Brooks in *Defending Your Life,* in which you must defend to a court in Judgment City that you were able to overcome your fears in your past life. The luxuriousness—or lack thereof—of your accommodations in Judgment City reflects how well you did. And you get sent back to a new life to have another chance at doing it right.

## Can't Take It with You

It's a terrible irony that we can't carry all the knowledge we acquire from one life to the next. Wouldn't it be so much easier if we could remember all the mistakes we have already made and never have to make them again? Well, this might not be such a good thing because some of the knowledge would hinder us. For instance, we might have trouble relating to spirits in our soul group who have hurt us in past lives. We might struggle to form relationships on new terms. Maybe, Wendy suggests, the little bits we remember are enough.

When we reincarnate, we are only given a slice of consciousness. Call it selective memory. Knowing the answers to the test would be cheating. We have to be tested. By undergoing our tests without full knowledge of how and why we failed, we can face our challenges honestly. We get to start out the new life free of baggage. No grudges, no preconceived notions—a true test.

> **Crystal Clear**
>
> Forgiving does not erase the bitter past. A healed memory is not a deleted memory. Instead, forgiving what we cannot forget creates a new way to remember. We change the memory of our past into a hope for our future.
>
> —Louis B. Smedes, professor of Christian ethics

## Choosing to Be Here

When a wise soul reincarnates, many believe, it gets to choose from among assignments at a certain level. The phenomenon of Indigo Children being born in high numbers at this moment in time tells us that they are choosing to be here. Not only that, they are choosing their parents. That may stun you, or it may seem like the simplest truth you have read in this entire book. Remember, your child *chose* you because you were equipped with the precise attributes he needed to fulfill his spiritual mission here.

Often souls cluster together to strengthen their mission by sheer fact of their numbers. It's the power of like-minded people banding together to change the world.

Indigos are here to bring about change. They seem to have little or no sense of a personal future—part of that exalted consciousness again. Their function is to serve as a bridge from our present age to the next.

# The Fifth World

According to many Indigo Children experts, they fit into the next step in human evolution. Many of their theories are based on the end of the Mayan long count calendar, which predicts that on Winter Solstice in 2012, the human race will progress to a new level. This is the Fifth World. In this scenario, there is a whole new kind of human, the Fifth Root Race. Some Indigo experts believe that Indigos are this root race. That is, from Indigos will descend new, highly evolved humans that will rule during the new era.

One person who has written predictions about the Fifth World is Aluna Joy Yaxkin. Based in Sedona, Arizona, Yaxkin describes herself as a sacred site guide, mystic, and author.

She predicts in this time, human, mineral, plant, and animal life will be equally respected, and there will be intelligent communication between each of their realms. Misuse and abuse of our mineral resources will cease; instead, we will recognize the healing energy of gems. Gems won't be for jewelry; they will be for healing. We will also have greater respect for plants and animals, protecting the environment.

This higher understanding of the value of all life will extend to human-kind. Our social structures will not be built around power and domination, but rather cooperation.

Yaxkin says several cultures have predated this Fifth World, and she counts among them Atlantis (which she locates in Santorini, Greece, or the Bahamas in the Caribbean), the Peruvian Andes, and places in the Himalayas. These cultures put into practice some of the belief systems she says will prevail in the Fifth World.

Some Mayan calendar watchers also believe the end of the calendar is the end of the world; others believe it's the end of an era, the beginning of another. The end of the world group believes that one way the world might end is through a meteorite that hits the earth. One insight comes from Indigo expert Lee Carroll, who professes to channel the entity Kryon. Kryon, Carroll says, explains that we have changed our course already. Kryon says Indigos have already shifted the energy of the earth so much that this dire event has been averted. Many changes will still happen before 2012, but not the destruction of the planet, Kryon says.

No matter which side you come down on, it is true that all children represent the hope for the future, and clearly the Indigos have made their presence felt thus far on the earth. They are magnificent. They are turbulent. And they are already changing the world.

## The Least You Need to Know

- ◆ Indigo Children may be wise souls who have been incarnated on this earth before, though some younger Indigos may be brand new souls.

- ◆ One attribute of a wise soul is that he or she has collected many lessons and is not willing to repeat the same painful experiences.

- ◆ People who have been reincarnated often come into the next life with a spiritual assignment. That's why many who believe in past lives think Indigos have been here before.

- ◆ What some describe as a past life might be cellular memory, genetic memory, or the collective unconscious. Not all spiritual traditions believe in them.

- ◆ Some people see a connection between Indigo Children and the lost kingdoms of Atlantis and Lemuria, possibly being reincarnated from those civilizations.

- ◆ Some theorize Indigo Children are part of a Fifth Root Race, here to lift humankind to the next level of evolution. They tie this to the end of the Mayan long count calendar on Winter Solstice in 2012.

# Chapter 21

# A Spiritual Evolution

## In This Chapter

- ◆ Meditating with your child
- ◆ Tapping into your child's psychic ability
- ◆ The twenty-first century child: a new creation
- ◆ High consciousness, high authenticity

Believe us, the work you are doing to understand your Indigo child will pay off. Not only are you helping your child, you are helping your child prepare to participate in a new evolution of the world.

Our future sharing the planet with Indigos means more spiritual advancement, a better understanding of the esoteric, and an ascendance of mystic consciousness. But above all, one revolution Indigos have already brought about is that of cherishing the child. In this chapter, we'll come full circle, weaving inspiring and practical advice in a new ethic for children of the near earth. And we'll look ahead to a more exalted (and less turbulent) future.

# Higher Spiritual Awareness

In the future, the spiritual will infuse all institutions—schools, government, corporate workplaces, even the highest bastions of science. As Indigo Children teach us to respect children, they teach us to respect the dignity—and diversity—of all human life.

This spiritual evolution may not look like a hierarchy, as in Maslow's pyramidal view of human needs. His theory is that at the bottom, we have physical survival needs—food, shelter, security. As we progress upward through the needs, getting our needs met, we are able to give mindspace to spiritual matters.

Author David Spangler (*Laws of Manifestation*, see Appendix B), who describes himself as an incarnational spiritualist, has a different view. He thinks consciousness infuses all levels. It's not as if we are down here and God is up there, and we have to leave the physical world to find Him. Spangler sees the spiritual and physical as interacting in interdependent ways to create new evolutions. So in Spangler's view, it's not about denying or overcoming the physical world to achieve spiritual enlightenment, but the earthly life is the *way* we make a spiritual contribution, and therefore, deepen our spiritual understanding.

## Consciousness Education

This new way of thinking is not compartmentalized. Spirituality for an Indigo is not sectioned off from the rest of life; neither is it something people will develop only after they have achieved certain levels of enlightenment. It's something that will develop from the beginning of life (and perhaps before incarnation). This is Indigo Children's purpose—and that of the Crystals who have come to help as well as people like you who have been chosen to participate with Indigos. It is the next step of human evolution.

Expect to see many more schools—private, alternative, and even public—embrace curricula that develop the heart and spirit as well as the mind and body. One such curriculum, embraced by Indigo advocates Carroll and Tober, is the Consciousness-Based Education Association, a nonprofit educational resource that works with new and existing schools, as well as after-school programs, to provide programs that help cultivate creativity and inner advancement in children. The program uses transcendental meditation and was developed by Maharishi Mahesh Yogi, though it touts itself as nonsectarian.

The consciousness approach emphasizes inner calm and deepening self-awareness. Its proponents say it significantly reduces stress. Children learn about natural law, which advocates say increases creative intelligence.

Whether it's this curriculum or another spiritual program, it's a good idea to look for ways to cultivate your Indigo's spiritual awareness early on. Take the time to do the research and find a program that fits.

## Teaching Your Child to Meditate

Even if your child's school doesn't offer a program like the consciousness program, you can introduce your child to meditation. Try to find classes in your community by checking with community centers, yoga studios, health clubs, or spiritual centers. If you already meditate, you can teach your child, and the two of you can do it together.

Many communities have *mindfulness-based stress reduction* programs through university medical schools that emphasize integrative medicine. Mindfulness-based stress reduction uses daily meditation and yoga to increase mindfulness—the awareness of the present moment—and reduce stress. By practicing mindfulness, you become aware of more than your mind and body and connect to something larger than yourself.

**def•i•ni•tion**

> **Mindfulness-based stress reduction** uses simple techniques from yoga and meditation to relieve stress. Mindfulness is present moment awareness using the five senses—smell, touch, taste, seeing, and hearing. Practitioners use yoga and meditation breathing techniques to calm the body and mind.

Meditation is quieting the mind, intentionally emptying it of distractions by focusing on the present moment. Though meditation practices exist in almost every spiritual tradition and every culture, meditation is usually grouped into two styles:

- **Concentration.** Focus on one simple thing such as the sensation of breath, body awareness, or a chant, such as "om." When your attention wanders, return your focus to that thing.

- **Mindfulness.** Keep your awareness in the present moment. Mindfulness is open, aware, and gentle; it does not evaluate the present thoughts or engage with them. It is awareness that is not thinking, yet you are aware of thought. Mindfulness uses sensory awareness—smell, taste, hearing, seeing, and touching—to maintain this open state of awareness.

When Wendy meditates, it's often focused, an emptying of the mind followed by a quiet, open awareness. Often it's a prelude to creative visualization. She may focus her meditation by asking a question, as though she's checking in to psychic voice mail. "How do I prepare for my baby?" and "What will he look like?" were the questions she posed during her pregnancy as she was writing this book. Answers come to her as thoughts, as though they have been spoken to her, but not heard so much as coming into her awareness. When she asked the baby his name, she saw it written and saw an image of him. Through these meditations, she has had telepathic communication with her baby.

## Creative Visualization

Wendy uses meditation to create that state of peaceful mind that is the foundation of creative visualization. You may use creative visualization with your Indigo child as a way to reduce some of the turbulence she experiences with her challenges. Here are some questions you and your child might pose and visualize the outcomes of:

- How can I gain more focus in the classroom?

- How can I develop more meaningful friendships?

- How can I be happier in school?

- How can I balance discipline and creativity?

- How can I create more fairness?

- How can I find more peacefulness at home?

Once you and your child create a visualization, write it down. Describe the scene. Flesh it out in vivid detail. If your child likes to draw, have her draw a picture of it. Or have her list adjectives that describe it. (She may be more writer than illustrator!) What does it look like when you have friends who understand you and appreciate you for who you are? (Your appreciation of your child may be the best and first role model for this.) Some words to use might be "comfortable," "smooth," and "easy."

Write an intention: *It is my intention that people will understand and appreciate my gifts.*

Write an affirmation: *I am a unique child of Spirit (use your word), and I am expressing my gifts to the world.*

(See Appendix C for a sample visualization, as well as a list of activities and affirmations that validate Indigo gifts.)

# The Child of the Twenty-First Century

Perhaps the most significant contribution Indigo Children are making toward our future is solidifying our culture's commitment to the worth of a child. At the dawn of the previous century, educators such as Marie Montessori and Rudolf Steiner were only beginning to understand how important it was to cultivate the creativity and spirit of a child. At that time, children were seen as adults in small bodies, and very little was understood about human emotional development. Children worked long hours in factories until child labor laws were enacted. As the century rolled along, we began to value childhood and develop a better understanding of adolescence in the stages of human development.

Indigo Children will get us to the next level in cherishing the gifts of all children.

### Patience

Even though we have come a long way in our viewpoints about children, we need to sound a note of caution. Though we no longer view children as adults in small bodies, it's possible to fall into the same trap with Indigo Children. That's because Indigo Children possess a spiritual maturity and emotional intelligence that's incongruent with their small bodies. Be careful not to put too many adult pressures on them, even when they seem wise enough to take them on.

# Equal, But Different

The Indigo child's emotional intelligence and advanced spiritual knowledge may be one of the biggest challenges in understanding an Indigo child. They are still developing emotionally and physically. They need respect—not full-ranging adult responsibility, just respect. They are not inferior because they are children. They need to be treated like equals, but they are different—because they are still young ones in this lifetime.

Get this paradox, and you have grasped the complex new way of thinking that Indigo Children will—and have—ushered us into. This complexity presents lessons in tolerance. We have to see them as different—not odd, not foreign, not strange, but diverse and complex wonderful beings. They have some superior abilities and some developing abilities—which is to say, they are like anybody else. Even grownups have strengths and weaknesses, and they are always learning.

So even though Indigo Children are not ready for adult responsibilities, they are ready for *some* responsibilities. They are ready to contribute input—about spiritual matters, about their understanding of the psychic world, about their own diet and nutrition, about their education environment. Give them that opportunity, and empower them to do what they can safely and reasonably do. Remember to keep the lines of communication open and to stay tuned in to your child's developing abilities.

> **Crystal Clear**
>
> We need a new, wiser, holistic, and more spiritual attitude toward children.
>
> —Anthony Gregorc, educator and developer of Mind Styles Theory

# Two-Way Connection

Children are not our lumps of clay, to be molded by us. Nor are they blank tablets on which we etch our preconceived ideas of who they will become. These children come into this world as defined souls, many of them with a unique spiritual mission. Indigo Children have their own agenda, and it's not the one we set for them. (But then, if you're living with one, you probably already knew that!)

Educator Anthony Gregorc urges us in general to become more "child-wise." He urges us to see them as "spirited beings, complete at every given moment and age." This is a shift from seeing them as adults-in-the-making. As 3-year-olds, they are complete 3-year-olds; as 7-year-olds, they are complete 7-year-olds. And that is true even when your 7-year-old has not developed the same skills of other 7-year-olds, while he has developed more skills than yet other 7-year-olds. Each child has a differentiated mind, special abilities, and unique gifts.

We must see the relationship of parent and child as one of co-creation. Again, this doesn't mean that you as the parent are not in control. This statement is not a license for permissiveness. You are responsible for recognizing and cultivating these differentiated minds, special abilities, and unique gifts. They need you to see what they are too young to see. They need you to guide them. You are the primary person in a web of influences that will shape them.

But they are creating this, too. Indigo Children are not only teaching us who they are; they are teaching us about *all* children. As Gregorc says, "it is the children who will write, rewrite, and edit our scripts of life."

# The Ascendance of the Mystic

Indigo Children, with their psychic ability, high emotional and physical sensitivity, and spiritual awareness, will spark an ascendance of mysticism in our lives. We, as a culture, took a giant leap toward more spiritual awareness as the millennium turned. After 9/11 (2001), we took another giant leap toward more tolerance and more compassion. Another came in the aftermath of the 2004 tsunami in the Indian Ocean, where the death toll exceeded 250,000. Again, months later, compassion was unleashed and tolerance tested in the aftermath of Hurricane Katrina, the costliest and one of the deadliest hurricanes in the history of the United States.

As the twenty-first century rolls along and some of our costliest conflicts such as the Middle East and Iraq persist, the awareness of spirit will increase as well. Perhaps that will come in a big energy shift in 2012, as proponents of the Fifth World viewpoint suggest. Or perhaps it will be as psychic Sylvia Browne says. After 2050, she says, there will be an "Age of the Messiah," in which masses will turn to spirituality and peace will reign. Perhaps we will come to a full understanding on how to act on what Chief Seattle said: "Man did not weave the web of life; he is merely a strand in it. Whatever he does to the web, he does to himself." Or perhaps, in the words of Jesus, from *The Complete Jesus* (Steerforth, 1998), we will see that "the Kingdom is inside of you and it is outside of you. When you come to know yourself, then you will become known."

### Good Counsel

We can't say enough about letting your Indigo child be with other Indigos. There is a center in Leicester, Massachusetts, called A Place of Light (placeoflight.net) that provides a place for Indigos and other psychic children to gather. It's vital for Indigos to gain a sense of who they are. Look for gathering places in your community for your child to get to know other Indigos and cultivate their psychic gifts.

## Live from the Esoteric!

We do believe the rest of the world is coming around to understanding the esoteric, and Indigos, by their sheer numbers, will usher this in. It's not merely the Harris poll (from Chapter 6) that shows most Americans have consulted a psychic, nor is it simply the plethora of television shows about mediums. It's the recent strides science has made as it has taken on explaining consciousness or intuition, for instance. Even one of the leading past lives scholars, Stephen Leberge, is based at Stanford University. Then there is the rising tide of research confirming some of the practices of integrative and alternative medicine, traditional Chinese medicine, and ayurveda.

The growing interest in the esoteric shows us there is so much we don't know. Some of us will embrace it—after all, if it works, why do we need to know how it works? Still others will wait it out for proof. But here's the thing: Indigo Children are going to teach it to us, anyway. As we learn to use and nurture their gifts, we'll learn how to work with the esoteric on a practical level.

Your Indigo child needs to be around other children with developing psychic abilities. He needs people to talk to who don't think he's crazy because he sees angels or talks to trees. He needs to know that it's a gift when he can "see" inside a person and know what's causing a physical ailment.

To cultivate telepathy, you may do this simple "linking" exercise. We have modified this from an exercise done at A Place of Light, a center for intuitive children in Massachusetts. Even if your psychic abilities are not developed, you may try this with your child. She can practice "receiving." For her to practice "sending," she needs to practice it with another psychic person. This linking exercise can also be done online or on the phone.

In linking, you and your child sit back to back, holding three differently colored but similar items, such as crystals or marbles. (Carolyn did this with her twins, using rings they won as carnival prizes.) The sender chooses one of the three and holds it clasped in her hand; the receiver concentrates on the sender and selects the item he senses the sender is holding. When the receiver has made her choice, she gives a signal, and both people reveal the object. The sender or another observer can keep track of the number of matches, to allow you to measure improvement over time.

After practicing linking, discuss how it went. What emotions came up when your child linked with you? What, if anything, was distracting her from choosing? What other messages did your child get about you? Often psychic children will pick up on other psychic messages. Be sure to talk about how your child felt about doing this activity, and check in to see if she'd like to do more activities like this.

After this exercise, Carolyn tried another, simply sending a message to her children by concentrating on it. The first time, she was thinking "angel," and her daughter Emerald said, "duck." Not perfect. Emerald got the white fluffy wings, but not the whole picture. (Carolyn compared this to being a little like Harry Potter's classmates' first attempts to apparate—transporting themselves to another place by concentrating on it—in which they got mostly there but left a leg or a shoe behind.) But the next time she sent a message, Emerald got it right away: butterfly. Carolyn did the same with her son, and right off the bat, he said "Hawaii." That was the answer. Obviously this was too easy! She tried

sending a number. She told Lucas it was a number, but gave no parameters, such as number under 10 or number under 100. Without missing
a beat, Lucas said, "45." That was it!

During this exercise, Carolyn felt a mysterious but gentle squeeze to
her shoulder, a benevolent presence. They were sitting in a busy restaurant, so Carolyn turned around to see who was there. No one. She had
the very strong sensation of pure white energy and nurturing love. She
believes it was an angel.

## Indigo Stars

When Joan of Arc was 13, she had visions and heard the voices of
saints, one of them Michael the Archangel, protector of France. The
saints urged to her to lend her support to the uncrowned King Charles
VII, organizing a French army that fought the English toward the end of
the Hundred Years War. Joan of Arc was instrumental in the victory. Even
as she was burned at the stake, she said she was guided by voices from
God, her united consciousness transcending her torturous physical death.

# Exalted Consciousness

Many Indigo Children will have the ability to achieve an exalted consciousness. An exalted consciousness is a state of high awareness and
high authenticity in which one is profoundly alive. A near-death experience may produce this, coming to the brink of suicide, or experiencing war or captivity. Some Indigos live as though this has happened,
though it has not. (Of course, we do not advocate trying to achieve this
consciousness by tempting death!)

French philosopher Jean Paul Sartre describes his experience of working for the French Resistance during World War II, knowing that at
any moment, he could be caught and executed. He says he never felt so
free. He was liberated from the trivial, dulled robotic state of awareness
that many of us function in day-to-day.

As we mentioned in Chapter 17, P.M.H. Atwater sees many similarities between Indigo Children and the children she has studied who
have had near-death experiences. Not only do they have a higher intelligence, but they have a heightened awareness—unusual sensitivities to

taste, texture, touch, smell, light, or sound. Both groups were highly intuitive, have a high intellect (and a high IQ) and are less competitive and more win-win oriented. Both groups are remarkably empathetic.

Colin Wilson, a prolific British author who writes about existentialism and many other topics, talks about the way he has chosen to live after experiencing so much angst as a teenager that he nearly committed suicide by drinking cyanide in his high school science class. In an interview, he recalls a dual awareness of that moment, of being aware of being outside of his body, looking at himself about to do the deed, evaluating himself with a mind of higher consciousness. Eckhart Tolle, author of *The Power of Now* and *Stillness Speaks* (see Appendix B), writes about having a similar dual awareness experience. As a young man, he experienced a lot of inner turbulence, and that led him to discovering this exalted state, in which the higher mind begins to speak more authoritatively than the ego-mind. This is a state that can be achieved through mindfulness.

The common theme through these experiences—exalted consciousness from a near-death experience, a white lightning revelatory moment, or a past life—is achieving some sort of rarefied connection with a higher mind—one that you cannot turn off. We can't exactly explain the source of this awareness for Indigo Children—it's unique to each individual child—but collectively they most certainly do have it.

## An Ego-Free World

What might this kind of consciousness mean for the world? Imagine how the world might operate without the trappings of the ego. Imagine being free of the protections we have to set up just to protect our egos. Imagine being free of the idea that our skin separates us. Indigos already have imagined this.

As John Lennon suggested in his song, "Imagine," try to imagine a world where all people are living in peace, with no greed or hunger. It is a brother- and sisterhood of humans, and the world is living as one. Can you imagine? In that kind of world, there is no ego to be threatened. Pride does not impede the innovation and collaboration we need to find better solutions. Higher mind rules.

Your challenge is to help your Indigo child understand that this idea of being a separate being in a separate body can be useful from time to time. Sometimes it's necessary to set boundaries with energy shielding, for instance. Your challenge, because they *are* children, is to teach them when and how it's appropriate to assert themselves as an individual force. Help your Indigo make that distinction—identifying instances when she should assert herself as an individual versus when she should be united as one with others.

The Indigo child's challenge is to open your mind to another way of understanding—to experience yourself as connected to something outside of yourself, to see that we are all connected. This is what we mean when we say the parent-child relationship is one of co-creating.

# Simply Extraordinary

Psychologist Dawna Markova, who has written many books about perception and learning, sees the role of parents as that of asking more of our children than they know how to ask of themselves. While Indigo Children have come here to change the world, they cannot do it without the wisdom of their parents and the others who guide them and love them. Markova urges us to "foster their open-hearted hopefulness, engage their need to collaborate, and be an incentive to utilize their natural competency and compassion." When we help them by showing them ways to weave themselves into the fabric of twenty-first century life, we empower them as agents of change.

Their gifts are rare, but not really. As we all open up to cultivating the values Indigo Children hold and the skills they possess, we may find these Indigo attributes are not so rare. They may be normal 30 years from now. Adults will develop their gifts and awaken their spirituality because of the impetus of some Indigos. Many more Crystal Children will arrive in the next 30 years, too, as well as perhaps another level or two of spiritual evolution beyond Crystals. As someone who loves an Indigo, you are participating in the next evolutionary step. We hope you agree it's quite magnificent.

## The Least You Need to Know

♦ The future world Indigo Children are creating will be infused with spiritual awareness.

♦ Mindfulness and meditation are grounding for Indigos.

♦ Cultivate and support your child's growing psychic abilities by using games and by participating in communities where they can befriend other psychic children.

♦ Perhaps the biggest contribution Indigo Children have already made to our world is expanding our understanding of child development.

♦ In the future, we will be more child-wise, seeing children as spiritual beings who work with us to write the script of their lives.

♦ Indigo Children will lead us into a higher understanding of an exalted consciousness, a state in which one feels profoundly alive.

# Appendix A

# Glossary

**ADHD** Attention-deficit hyperactivity disorder, a condition defined by inattentiveness, impulsivity, and hyperactivity. People with ADHD tend to think randomly, not sequentially. They tend to be distracted easily by many stimuli. ADHD children have these behaviors more than is appropriate for their developmental stage.

**Asperger's syndrome** A severe developmental disorder characterized by major difficulties in social interaction, restricted interest, and unusual behavior. It falls on the autism continuum, but unlike autism, there are no delays in learning language, cognition, or coping skills.

**astral travel** The ability to transport your astral body—your spirit and psyche—to another place.

**autism** A developmental disability that affects social interaction, communication, play, and cognition. Autistic children are highly sensitive and may have unusual responses to people and strong attachment to objects.

**ayurveda** A holistic system of medicine that comes from India. It emphasizes harmony in the body, with a strong preventive emphasis. Ayurveda means "knowledge of life" in Sanskirt.

**bandwidth scanning**   Accessing information from multiple dimensions.

**bilocation**   In astral travel, this is the phenomenon of being in one place physically at the same time your spirit is in another place.

**channeling**   The ability to receive thoughts of enlightened spirits or angels.

**clairaroma**   Synonymous with clairscence or clairolfaction, the ability to smell as a precognition; a smell that indicates a future event or contains a message from the spirit world.

**clairaudience**   Clear hearing, the ability to hear sounds or voices from the spirit realm.

**clairempathy**   The ability to experience empathy as a precognition.

**clairgustance**   Clear tasting, the ability to experience taste as a precognition; a sensation of taste that predicts a future event.

**clairsentience**   Clear feeling, the ability to perceive feeling without a clear external physical cause.

**clairtangence**   Clear touching, more commonly known as psychometry. The ability to know, by holding an item belonging to a person, details about that person's history.

**clairvoyance**   Clear sight, the ability to see into the future.

**creative visualization**   A technique of imagining a desired goal, then using meditation and focused, positive energy to manifest something in your life. Intention and affirmations are key components. You must believe that what you visualize has already happened and then act as if it already has.

**Crystal Children**   The next wave of children after Indigos. They are more sensitive and fragile and will be the healers and peacekeepers.

**dyslexia**   A learning disability defined by inability to process letterforms into words and therefore to read effectively.

**energy shielding**   The technique of creating a psychic shield around oneself in order to protect oneself from negative energy.

**Fifth World**   A theory that the world will change at the end of the Mayan long count calendar in 2012.

**giftedness**   In the educational environment, a gifted child demonstrates exceptionally high intelligence or great special abilities. Gifted children show creative thinking, leadership, and academic aptitude. Most schools in the United States use the Marland standard or Renzulli's Three Ring Definition of Giftedness to determine if a child is gifted.

**homeopathy**   A holistic health treatment that uses natural remedies to stimulate the body's natural healing properties. The word comes from Greek—*homeo* means similar, and *pathos* means disease.

**homeschooling**   An educational method in which parents serve as teachers, sometimes using textbooks that can be obtained from various homeschooling organizations.

**hyperspeed thinking**   Understanding a situation from a multiplicity of perspectives in an instant.

**indigo**   A deep blue color, said to be prominent in the life aura of Indigo Children.

**Indigo Children**   Indigo Children is a term that embraces a broad range of attributes in children who are breaking the mold. These children are brilliant and imaginative, and they defy categorization in everything they do. Many of them have high psychic awareness or advanced psychic skills. They feel things deeply—emotionally and physically. Some may have attention-deficit hyperactivity disorder (ADHD) or a learning disability. Some may tend toward a righteous anger or stubborn nonconformity; others may exhibit exceptional tolerance or compassion. (The same child may be both a stubborn nonconformist and a compassionate humanitarian—go figure!) Indigo Children are often spiritually advanced. As a group, they are here to change the world.

**Indigo overlay**   A person who has an Indigo overlay is not an Indigo child or adult Indigo, but this person may exhibit Indigo traits in certain situations. There is much debate about whether the Indigo overlay exists or if some adult Indigos (in particular) are simply Indigos who have suppressed their Indigo attributes. Some Indigo experts have observed the Indigo overlay in parents of Indigo Children. A person with an Indigo overlay could exhibit symptoms only for a certain cycle of life, such as parenting an Indigo child.

**karma**   The universe's balancing energy. All energy—good and bad—that goes out comes back. Karma is about sending and taking. Whatever you send out into the world returns to you in another form. Though karma is neutral—it does not make value judgments—many people ascribe value to it: good deeds bring good rewards.

**learning disability**   A neurological disorder that usually affects the child's ability to read, use language correctly, process numbers, or do math.

**lucid dreaming**   A dream state in which you are simultaneously dreaming yet aware of the fact that you are dreaming. You understand you can take control of the events in the dream from that point.

**Merkaba**   A star-shaped double tetrahedron, also called a stellated octahedron, while comes from ancient Egypt. A Merkaba is two inter-locking tetrahedra of light, with one pointing up, the other down. A Merkaba can be used for visualization, energy protection, and astral travel. *Mer* means light, *ka* means spirit, and *ba* means body. A Merkaba is often used as a symbol of ascending to heaven. It is linked to the Hebrew prophet Ezekiel.

**metagifted**   A term coined by Wendy H. Chapman, MA to mean metaphysically gifted, as well as having knowledge about one's own giftedness. Indigo Children are metagifted.

**mindfulness-based stress reduction**   A stress-reduction technique that uses yoga, meditation, and present-moment awareness.

**Montessori method**   An educational style created by Marie Montessori at the turn of the twentieth century. The method emphasizes the creativity and spontaneity of the child while teaching self-discipline and self-motivation. The method believes that freedom within limits gives children a lifetime love of learning.

**nonlinear thinking**   In nonlinear thinking, the thought process is not sequential but random. Nonlinear thinking is complex, and its conclusions are not predictable. It's not tied to logic or based on patterns built from prior experience.

**overexcitability**   Responding intensely to minor stimulus. Many indigos are have overexcitabilities to senses, emotions, and imagination, but also to physical and mental stimuli. This refers to Dabrowski's Theory of Overexcitability.

**past lives**   Rebirth of the soul in another body. Several belief systems say the soul reincarnates after death, choosing another form (a body) in which to live the next life.

**precognition**   The umbrella term for many types of psychic perception, precognition is the ability to know about events that have not yet happened.

**prosperity consciousness**   The positive state of mind that attracts prosperity.

**psychic**   An ability or talent to sense things beyond the physical and beyond the normal five senses.

**psychic teleportation**   This terms comprises astral travel in dreams as well as bilocation. It's the ability to transport oneself psychically.

**quantum intelligence**   Thinking beyond the norm, connecting with higher dimensions. It is characterized by hyperspeed and high bandwidth thinking. It's what Indigos are here to contribute.

**Reggia Emilio**   A preschool educational method that responds to the interests of the child and allows the child to select activities. The method emphasizes parental and community involvement.

**Reiki**   Energy healing that uses certain symbols and hands-on touch healing to help channel chi into a person and help them heal. There are many varieties of Reiki.

**reincarnation**   The belief that when a person dies, his or her soul incarnates in another body and another life at another time. Reincarnation is part of the belief system of some religions, but not all.

**sapience**   Self-awareness or consciousness. It's an awareness of your knowing, or an awareness of yourself as a being who knows ("I think therefore I am").

**sentience**   The quality of sensing through taste, smell, touch, hearing, or sight.

**Shamballa**   A type of high frequency energy healing in which chi is channeled into someone or something living to help them balance and heal.

**soul intelligence**   Also called holistic intelligence; knowing another person's soul by picking up on their energy field. This is the deepest level of empathy possible.

**super creation**   The ability to work in high bursts of creativity using nonlinear thinking.

**synchronicity**   The occurrence of two seemingly unrelated things at the same time.

**synesthesia**   Receiving sensory input with perception of additional sense, such as hearing colors, tasting sounds.

**telekinesis**   The ability to move objects with your thoughts.

**telepathy**   The ability to send messages from one mind to another.

**unschooling**   An educational method that does not follow a curriculum and does not have scheduled classes. Students set the curriculum by their interest, using teachers as resources to gather information for learning about a particular topic.

**vibrant multiplicity**   Remaining vibrantly engaged with multiple projects, while maintaining focus and vision for each one.

**Waldorf method**   An educational method developed by Rudolf Steiner that emphasizes the whole child, developing heart, hands, and mind. The Waldorf method emphasizes artistic expression, hands-on creation, and social responsibility.

# Resources

## Wendy Can Help!

Wendy H. Chapman, MA started her website, www.metagifted.org, in 1998 to spread the word about gifted children of all kinds from the academically gifted to metaphysically gifted (metagifted). The topics of Indigo Children and Indigo Adults are well covered on this site with lots of information regarding how to identify, work with, and help Indigos. At metagifted.org/services, Wendy offers Indigo consultations for parents and other caregivers of Indigos, as well as teen and adult Indigos, available via email and phone. She also offers Shamballa Multidimensional Energy Healing training and healing sessions and Psychic Readings. She will travel to present workshops on Indigos or teach Shamballa to groups of people. To get in touch with Wendy, e-mail her at Director@metagifted.org.

# Further Reading

## ADHD

Emery, Kevin Ross. *Managing the Gift: Alternative Approaches to Attention Deficit Disorder.* San Diego, CA: New Century Press, 2005.

Hallowell, Edward M., and John J. Ratey. *Driven to Distraction: Recognizing and Coping with Attention Deficit Disorder from Childhood to Adulthood.* New York: Touchstone, 1995.

## Anger

Hanh, Thich Nhat. *Anger: Wisdom for Cooling the Flames.* New York: Riverhead Books, 2002.

Lancaster, Diane. *Anger and the Indigo Child.* Boulder, CO: Wellness Press, 2002.

Warren, Neil Clark. *Make Anger Your Ally: Harnessing Our Most Baffling Emotion.* New York: Doubleday, 1983.

## Body, Mind, and Spirit

Chopra, Deepak, M.D. *Quantum Healing: Exploring the Frontiers of Mind/Body Medicine.* New York: Bantam Books, 1989.

Flynn, Carolyn, and Erica Tismer. *Empowering Your Life with Massage.* Indianapolis: Alpha Books, 2004.

Flynn, Carolyn, and Shari Just, Ph.D. *The Complete Idiot's Guide to Creative Visualization.* Indianapolis: Alpha Books, 2005.

Fontana, David, and Ingrid Slack. *Teaching Meditation to Children: A Practical Guide to the Use and Benefits of Meditation Techniques.* Shaftesbury, Dorset, Great Britain: Element Books Ltd., 1997.

Friedman, Robert Lawrence. *The Healing Power of the Drum.* Gilsum, NH: White Cliffs Media Inc., 2000.

Garth, Maureen. *Moonbeam: A Book of Meditations for Children.* New York: Harper Collins, 1993.

——. *Starbright: Meditations for Children.* San Francisco, CA: Harper San Francisco, 1991.

Rozman, Deborah, Ph.D. *Meditating with Children: The Art of Concentration and Centering.* Boulder Creek, CA: Planetary Publications, 1994.

Ruiz, Don Miguel. *A Practical Guide to Personal Freedom, The Four Agreements:.* San Rafael, CA: Amber-Allen Publishing, 1997.

——. *The Mastery of Love: A Practical Guide to the Art of Relationship, a Toltec Wisdom Book.* San Rafael, CA: Amber-Allen Publishing, 1999.

# Education

Adderholdt-Elliot, Miriam. *Perfectionism: What's Bad About Being Too Good.* Minneapolis, MN: Free Spirit Publishing, 1987.

Bagley, Michael T. *Using Imagery in Creative Problem Solving.* New York: Royal Fireworks Press, 1999.

Bagley, Michael T., and Karin K. Hess. *200 Ways of Using Imagery in the Classroom.* Unionville, NY: Trillium Press, 1984.

Greenberg, Daniel. *Free at Last: The Sudbury Valley School.* Framingham, MA: Sudbury Valley School Press, 1987.

Pearce, Joseph Chilton. *Magical Child.* New York: Penguin, 1977.

Penrose, Roger. *The Emperor's New Mind: Concerning Computers, Minds and the Laws of Physics.* New York: Oxford University Press, 2002.

Reis, Sally M., and Joseph S. Renzulli. *The Schoolwide Enrichment Model: A How-To Guide for Educational Excellence,* 2nd ed. Mansfield Center, CT: Creative Learning Press Inc., 1997.

## Indigo Children

Aron, Elaine N. *The Highly Sensitive Person: How to Thrive When the World Overwhelms You.* New York: Broadway Books, 1996.

———. *The Highly Sensitive Child.* New York: Broadway Books, 1996.

Atwater, P.M.H., Lh.D. *Beyond the Indigo Children: The New Children and the Coming of the Fifth World.* Rochester, VT: Bear & Co., 2005.

———. *Children of the New Millennium: Children's Near-Death Experiences and the Evolution of Humankind.* New York: Three Rivers Press, 1999.

———. *The New Children and Near-Death Experiences.* Rochester, VT: Bear & Co., 2003.

Carroll, Lee, and Jan Tober. *An Indigo Celebration: More Messages, Stories, and Insights from the Indigo Children.* Carlsbad, CA: Hay House, 2001.

———. *The Indigo Children: The New Kids Have Arrived.* Carlsbad, CA: Hay House, 1999.

Condron, Barbara. *How to Raise an Indigo Child: 10 Keys for Cultivating a Child's Natural Brilliance.* Windyville, MO: School of Metaphysics, 2002.

Day, Peggy, and Susan Gale. *Edgar Cayce on the Indigo Children.* Virginia Beach, VA: A.R.E. Press, 2004.

Dosick, Wayne D., and Ellen Kaufman Dosick. *Spiritual Healing the Indigo Children (And Adult Indigos, Too!): The Practical Guide and Handbook*. San Diego, CA: Jodere Group, 2004.

Kurcinka, Mary Sheedy. *Raising Your Spirited Child: A Guide for Parents Whose Child is More Intense, Sensitive, Perceptive, Persistent, Energetic*. New York: Harper Collins, 1991.

Schweizer, Jean, Ph.D. *New Children of Earth Reach, Teach and Inspire; The Indigo Children*. Victoria, BC, Canada: Trafford Publishing, 2005.

Tappe, Nancy Ann. *Understanding Your Life Through Color*. Carlsbad, CA: Starling Publishers, 1982.

Virtue, Doreen, Ph.D. *The Care and Feeding of Indigo Children*. Carlsbad, CA: Hay House, 2001.

———. *The Crystal Children*. Carlsbad, CA: Hay House, 2003.

———. *Indigo, Crystal, and Rainbow Children*. (Audio CD). Carlsbad, CA: Hay House, 2005.

## Psychic Intuition

Andrews, Ted. *Animal-Speak: The Spiritual and Magical Powers of Creatures Great and Small*. St. Paul, MN: Llewellyn Publications, 1996.

Choquette, Sonia. *The Wise Child: A Spiritual Guide to Nurturing Your Child's Intuition*. New York: Three Rivers Press, 1999.

———. *The Psychic Pathway: A Workbook for Reawakening the Voice of the Soul*. New York: Three Rivers Press, 1994.

Dennis, Caryl, with Parker Whitman. *The Millennium Children: Tales of the Shift*. Clearwater, FL: Rainbows Unlimited, 1997.

Dong, Paul, and Thomas E. Raffill. *China's Super Psychics.* New York: Marlowe and Company, 1997.

Flynn, Carolyn, and Arlene Tognetti. *The Intuitive Arts on Health: Using Astrology, Tarot, and Psychic Intuition to See Your Future.* Indianapolis: Alpha Books, 2003.

———. *The Complete Idiot's Guide to Tarot Spreads.* Indianapolis: Alpha Books, 2006.

Flynn, Carolyn, and Gary R. McClain, Ph.D. *The Complete Idiot's Guide to Oracles.* Indianapolis: Alpha Books, 2006.

Goldman, Karen. *Angel Voices: The Advanced Handbook for Aspiring Angels.* New York: Simon & Schuster, 1993.

Hurwitz, Sue. *The Library of the Five Senses & the Sixth Sense: Intuition.* Danbury, CT: Franklin Watts, The Rosen Publishing Group Inc., 1998.

Pliskin, Marci, CSW, ACSW, and Shari L. Just, Ph.D. *The Complete Idiot's Guide to Interpreting Your Dreams, Second Edition.* Indianapolis: Alpha Books, 2003.

Powell, Dr. Tag, and Carol Howell Mills. *ESP for Kids: How to Develop Your Child's Psychic Ability.* Key Largo, FL: Top of the Mountain, Publishing, 1993.

Romaine, Deborah S., and Arlene Tognetti. *The Intuitive Arts on Work: Using Astrology, Tarot, and Psychic Intuition to See Your Future.* Indianapolis: Alpha Books, 2003.

Sandoz-Merrill, Bobbie. *In the Presence of High Beings: What Dolphins Want You to Know.* Tulsa, OK: Council Oak Books.

Sisk, Dorothy Ann. *Developing and Increasing Intuitive Thinking: Activity Cards to Help.* Unionville, NY: Trillim Press, 1991.

Thibodeau, Lauren, Ph.D. *Natural-Born Intuition: How to Awaken and Develop Your Inner Wisdom.* Franklin Lakes, NJ: New Page Books, 2005.

Virtue, Doreen. *Angel Medicine: How to Heal the Body and Mind with the Help of Angels.* Santa Monica, CA: Hay House, 2004.

———. *Healing with Angels: How the Angels Can Assist You in Every Area of Your Life.* Santa Monica, CA: Hay House, 1999.

———. *Messages from Your Angels: What Your Angels Want You to Know.* Santa Monica, CA: Hay House, 2002.

## Spirituality

Bhaumik, Mani. *Code Name God: The Spiritual Odyssey of a Man of Science* New York: Crossroad, 2005.

Dalai Lama. *The Universe in a Single Atom: The Convergence of Science and Spirituality.* New York: Morgan Road, 2005.

Fromm, Erich, *The Art of Loving.* New York: Harper Perennial, 2000.

Hicks, Esther and Jerry, and Abraham. *Sara and the Foreverness of Friends of a Feather: An Inspired Narrative of a Child's Experiential Journey into the Knowingness that All is Well.* San Antonio, TX: Abraham-Hicks Publications, 1995.

Jenkins, Peggy. *Nurturing Spirituality in Children: Simple Hands-On Activities.* Hillsboro, OR: Beyond Worlds Publishing Inc., 1995.

Kryon, channeled by Lee Carroll. *The Parables of Kryon*. Carlsbad, CA: Hay House Inc., 1996.

Millman, Dan. *Quest for the Crystal Castle: A Peaceful Warrior Children's Book*. Tiburon, CA: H.J. Kramer, Inc, Starseed Press, 1992.

————. *Sacred Journey of the Peaceful Warrior*. Tiburon, CA: H.J. Kramer, Inc., 1991.

————. *Way of the Peaceful Warrior*. Tiburon, CA: H.J. Kramer Inc., 1984.

Myss, Caroline. *Anatomy of the Spirit: The Seven Stages and of Power and Healing*. New York: Three Rivers Press, 1996.

————. *Invisible Acts of Power: Personal Choices That Create Miracles*. New York: Free Press, 2004.

————. *Sacred Contracts: Awakening Your Divine Potential*. New York: Harmony Books, 2001.

————. *Why People Don't Heal and How They Can*. New York: Three Rivers Press, 1998.

Redfield, James. *The Celestine Prophecy: An Adventure*. New York: Warner Books, 1993.

Spangler, David. *Everyday Miracles: The Inner Art of Manifestation*. New York: Bantam, 1995.

————. *Laws of Manifestation*. Forres, Scotland: Findshorn, 1981.

Tolle, Eckhart. *The Power of Now: A Gateway to Spiritual Enlightenment*. Novato, CA: New World Library, 1999.

————. *Stillness Speaks*. Novato, CA: New World Library, 2003.

Williamson, Marianne. *A Return to Love: Reflections on the Principles in a Course in Miracles.* New York: HarperCollins, 1996.

Wilson, Colin. *Beyond the Occult.* New York: Carroll & Graf Publishers, 1991.


## Miscellaneous

Atwater, P.M.H. *The Complete Idiot's Guide to Near-Death Experiences.* Indianapolis: Alpha Books, 2000.

Ausubel, Ken. *Nature's Operating Instructions.* San Francisco, CA: Sierra Club Books, 2004.

Cline, Foster W., and Jim Fay. *Parenting with Love and Logic.* Colorado Springs, CO: Pin[td]on Press, 2006.

Dreamhealer, Adam. *Dreamhealer.* Dreamhealer.com, 2003.

Florida, Richard. *The Rise of the Creative Class: How It's Transforming Work, Leisure, Community and Everyday Life.* New York: Basic Books, 2003.

Kohn, Alfie. *Unconditional Parenting: Moving from Rewards and Punishment to Love and Reason.* New York: Atria, 2005.

Pearsall, Paul. *The Heart's Code.* New York: Broadway, 1999.

Schulz, Mona Lisa. *The New Feminine Brain: Developing Your Intuitive Genius.* New York: Free Press, 2005.

# Also on the Web

## Education

**http://awsna.org.** Association of Waldorf Schools of North America.

**http://gregorc.com.** Educator and author Anthony Gregorc, who pioneered Mind Styles Theory.

**http://idodi.org.** This website features destination imagination challenges and can help you get in touch with local groups.

**http://montessori.org.** A guide to the Montessori educational method.

**http://sudval.org.** A guide to the Sudbury unschooling method.

**http://trust.wdn.com/ims/Mont.htm.** Information about Montessori educational method.

## Holistic Health

**http://all-natural.com/add.html.** Information about food additives, homeopathic remedies, and ADHD.

**http://AskKarenEck.com.** Website for Karen Eck, nutritional educator who often writes for Children of the New Earth.

**http://aura-soma.net/index.asp.** Website for aura-soma color therapy.

**http://bachflower.com.** Website that sells flower essences.

**http://diet-studies.com.** List of studies in medical journals about topics ranging from ADHD, Asperger's food allergies, learning difficulties, and behavior problems.

**http://ewg.org/reports/bodyburden2/execsumm.php.** Environmental Working Group site that includes research about how toxic substances affect people.

**http://feingold.org.** An organization of families and professionals that researches and advocates proven dietary techniques to improve learning and behavior in children.

**http://healing-arts.org/children.** A research project through the program in integrative medicine at the University of Arizona College of Medicine. It is geared toward children with ADHD, Asperger's, and other challenges.

**http://heartmath.org.** Institute of HeartMath researches the role the heart plays in our emotional management.

**http://mercola.com.** This site provides holistic health advice.

**http://nccam.nih.gov/health/backgrounds/energymed.htm.** The National Center for Complementary and Alternative Medicine site provides a guide to energy medicine.

**http://nmessences.com.** Provides flower essences for children, including "Children's Issues" Super Essence.

# Indigo Children

**http://childrenofthenewearth.com.** An online publication with articles and tips about Indigo and Crystal children.

**http://emissaryoflight.com.** Website of James Twymann that gives a great deal of information on his work and the children with whom he works.

**http://indigochild.com.** Site of Lee Carroll and Jan Tober.

**http://metagifted.org.** Wendy H. Chapman MA's comprehensive website about Indigo Children and Indigo Adults.

**http://sunfell.com/indigo.htm.** An exploration of the experience of Indigo Children emerging into the world.

**www.starchild.co.za/what.html.** This website, part of The Starchild Network, explains Indigo Children and Indigo Adults, as well as Crystal Children.

# Connecting with Other Indigo Parents

**http://groups.yahoo.com/group/indigo-parents.** Yahoo! group for Indigo parents.

**http://indigochild.net.** This multi-language networking site provides articles and discussions about Indigo Children.

**http://indigochildren.meetup.com.** Indigo Meetup Day is a monthly worldwide event worldwide that brings together parents to discuss topics related to raising intuitive children.

**http://psykids.net.** Yahoo! group for those interested in sharing experiences about their intuitive children.

## Other Resources

*Indigo* (2003). Feature-length movie about an Indigo child; Indigothemovie.com.

*The Indigo Evolution* (2006). Documentary in which Indigo Children and experts are interviewed about the Indigo phenomenon; theindigoevolution.com.

# Activities and Affirmations of Indigo Gifts

Use these activities and affirmations as a way of cementing your Indigo's appreciation of his or her gifts. These practices can be a great way to keep you mindful about ways to cherish your Indigo child. When Indigo Children have this kind of support, they flourish.

## Compassion

Activities: Community projects; volunteer at food banks; make creative arts for group fundraisers; plan free time to first get your own work done, then make time for others and group projects.

Affirmation: *I care about others' feelings and want them to be comforted.*

Or for those who are overly compassionate at their own expense:

*I remember to put my own needs first and not be too distracted by others' feelings. I strive to stay focused and get things done while also maintaining my connection with others.*

# Tolerance

Activities: Practice giving compliments to others and restricting judgment; visit places where people are different from you and discuss with your child afterward; do "what is similar" games, not "what is different" study of other cultures.

Affirmation: *I accept others as they are. I try not to make judgments of other people.*

# Nonconformity

Activities: Create a game with your own rules; find safe ways to show your differences, such as hairstyles, clothing, and creative projects; write to legislators to propose new laws or modifications of existing ones.

Affirmation: *I am a unique, special individual, not just one of the crowd. Some rules can be challenged and improved.*

# Sense of Fairness

Activities: Practice dividing food, time, and prizes into equally shared parts; work to help people who have less than you; study inequality in history—slavery and caste systems.

Affirmation: *I want things to be fair for all people. I will do what I can to make things fair for everyone.*

# Strong Sense of Self

Activities: Enroll your child in a class for self-defense, tai chi, or yoga; role-play with your child; have her stand up for herself and say no when faced with peer pressure to do something she knows is wrong; take turns modeling the behavior; try different scenarios.

Affirmation: *I am a strong, healthy person and I know my own mind.*

# Psychic Abilities

Activities: Practice linking and telepathy with friends; try guessing who is on the phone before you answer it or look at caller ID; study Tarot or other psychic tools; meditate daily.

Affirmation: *My psychic abilities are developing and getting stronger. I can control my psychic skills better every day. I value this talent.*

# Creative Thinking

Activities: Create an invention; make creative art; practice creative visualization techniques.

Affirmation: *I can find creative solutions. I have fun! I am a creative thinker. I can manifest things with my creative visualizations.*

# Righteous Anger

Activities: Practice grounding out negative energy; do yoga; exercise regularly; use talking a walk or other vigorous exercise to release anger; take action to improve the world; write to newspaper editors or elected leaders; talk to school counselors; talk to other Indigo parents.

Affirmation: *I will do my best to improve things in the world. I will release my anger when it is not beneficial or when it distracts me from my purpose.*

# Random, Out-of-the-Box Thinking

Activities: Develop unique solutions to problems; challenge children to solve problems creatively—move a raw egg from the table to the floor without touching it or cracking it, for instance, using only two sticky labels, four straws, and two pieces of paper; try destination imagination challenges or join a local destination imagination group challenge (idodi.org).

Affirmation: *I am not held back by expectations. I can see beyond the box.*

# Spiritual Intelligence

Activities: Meditate daily; collect crystals that resonate for you and tune in with them; attend church as a family; explore spiritual traditions; use feng shui in your home.

Affirmation: *I connect with my higher self and with other dimensions of life.*

# Respect for All Beings

Activities: Take weekly nature walks; go to the growers market in your community; start a butterfly pavilion (insectlore.com).

Affirmation: *Together, we cherish the living spirit of all things on this earth.*

# High Sensitivity

Activities: Study Reiki, Shamballa, or other energy healing; practice energy shielding when entering busy places or emotionally draining situations; remove clothing tags; wear natural fabrics; eat organic foods without additives such as MSG; use flower essences.

Affirmation: *I activate my energy shielding to keep out negative energy and let in positive energy. I am protected.*

# Win-Win Thinking

Activities: Put your child on the school debate team; play games in which everyone wins; bake and decorate a cake together; draw a mural together; go on scavenger hunts.

Affirmation: *I appreciate your helping to make sure everyone feels valued and appreciated.*

# Creative Visualization

Creative visualization is using the power of your imagination to manifest what you want in life. Creative visualization has three essential steps: imagining it, believing it, and affirming it.

With your child, create a visualization about an area of life in which he has a challenge.

**1.     Imagine It**

Describe what he wants, what it looks like, how he feels when it's accomplished. Fill in the picture in vivid detail.

_____

_____

_____

_____

_____

**2.     Believe It**

Using focus, meditation, and support of others, continue to be devoted to developing your visualization until you reach the point that you believe it will happen. Act as if this goal has already been achieved. Believe it with conviction. Take your meditation focus now to expand the feeling of experiencing your vision as if it had already happened.

_____

_____

_____

_____

_____

**3.     Affirm It**

Every day, use affirmations to cement your visualization. Affirmations are simple, positive statements. They are not about what will happen or what you will become; you _are_ that person. You possess those attributes.

Affirmations are always in present tense.

_____

_____

_____

_____

_____

# Index

## A

abstract random learners, 178
abstract sequential learners, 178
abstract thinking, 74-75
abundant Indigo
   prosperity consciousness,
     162-163
   prosperous spirits, 165
   types, 163-164
Abzug, Bella, 9
Adam, 19
ADD (attention deficit disorder),
  53-55
   dealing with, 59-63
   determining, 55-57
ADHD (attention-deficit hyperactivity disorder), 13, 53-55
   dealing with, 59-63
   determining, 55-57
Affective Computing, 222-223
Alex's Lemonade Stand, establishment of, 21
*Alice in Wonderland*, 9
Allen, Woody, 34
alternative education, 180
   gifted programs, 185
   home schooling, 184-185
   Montessori method, 182-184
   Reggio Emilia method, 182
   resources, 185
   unschooling, 183-184
   Waldorf method, 180-182
alternative medicines, 188-190,
  194-197

altruism
   global communities, building,
     246-248
   importance of, 243-246
Amos, Tori, 34
*Anatomy of the Spirit, Sacred
  Contracts*, 9
anger, 45
   compression and release, 41-43
   love, transforming anger
     through, 46-48
   physical solutions, 43-44
   rage, preventing, 48-50
   rules regarding, 50-51
   signals, 51
   sources for, 40-41
   vocal solutions, 45
Anger, 43
Anthony, Susan B., 9
Armitage, John, 62
Armstrong, Heather, 172
Aron, Elaine N., 31
*Art of Loving, The*, 96
Ask Eric, 88
Asperger's Syndrome, 13, 53-55,
  59
astral dimensions, dreams,
  223-226
Atlantis, 258
   Santorini, possible connection
    to, 254
attention-deficit hyperactivity
  disorder (ADHD). *See* ADHD
  (attention-deficit hyperactivity
  disorder)
attributes, Indigo Children, 7-8
Atwater, P.M.H., 218, 222, 272
Austen, Jane, 9
Ausubel, Ken, 243
autism, 13, 53-55, 59
ayurveda, 189-190

Tew, Alex, 171
Theory of Overexcitabilities, 31
Thich Nhat Hanh, 189
Thoreau, Henry David, 9
Three Ring Definition of
  Giftedness, 180
Ticket2Ride, 206
Tober, Jan, 6, 135
tolerance, importance of, 86-88
Tolle, Eckhart, 273
touch, healing power of, 197-198
touch therapy, 85-86
Tubman, Harriet, 9
Twain, Mark, 9
Twyman, James, 6-7

unconditional love, importance
  of, 119-124
*Understanding Your Life Through
  Color*, 6
*Universe in a Single Atom: The
  Convergence of Science and
  Spirituality, The*, 23
unschooling, 183-184

van Gogh, Vincent, 9, 34
Virtue, Doreen, 56
vocal solutions, anger, 45
von Schelling, Friedrich, 222
von Stradonitz, Friedrich August
  Kekule, 216

# W-X-Y-Z

Waldorf educational system, 59
Waldorf education method,
  180-182
Wales, Jimmy, 183
Walsch, Neale Donald, 6
water, power of, 245-246
Weir, Johnny, 22

"What the Bleep Do We Know?,"
  23
White, Shaun, 8, 9
whole parenting, 188-189, 198
  environmental protections,
    193-194
  holistic health practices,
    194-198
  nutrition, 191-193
  physical fitness, 190-191
Williams, Robin, 9
Williamson, Marianne, 9, 34
Wilson, Colin, 221-273
Winfrey, Oprah, 9
work environments, changing, 21
Wright, Machaelle, 195

Yaxkin, Aluna Joy, 261
Yeats, William Butler, 34
yoga, benefits of, 190, 191
Yoga Sutras, 191
Younger, Nathaniel, 172

zeitgeist, 18